The negro, the black, the MOOR

Rommani M. Amenu-EL

Edited by Elaine Myrick-Bey

GATEWAY PRESS, INC.
Baltimore, MD   2008

Please direct all correspondence and book orders to:
AmeNu Publications and Productions
P.O. Box 2042
Baltimore, MD 21203

Library of Congress Control Number 2007942740
ISBN 978-0-615-17332-0

Published for the author by
Gateway Press, Inc.
3600 Clipper Mill Rd., Suite 260
Baltimore, MD 21211-1953

www.gatewaypress.com

Printed in the United States of America

DEDICATION

This book is dedicated to my son Rommani II, his mother, (Florence) for blessing me with a son, my two daughters Mia and T'pyge and their mother (Saisa) for blessing me with a deceased son Mulai and my present soul mate Cydney and her son Ronday. I further dedicate this book to my deceased parents and Grandparents, my biological brothers, sisters, nieces, nephews and all of my grandchildren of whom my son Rommani II is the father and his wife Rhonda who is the mother.

This book is especially dedicated to all Moorish Americans throughout this hemisphere and to thank those who are keeping the Moorish culture and history alive through writing books, publishing pamphlets, conducting seminars and lectures guided by and standing for the principles of Love, Truth, Peace, Freedom and Justice.

The cosmic spirit within compels me to above all else dedicate this work to the Honorable Noble Drew Ali, Prophet (January 8, 1886-July 1929). The concept of a prophet can be viewed in many ways by the public. The teachings of Noble Drew Ali espoused that a Prophet was a thought of Allah (God) manifested in the flesh. I find it note worthy to mention of the several definitions of a prophet the two below seem most appropriate from my perspective.

> A. teacher and a leader
> B. chief spokesman for a cause or a movement

I do know that his teachings provided many with a solid foundation and inspiration to research, study Moorish history, US Constitution, civil war, metaphysics or ontology and several other Sciences all under the ancient wisdom of "Man Know Thy Self".

I felt some of the above within, but was not motivated to pursue until I was awaken to the lessons of Noble Drew Ali. I am certain that Moorish Americans everywhere would agree that we are highly enlighten by his teachings.

I trust that this historical work will benefit all and be preserved in the Moorish American legacy for years to come.

ACKNOWLEDGMENTS

It is with great pride that I give honor and remembrance to those who have passed on through transition and contributed so much to the creation and organization of the original Moorish School of Law and History, Incorporated # 13. I give special thanks and gratitude to its founder the Honorable Richardson Dingle-El born in Manning South Carolina. He lived from 1910 to 1992. I'd also like to thank his younger brother Timothy Dingle-El who introduced me to Moorish Science and issued to me, my original Nationality Card.

Dedicated instructors/administrators who passed on are Carolyn L. Reynolds-EL, Alfred Collins-El (Al-Mansur), Leon Smith-Bey (Musa Pratabulu-Bey), and Malbert Brown-Bey. Other dedicated deceased staff is Sarah Ferrell-EL, James and Helen Richardson-El.

I am also very grateful for our attorney Jacques E. Leeds-Bey now (retired judge, Maryland Workmen's Compensation Commission). Aside from the many contributions too numerous to mention here, attorney Leeds-Bey along with researchers from the Moorish School of Law and History litigated a case all the way to the supreme court . The case involved former slaves and the Executive Will of Abraham Lincoln. The case can be found in this book. Moreover, I am equally grateful to Martha Leeds-Bey (Polly) Jacques Leeds-Bey's wife for her support and sacrifice during very trying times.

I am exceptionally thankful for our own printer, Khalil Adolemiua-Bey, for all of his contributions over the years to the Moorish School, Community and related organizations.

The success of any major undertaking depends upon the diligence, hard work and commitment of many individuals. I extend our deep gratitude to Dr. Herbert Joiner-Bey, former Director of the dept education and research and special assistant to the chairman. I wish to thank other instructors, staff and original trustees/directors as follows: Isisara Adolemiua Bey (known then as Niki Jones Bey), Emim Ankh Unu-Bey (known then as Eric Agee-Bey) Bobby C. McQueen-Bey, Chefreen El Ontu-El, (known then as Anthony Leak-El) and Micha-El Oneferu-Bey, Treasurer (known then as Michael Baker-Bey). Special acknowledgement to the Most Puissant Sovereign Grand Commander, Supreme Free Masonry of the Southern and Western Hemisphere Inc., the Illustrious Bro Clifford Hazel Bey for over 30 years of continued support, assistance and unselfish referrals of those seeking Moorish light.

I would like to thank Elaine Myrick-Bey and Claud Myrick -Bey for their editorial and technical assistance.

Lastly, I would express my gratitude to Wajid Ebenufu-Bey (known then as William Wellington-Bey) and Sunni Karnatu-Bey (known then as Clifton R. Brown-Bey) for their continued support over the years in a wide range of areas.

TABLE OF CONTENTS

PREFACE

The content of this work is a compilation of research, documents, newspaper and magazine articles, excerpts from books, quotes from authors and a brief history of the incorporation of the Moorish Science Temple of America and the establishment of the Moorish School of Law and History, Inc. It was formulated and directed by the Moorish School of Law and History, Inc. #13 during the period of 1972 through 1980. During this period of time, some of the goals of the members of the Moorish School of Law and History attempted to attain are as follows:

1. To established their nationality as Moorish–American and eliminate the designations of black, colored, negro from all governmental records i.e. Motor Vehicle Administration, Bureau Vital Statistics etc.

2. To have national Recognition of Moorish-American Citizenship and all respective birthrights restored.

3. To have executive, legislative and judicial enforcement of Lincoln's Executive Will (Compensated Emancipation).

4. To exempt conscious Moorish-Americans and so-called blacks from the imposition of illegal taxation via communication with the National Director for the Internal Revenue Service, until such time as Moorish–Americans were compensated for their ancestors' period of servitude.

5. To litigate the resulting case within the U.S. 4th Circuit Court of Appeals and Supreme Court of the U.S. (See appendix for relative IRS correspondence and appellant brief).

Several letters and responses to and from state and federal agencies, US Congress as well as the Justice Department can be found in the appendix, as well as, newspaper and magazine articles relative to Moorish Americans and the so-called black, colored and negro. Listed below are several topics which will be discussed:

- How the term negro and black was placed upon the Moors and its derogatory meaning and psychological affect.
- The systematic disconnection of negroes and blacks from their Moorish culture and contributions to world civilization.
- The deliberate disconnection and disenfranchisement from the human family of nations.

- The legal definition of the negro as a chattel slave and the distinction between a person and a thing.

- The Dred Scott Decision—Chief Justice Roger B. Taney and concurrence of Justice Daniels.

- The dissenting opinion Justice Curtis.

- The Initial Emancipation Proclamation (Compensated Emancipation), September 22nd 1862

- President Lincoln's second annual address to congress December 1st 1862

- December 15th 1862 US House of Representatives (Senate concurring) passing of the policy of Compensated Emancipation

- Supplementary Emancipation Proclamation January 1st 1863 specifically Emancipating the slaves in the rebellious parts of the United States

- The 13th Amendment with 20 sections vs. the 13th Amendment with 2 sections

- The judicial nullification of civil rights cases and the 14th Amendment via the Supreme Court Decision of 1883

It is anticipated that many readers of this work may not be familiar with the Moorish Science Temple of America, the Moorish School of Law and History or the Moorish American Movement. Suffice to say, there are several books in print about the Moorish Science Temple of America (MST of A) and its founder The Honorable Prophet Noble Drew Ali. Some of the books were written by members of the organization and some were not. Depending on the source, some of the information is factual and some is legendary.

It is not the intention of the author of this work to present a comprehensive history of the Moorish Movement. However, a very brief history of the establishment of the MST of A is necessary in order order for the readers to gain an understanding and appreciation of the creation of the Moorish School of Law and History and its contributions not only to the Moorish Movement, but to persons of African descent namely negroes and blacks. Trying to educate people, who have **customarily** accepted the terms **Negro and black** as their **national identity,** to value the importance of reconnecting with its glorious past, both historically and geographically is a very challenging task.

CHAPTER 1

This book is, in a primary sense, formatted for all Moorish Americans. Moorish Americans are persons who are born in this country and are descendants of ancient Moroccans who have been improperly labeled as Negro, colored or black and have publicly proclaimed their nationality as Moorish Americans. However, in a broader sense, this work is a must read for **all persons of African descent** since our collective ancestors were **Moors.**

Moors were held as slaves in the western hemisphere under the terms and designations of Negro, black and colored. I intend to demonstrate that the terms Negro, black and colored are incorrect, inappropriate and misleading. Most African American scholars and historians have some knowledge of the Moors who invaded Spain in the year 711 AD, but for some reason, are unable to link these Moors to the (derogatory) terms of negro and black and understand the importance of its relevance as it appears in today's society.

Many African American scholars have also failed to research who the Moors really were and still are. These scholars and historians erroneously think that the Moors were all Arabs. However, Dr. Martha Cobb, Howard University writes otherwise. (biography in appendix) She states, in her article, *An Inquiry Into Race Concerns in Spanish Literature,* (Black World Journal) (see figures 1.1-1.5).

> "Some modern writers like to call The Moorish Invaders Arabs, but the term is wrong... others from the Zenaga Berbers who gave their name to Senegal, and a mixture of many more, most of whom were so dark that they were called **blackamoors by the Europeans.**"

Incidentally, you can find the word blackamoor in old dictionaries, but the question is why has this link been deliberately omitted in newer dictionaries? For instance, *Webster's Collegiate Dictionary, Fifth Edition* (G&C Merriam Co 1942) defines blackamoor as follows: n. a black; esp., an African black. If we look for the same definition, from Webster, twelve years later, we will find the following:

n. a Negro . Look at the next paragraph from *Wikipedia*- encyclopedia-internet.

> "According to the older versions of the Oxford English Dictionary, the Moors, during the Middle Ages and as late as the 17th Century, were described as being black, dark skinned, or swarthy in complexion. Modern text, such as Webster's New World Dictionary, groups all Moors together under the terms Arab and Berber which has caused individuals to **omit** the association with Africans that are racially considered black... Historically, European scholars have divided the Moors into two groups: African and European-Arab Moors. Arabs invaded North Africa during 640 and are nomads of Arab-Berber origin. This represented the smallest group within the Moorish population. Moors were all one class and culture...Although the darker skinned African Moors made up the majority of this group, race and ethnic division did not exist amongst Moors and there was no distinction in regards to race- Stanley Lane Poole."

Afro-Arabs
Blackamoors
and Blacks

AN INQUIRY INTO RACE CONCEPT
THROUGH SPANISH LITERATURE

BY MARTHA COBB

FOR a long time history and literature, dominated by the orientation and attitudes of European scholarship, have conspired to hide the impact that Africa once had on the development of culture and civilization. To deny this past is to ignore a significant part of both African and European history, to be unaware of the constantly changing human relationships of the past that have evolved into attitudes and concepts about Black people in the modern world.

From ancient times Spain served as a bridge between Europe and an Eastern world whose cultural crossroads was Africa. Situated the extreme southeast of the European continent, the Iberian penin-sula very nearly touches Africa in the Straits of Gibraltar. Bearing out this reality, we can still see in the Alpera Caves in the southeast of Spain a treasury of stylized drawings of African origin that represent men and women and animals. These sophisticated drawings of figures in movement are focused on the central themes of hunting and the dance. On the other hand, in the Altamira Caves in the north of Spain are found the simpler drawings of animals on the walls that are European in origin. It is interesting to note that scholars now admit that it is the representations of African origin on the walls of the southeastern Alpera Caves which are the first cultural document of European life rather than those that lack human figures found in the northern Altamira Caves.

Successive waves of human beings entered Spain, but the indigenous population was composed of the Iberians, a dark people, considered to be of African origin, a fact that the Caves of Alpera sustain. The people who are the concern of this study, however, were the Moors, who came into Spain in 711 A.D., defeating the Visigoths and initiating a struggle between Christianity and Islam that lasted until 1492 with the triumph of the Catholic monarchs, Ferdinand and Isabella. During this time, a second Moorish invasion, under the African general Yusuf in the 11th century, extended Moslem rule for approximately 100 years from the Senegal River in West Africa to the Ebro River in northern Spain.

Some modern writers like to call the Moorish invaders Arabs, but this term is wrong. What actually happened, as the writings of the time can testify, is that a minority of Arabs (themselves an interracial group) left their homeland to push the Moslem religion westward and to gain new lands. They converted the people in their path to Islam—the Mohammedan religion. Their converts were Africans: East and North Africans, Egyptians, men from the Sudan—the "land of the Blacks," others from the Zenaga Berbers who gave their name to Senegal, and a mixture of many more, most of whom were so dark they were called blackamoors by Europeans.

During the Moorish domination, Spaniards themselves used the term *Moors*, which indicates more accurately that the invaders crossed into Spain from the continent of Africa and that it was Mohammedan Africans rather than Arabs who defeated Spain. Yusuf's warriors, who were drawn from both West and North Africa, were called Almoravids, which may give a linguistic clue to the origin of the term Moor. As we shall see, literature expresses the profound influence of these historical facts on Spanish culture, and as a result, through Spain, on the culture of other parts of the European continent.

We must bear in mind that during this epoch of Islamic invasions and Moorish power in Spain, Black civilizations, flourished in West

Martha Kendrick Cobb, who contributed "Afro-Arabs, Blackamoors, and Blacks: An Inquiry into Concepts Through Spanish Literature," completed her undergraduate work and M.A. in Romance Languages at Howard University. She studied abroad—in France, Mexico, Spain, Puerto Rico, the Caribbean, and Africa—researching African themes in Hispanic literature, a topic about which she has also written and lectured. At Howard in early 1971, Mrs. Cobb inaugurated, and is presently teaching in, a program leading to post-graduate degrees in the field of Afro-Spanish literature and culture.

Figure 1.1

2

Africa and extended their influence northward. The empires of Ghana, Mali, and Songhay advanced to successive heights of civilization in Africa during the "dark" ages of medieval Europe. Between the Africans of these empires and the Islamic Arabs there flourished a commercial, religious and cultural interchange which included matrimony between Arab and African and the development of education in African universities, such as that of Timbuctu, which attracted scholars from all parts of the Moslem world.

Thus, the Moslems who dominated Spain were not a homogenous people. On the contrary, to the Arabs were united the African peoples—on an equal basis if they converted to Islam, otherwise enslaved if they were conquered, as many white Europeans were enslaved during the same epoch for the same reasons. Modern studies as expressed in many American textbooks have eliminated references to Africans, using the word Arab as if Arabs were a pure (unmixed) race, or perhaps a white race. In neither case is this true.

One of the most distinguished Afro-Arabs, honored and well-known in the Eastern world, was Antar. His full name was Antar Ibn Shaddad al 'Absi, and he lived before the Islamic era and the invasion of Spain. The son of a Black woman from the African continent and a Berber Arab, Antar was renowned as warrior, poet, and the ideal representative of a chivalric

code which, according to the legends that followed his death, he formulated. His *Mo'allaqua*, or "Praise Song," which hung in the Mosque at Mecca, is considered a masterpiece: one of the seven golden odes of the Arab world. Typical of the poetry of those feudal times, Antar wrote about the glory of his conquests in war and love, as the following lines illustrate:

> Before the spearmen's deadly thrust she tried to rouse my fears,
> As if I were defenceless and unarmed against their spears.
> I answered her, "Now surely death is no more than a pool,
> And some day I must drain the cup dipped in its waters cool.
> So fare thee well, care for thy young, and tell thyself once more
> That I'm a man who's either making love or making war.
> Privation many nights and days I easily can bear,
> Knowing that in the end I'll gain of noble food my share."

It is also interesting to discover that Antar took pride in his Black pigmentation. Thus:

> In blackness there is great virtue, if you will but observe its beauty . . .
> Black ambergris has the purest fragrance . . .

After his death in 615 A.D., the tradition of Antar spread because of the honor accorded his celebrated career and writings, perpetuated in song and story through

the efforts of a group of story tellers and poets, his disciples, who called themselves Antaristas. In the course of time, Antar legend and poetry flourished in the Eastern world, similar in manner to the tales of chivalry that took root at a later time in Spain and France, or the King Arthur legends in England. It was this Antarista tradition that entered the Iberian peninsula with the Moorish invasion, to form the base of many European romances of chivalry and later to influence the development of the codes of chivalry of the European medieval period. According to one scholar, "the Antarah was the most important of the oriental originals on which some of our own Christian romances of the Middle Ages were founded."[1] Joseph Freiherr von Hammer-Purgstall writes: "This is the work, and not, as is generally supposed, the *Thousand and One Nights*, which is the source of the stories which fill the tents and cottages in Arabia and Egypt."[2] In this same context he adds that ". . . the very spirit and substance of chivalry migrated with the Arabians from the East, through Spain to Europe."[3]

A contemporary Spanish scholar and critic notes in his book on Arab literature that the Antar tra-

dition has a parallel in the cycle of stories based on the French hero Roland, and that this needs to be investigated further to verify the former's influence on the later epic poem, *Song of Roland*.[4]

Following Antar, Islamic Arabs who were recognized as Black men were to contribute, through Spain, to medieval scholarship and literature which Europeans would utilize later. For example, there were Abu Dulama Ibn Al Djaun, poet in the court at Baghdad in the 8th century, and Ziriab (Zirvab), better known to his contemporaries as the "Black Nightingale," who arrived in Spain in 822 where he resided at the court in Cordoba. Others were Ibn Darray, poet; Abu Bakr, warrior and poet; Ben Said Al-Magribi, geographer, traveler, scholar, poet, a writer of note. Serious inquiry into the lives and works of any of these men suggests the possibility of significant contributions that can be made in the scholarly field.

A historical figure who further indicates the confluence of the Arab, African and Spanish worlds in the early Middle Ages was Tariq. He was an African warrior converted to Islam when the Arabs moved across North Africa, and was made a general to support Arab troops with his African army. When Tariq discovered the possibilities of invasion, he crossed over into Spain twice in 711, the second time in command of an army of

1) Janheinz Jahn, *Neo-African Literature, A History of Black Writing*, tr. from German, Grove Press, N.Y., 1968. (Quotation from Wilfred Scawn Blunt, British orientalist)
2) *Ibid.*, quotation from Hammar-Purgstall, p. 29.
3) *Ibid.*, p. 29

4) Juan Vernet, *Literatura Arabe*, Editorial Labor, S.A., Barcelona, 2nd ed., 1968.

Figure 1.2

3

7,000 Africans that defeated the Gothic king of Spain, Rodrigo. He was later joined by Musa ben Nusayr, leading Arab troops to reinforce that victory. Together they pushed further into Spain, but the initial conquest belongs to Tariq and his Africans. Mons Calpe, where Tariq had built an encampment and left a garrison to secure his communication with Africa, was renamed Gebel Tariq by his troops in his honor, a name which meant Hill of Tariq. It was this name, Gebel Tariq, which later was transformed by the Spanish into Gibraltar.

On the European continent, literature, folklore, and fine arts bear out the historical reality. The Spanish language also reflects a cultural amalgam that existed nearly 800 years. Semanticists might take note that the word for *blackberry* still in use in present-day Spain is *mora*, feminine noun whose original meaning is Moorish woman, and that the adjective for *dark-complexioned*, later evolving into the meaning of brunette, is *moreno* (that is, Moorish).*

At this point a basic division in concepts with reference to Africa and Africans must be indicated. On the one hand, both in antiquity and especially during the Middle Ages, the image of Africa and Africans was generally characterized by respect, largely dependent on the fortunes of war. In Spanish literature the African in the person of the Moor is usually of the ruling or upper classes. He is frequently characterized as a wealthy person, or a learned person to whom Spaniards often went for counsel. Often he is pictured as greedy for wealth and power, but in any case to be respected and more than likely admired even when he was the enemy. On the other hand, the 16th century marked a turning point. The Moors were expelled from Spain after 1492. Christianity triumphed in Europe at last. Moors, folding back on African soil after their defeat and rout from Spain, were a major factor in the sacking and break-down of West African empires and civilization. For Europe the way was open for the age of discovery and exploration, initiated by Spain and Portugal, that was to result in the colonization and enslavement of Africa and the opening up of the Americas. As a result, Africans (and those of African descent) came more and more to be depicted as

primitives, as savages, as slaves. African humanity was denied. In Western thought and literature, Africa became a caricature for barbarism and backwardness, incapable of contributing to the ongoing evolution of world civilizations.

Stemming from these two concepts, and using the 16th century as the dividing line, the significance of Africa in Hispanic culture becomes evident, serving to clear away the old myths, stereotypes, and misinformation that have pursued Black men into the 1900's.

Literature and the arts in Spain, as well as other European countries prior to the 16th century, substantiate the view of Africans in elevated positions and Africa as a land that evoked both respect and curiosity. Statues of Black kings and the painting of Black Madonnas can still be seen in European churches. The Moor, noble and authoritative figure, has literary counterparts of which Shakespeare's Othello and the Moors of *Titus Andronicus* are major examples. References to Ethiopians and their land as the land of the Blacks and symbol of learning and wealth, the legend and search for Prester John —mythical figure whom medieval Europe, fighting Islam, idealized as the image of Black Christianity in Africa—the symbol of Black Saint Maurice in Germany, are as indicative of the African image in Western consciousness at one point in history as the slave, flooding the markets of Seville and Lisbon, was to become during the 1500's.

A primary source for Spanish writers on Moorish themes is the work entitled, *Guerras Civiles de Granada*, by Ginés Pérez de Hita. It describes the frontier wars between Moor and Christian that took place on Spanish soil. Dramatists and poets used this book as a source for the colorful Moorish romances and "frontier" stories that became popular in the 16th and 17th centuries as Spain looked back to her past. One chapter tells of the exploits of a Black named Captain Farax whose furious fighting gave him the reputation of being a hero in the region around Lorca. When at last forced to retreat, he burned the fields around him and in other ways attacked Christians, who fell in great numbers or who were made slaves. In retaliation, the Christians tried to burn him alive, but according to the accounts, Black Captain Farax escaped and is said to have fled to Africa and planned other assaults from there. A 16th century playwright, Diego Jiménez de Encisco, in one of his plays, modeled a character whom he called Cañeri on this personality, the Black warrior Farax. Other Spanish writers, especially those of the 16th and 17th centuries, were to use similar episodes for the elaboration of the popular Moorish romances of the era.

Margaret Sampson, in her studies on *El Caballero Cifar* notes

---

* During my own studies in Madrid, Spain, in the summer of 1970, I was often pointed out on the streets and in the parks as "la mora" or sometimes "la morena." There was no derogatory intent evident, simply that "the Moor" or "Moorish" took precedence over the use of the word "negro" (feminine "negra"); Spanish adjective meaning black.

5) Margaret Sampson, "Africa in Medieval Spanish Literature: Its Appearance in El Caballero Cifar," *Negro History Bulletin*, Dec. 1969.

Figure 1.3

that in this prose romance of chivalry dating back to the 13th century Africa is often referred to either geographically or mythically. In addition, the work includes didactic tales and adventure stories which confirm the authoritative position of the Moor in the society of the time.

Much the same can be said for the 14th century tales written by Don Juan Manuel in his masterpiece, the *Libro de Conde Lucanor*. The author utilizes the framework of a storyteller—in this case a counselor named Patronio—who tells moral tales, usually with Moorish protagonists, to illustrate solutions to problems that his master, the Count Lucanor, presents to him. The stories spin on, many of them having their base in tales brought into Spain with the Moorish invasion.

Advancing to the 16th century, a different kind of Black personality marks Spanish literature. Moorish leaders and warriors had been routed and expelled. Those who were left were of a lower class and called "Moriscos" rather than "Moros." They were poor agricultural laborers needed to work in the fields of Andalusia; they were often peddlers and vagrants who lived by their wits. A triumphant Spanish nobility learned to look down on this dark-skinned people. Furthermore, slaves from Africa were being imported into Spain in increasing numbers. Cities like Seville and Granada now became accustomed to associating Blackness with the inferior slave.

Juan Latino stands out as an unusual representative of this new kind of Black. In 1528 he was brought from Africa (possibly Guinea) to Spain as a slave. Growing up in slavery, he adopted Christianity and learned Latin and Greek from the books of his master's son, eventually becoming the boy's tutor. He graduated from the University of Granada with honors in 1557 and was appointed a professor in the same university. He was so outstanding in Latin that he renounced his slave name to call himself Juan Latino. He was received with acclamation and great respect by the Spanish people throughout a long life that spanned Spain's Golden Age. Both Cervantes and Lope de Vega referred to him or used incidents from his life in their works.

For the most part Juan Latino expressed in his written works a personality that was essentially Spanish in nature. He wrote like a white Spaniard with no central theme that concerned itself with his African origins nor with the conditions of slavery that he not only must have witnessed but must himself have been subjected to. His marriage to a white Spanish woman, noted and referred to by writers of his time, served to enhance his position. His major literary work was the *Austrias*, whose verses are erudite in language and academic in style, revealing a patriotic commitment to Spain. Written in Latin, this work by the ex-slave Juan Latino celebrates the Spanish victory at the Battle of Lepanto.

The success of Juan Latino was achieved despite the fact that he was African. The price exacted was that he convert to Christianity, cut loose from his African origins, and adopt the Spanish way of life. By Spanish standards, therefore, he was judged a worthy individual. Thus the balance had tipped against Africa and in favor of Europe. The erudite Ethiopians, fierce Moorish warriors, Black kings, knights and saints, the mysterious Prester John—all who had set standards of culture and chivalry on their own terms—were disappearing from Western consciousness. Juan Latino was himself symbolic of the new age: he was brought into Spain as a slave and he learned to read and master the Latin language through the indulgence of his owners.

For a while the Moor was to linger on in Spanish literature through the popular Moorish romances of the 16th and 17th centuries that were the themes of such poets and dramatists as Lope de Vega, Louis de Góngora, Francisco de Quevedo, Lope de Rueda and others. Their writing, as in the case of Quevedo, often expressed a duality in concept. His "Boda de Negros," for example, exaggerates and burlesques the Blackness of a wedding party, the gestures and manners of the participants, to the point of making fun of them, ridiculing their Blackness. On the other hand, in his "La Hora de Todos," he expresses compassion for Black slaves in their unfortunate condition. Góngora also demonstrates a dual point of view: he uses the speech patterns and jargon of 16th century Blacks in creating images of their lower-class lifestyle in some of his poetry; in other poetry he goes back to the traditions of medieval Spain in retelling stories of interracial romance between African and Spaniard and recreating the splendor of the chivalric code upheld by noble Moor and noble Christian alike.

However, the effect of the Renaissance and the age of discovery and exploration in Europe were irreversible in literature. A new era opened up after 1492 in which men of African origin suffered the final collapse of their culture and the indignities of chattel enslavement which stripped them of their rights as human beings. The African of the medieval world was rejected for a different image that must satisfy the economic needs that the new age demanded. Literature would do no less than reflect these changes.

The African—whether called Moor, Ethiopian or Black—gradually disappeared from Spanish peninsular culture. Neither art nor literature took serious note of him. Royalty occasionally made him

Figure 1.4

5

a court pet. Slaves were sometimes elevated to positions of trust in Spanish households or artists' workshops. Even more significantly in terms of New World history, they often served as right-hand men, guides, and explorers to Spanish conquerors as they advanced through forest, jungle, and Indian territory in both South and North America. Estevanico is just one example of this breed of slave upon whom Spaniards in America depended. Sometimes references were made to the Moorish past, but more often 16th and 17th century literature portrayed its Black element as buffoons or rascals. Spain was too occupied with setting up a slave trade for pumping wealth out of her colonies to perceive the African as anything more than a sub-human species to be exploited.

To continue to trace the literary presence of Africa in Hispanic cul-ture, interested scholars must proceed to the Americas. Spanish American culture reveals that the African way of life found expression in folklore, in the syncretism of African religious practices with the Catholic Church, in music and dance, and in language, all of which were to flower ultimately in the expressive Black poetry of the Caribbean, in the early 1920's. An examination of this culture must be the subject of another paper.

Meanwhile, a study of the concepts that mark the distance traveled from medieval Blackamoor to present-day Blacks offers a valuable tool in understanding and defining the African heritage of African peoples in the 20th century, wherever they are located. The dimensions of research in this field should open up to scholars and educators channels for more study and dissemination of knowledge.

Martha Kendrick Cobb, who contributed "Afro-Arabs, Blackamoors, and Blacks: An Inquiry into Concepts Through Spanish Literature," completed her undergraduate work and M.A. in Romance Languages at Howard University. She studied abroad—in France, Mexico, Spain, Puerto Rico, the Caribbean, and Africa—researching African themes in Hispanic literature, a topic about which she has also written and lectured. At Howard in early 1971, Mrs. Cobb inaugurated, and is presently teaching in, a program leading to post-graduate degrees in the field of Afro-Spanish literature and culture.

Figure 1.5

6

Let us pause for a moment and examine and research the meaning and origin of the word negro. Research will reveal that **negro means black in both Spanish and Portuguese languages, being derived from the Latin word niger of the same meaning**.

Charles Codman Hurd states in his book, *Law of Freedom and Bondage,* (See figures 1.6-1.7)

" ...and probably many Africans of the **negro** race were held as slaves in Europe **under the name of Moors** and their slavery ascribed to the same international usage"

As you will notice, Hurd elaborates on the term negro and the legal nature of the condition as defined by the Law of Nations. Ironically, the aforementioned book by Hurd though originally published in 1858 was reprinted by the Negro Universities Press in 1968, approximately 110 years later.

Another historian, George Bancroft writes in his book *History of the United States* the following two excerpts:

1." the first ships which sailed so far south as Cape Blanco, returned, not with negroes, but with **Moors**. The subjects of this importation were treated, not as laborers, but rather as strangers, from whom information respecting their native country was to be derived. Antony Gonzales, who had brought them to Portugal, was commanded to restore them to their ancient homes. He did so and the Moors gave him as their ransom, not gold only, but **"black Moors"** with curled hair. **Thus negro** slaves came into Europe; and mercantile cupidity immediately observed that negroes might become an object of lucrative commerce."

In the above excerpt observe the transition from Moor to black Moors and then the sentence beginning with the, word **"Thus"**. Take a look at the excerpt below.

2. " The final victory of the Spaniards over the Moors of Granada---an event contemporary with the discovery of America---was signalized by a great migration of the Moors to the coast of Northern Africa, where each mercantile city became a nest of pirates, and every Christian the wonted booty of corsair. Servitude was thus the doom of the Christian in North Africa: the hatred of Moorish dominion extending to all of Africa, an indiscriminate and **retaliating bigotry felt no remorse** at dooming the sons of Africa to bondage. **All Africans were esteemed as Moors ...The sins of the Moors to be ravished on the negroes."**

It seems being classified as a negro was the beginning of the retaliating bigotry Bancroft is describing. We went from being **Africans** to esteemed **Moors** to **negroes** in less than one sentence, or rather, the stroke of a pen.

Moors—the Arabian inhabitants of Africa, were still held as slaves by captivity, in Spain, France, and Italy; and probably many Africans of negro race were held as slaves in Europe under the name of Moors,[1] and their slavery ascribed to the same international usage. Domestic slavery, as part of the system of civil society, still remained, as at the present day, among Mohammedan nations, and the negro tribes of Africa; in which country it is believed to have been for many centuries the condition of a vast majority of the inhabitants.[2] It is probable that long after the ancient chattel slavery of Europe had been replaced by the serfdom of the Middle Ages, negroes had occasionally been brought as articles of commerce to Europe, and retained there as domestic slaves.[3] But it was not until the geographical discoveries of the Portuguese in the fifteenth century, that African slaves, in any considerable number, were made an article of commerce in Europe. The first recorded instance of the importation of African slaves by the Portuguese from the western coast of Africa, illustrates the principles of the *law of nations* exhibited at that time in the international intercourse of Christian nations with Mohammedans, Moors, and heathen negroes of Africa. In the year 1440, Antonio Gonsalez, sent out by Prince Henry of Portugal on a voyage of discovery, attacked a party of wandering Arabs or Moors, and carried off ten or twelve of them captives to Portugal, where, and in the Spanish portion of the peninsula, thousands of the subjects of the extinct Moorish kingdom in Spain were already enduring slavery, as the consequence of their defeat by the Christian princes. Three of these captive Moors, at the command of Prince Henry, and on their promise to pay ransom, were sent back with Gonsalez, on his second voyage to the African coast in 1442; and he received from their kinsmen, in exchange for his prisoners, a ransom consisting of gold dust and ten or twelve negro slaves, as ordinary articles of merchandise.[4] A similar

[1] Hüne, vol. I., pp. 128, 130, 211.
[2] Hüne, vol. I., pp. 148—175.
[3] Bancroft, vol. I., p. 165. Hüne, I., 150—163. Citing Edrisius and Leo Africanus, that accounts of a regular trade in negro slaves exist from about the year 990. Raynal's W. I., tom. 4, p. 43.
[4] Hüne, vol. I., p. 181. 1 Banc., 166, cites Navarete, Introduccion S. XIX., (see 2 Presc. Ferd. and Is., 114,) that Spain anticipated Portugal in introducing negroes

Figure 1.6

transaction became one of the objects of succeeding voyages. Moors and negroes were carried away, by force, by the Portuguese adventurers, until, after the exploration of the coast had been pushed as far south as the richer and more populous shores of the Gulf of Guinea, it was found safer and more profitable to procure only negroes, by purchase from the native slave merchants.

§ 166. This traffic, in negroes as merchandise, was at this time recognized as legitimate by European governments, without any direct sanction from positive legislation, but rested on the general custom among nations, known both in municipal and international private law,—that custom which, under the name of "the custom of merchants,"—meaning merchants without regard to nationality, was recognized in the English courts as a rule of law. Property in heathen negroes bought in Africa, being then regarded as the effect of *natural law*, so far as it is known in jurisprudence, or as an illustration of the distinction between persons and things, entering into all law, because founded in natural reason. The trade in that property was regarded as founded on existing relations between legal persons in respect to things, which might, like any other branch of commerce, be *regulated* by statute, without a previous act declaring the condition of the negroes who were the objects of those relations and of that commerce. Like many other branches of commerce at that period, it was an object of monopoly; being sometimes granted by the patent of the monarch to companies of discoverers, commercial adventurers, and colonists trading in and between those regions then recently made known, and popularly designated the Eastern and Western Indies. The conversion of infidels being always proposed as a prominent object, and declared to be the justifying motive for the forcible enslavement of barbarians and heathens, whenever contemplated in such enterprises;[1] if not also for the acquisition of purchased slaves. On the discovery of America, the same reasons which upheld the slavery of African Moors and negroes were held to

into Europe. That Sevillian merchants imported slaves from Western Africa,—Irving's Columbus, vol. II., p. 351.

[1] 1 Hüne, p. 304, cites Benezet, p. 58.

Figure 1.7

9

We will also discuss the relevance of the word negro in the Dred Scott decision, as well as the Fourteenth Amendment and 1883 Supreme Court judicial nullification of the Fourteenth Amendment later.

A great deal of the above information was quoted by these three highly credible authors. Two of whom published their books in1858 and 1859 respectively. The intent here is to demonstrate that the word negro has no **geographic, cultural, ethnic, ancestral meaning associated** with it. However, the term negro did have a beneficial meaning for persons employing the term to rob the Moors of all ties to geographical, cultural, ethnical and ancestral knowledge of self.

The extent of the term negroes in statues, are spoken of are as objects of commercial trade in the Law of Nations, long before being introduced in the American Colonies. The term only began to be capitalized, that is, used as a proper noun, in books in the late 1800s. On the other hand, Europeans recognize Moors and acknowledge their contribution to the civilization of Europe during its dark ages. Moors ruled an Empire, they represented sovereignty and royalty.

As we have seen, the word Moor takes precedent over the word negro. There are numerous derivatives of the word Moor in several different languages that trace back to ancient Kemit (Egypt). Moreover, the Moors are not extinct. The Moors in America who have not proclaimed and declared their Moorish nationality **still exist, but are historically still under the old umbrella of the terms negro, black and colored introduced in Jamestown Virginia as chattel slaves**. Professor Booker T. Coleman said at one of his lectures in New York that a person can not begin to study history correctly until he or she studies the history of the Moors.

We must also bear in mind that since negro is synonymous with **black**, that **black** in all dictionaries have most derogatory meanings i.e., **evil, wicked, gloomy, dismal, depressing, absence of light, incurring censure or dishonor, having no predominate hue, etc., thus the adjective black is an equally inappropriate name for persons of African ancestry as well application of the term to their rich history and culture.**

To further illustrate the above, I refer to a book written by Richard B. Moore entitled *The Name "Negro" Its Origin and Evil Use*, (Black Classic Press 1992) first privately published in1960. The following are quotes from the introduction by the editors of the recent publication:

> "Although the elimination of the term "negro" has been largely accomplished, the wide substitution of "black" failed to bring recognition of the connection of the Afro-American with an honorable land, history and culture...Millions of Afro- American children ranging in complexion of very dark to very light have been left in a state of confusion as to why they are referred to as "black" when their eyes tell them otherwise. It is obvious that there is no single color designation that could adequately serve to describe the

beautiful array of complexions in the Afro-American community...Our children need to be assured of their long historical and Cultural heritage as reflected in the collective identification used by society...The editors of this volume hope that the reissuance of this book will help to advance the day when our nation will move beyond the stage of naming people by any color and give proper recognition to historical, geographic and cultural heritage."

In an attempt to grasp a sense of new racial pride, particularly in the 1960's after Dr. Martin Luther King's assassination, James Brown introduced the phrase "I'm black and I'm Proud", and a heighten level of awareness; and what was termed **blackness** in the African American Community sprung forth. Many so-called black leaders and educators were trying to give new meaning and definition to the word black **without changing its definition in the dictionary.** This presented a real dilemma because most persons of African decent born in this country knew of no other way to link themselves back to their African heritage other then to accept this derogatory word **black** and impose an imaginary and fictitious definition to it. This was due to the lack of knowledge and thorough study of Moorish History prior to the year 1619, and chronologically back to 711 AD. Over time, by not understanding that they were, in fact, still Moors; the so-called African American educators and historians allowed the derogatory terms of negro, colored and black to take precedence over the term Moor.

Moorish Americans who are conscious of their African culture and heritage are not ostracizing African heritage or those who now, through lack of understanding, define themselves as black. The proclamation of Moorish decent links them to the Human family of nations (which will be explained later).

All persons of African decent, especially those who have not yet realized the importance of proclaiming their Moorish culture and heritage, should spend some time **researching the word black.** The question should also be asked: "why has it been embraced as identification of who they are as a people?" Europeans, whom have long ago selected the word White to identify their race, did so without assassinating the character of their people as a whole. For example, white, means among other things- **pure, perfect, without sin, or in other words God.** Europeans have never experienced the feeling of being labeled inferior by definition. To the contrary, because of the definition of white- meaning pure, perfect etc, they have always whether conscious or subconsciously felt superior. However, both the terms black and white are adjectives and can only be used to describe people not identify them.

Africans should not be described or categorized as **black for their race identity** and **Europeans should not be categorized as white** for their **race** as well. Just look at the psychological effect that the above definitions impose on civilized people whether consciously or subconsciously. Still persons of African decent continue to **perpetuate** the word black similar to a runaway train, like the ones in the **media** who use the word black and African American **interchangeably**, as if they are afraid to let the word go.

When describing certain world events, media in the western hemisphere often refers to people in various countries as "black". Here is an example, some people have made statements like—"blacks in Brazil, blacks in Puerto Rico, blacks in Venezuela, blacks in Morocco." Whether we like or not the peoples spoken about are all of one family bearing one free national name, whether they are Brazilians, Venezuelans, Puerto Ricans or Moroccans, all of them are spawned by the ancient Moors. There is a global assault of Moors being perpetrated by the most influential and wealthiest country on the planet. Yet, because the weapon used is vocabulary, it goes unchecked and remains lethal.

All members of the human family are represented in the United Nations. But there are no descendants of **blacks or negroes represented by any specific country from Africa or the United States of America in the United Nations**. There are many modern African countries registered in the United Nations and they all have flags representing their respective countries. However, the Moors in America are linked with Morocco, specifically with Ancient Morocco.

Another alarming fact is that a majority of African American scholars and educators are teaching the so-called black history began with the alleged importation of slaves in 1619 (some say 1620) when 20 negroes landed in Jamestown, Virginia whom had been purchased or caught in Africa. It is possible this is due to our scholars only associating "black" with America. Therefore, it is impossible to discuss "black" history prior to 1619 since "black" had not existed. If it were attempted, wouldn't they be discussing African history?

Before going any further, research has confirmed that the name of the continent Africa came from the Roman Military General Scipio Africanus. Africa has more ancient names such as Amexem, Kemet and Eurasia. Nevertheless, as to the twenty negroes, the question would be: "where were they bought or caught and who was the seller"? If this transaction actually occurred-- where is the parchment, documentation, bill of sale or ship manifest? Yet because of this so-called event, negro history, as it has been taught for many years, began in America.

A quick glimpse or bird's eye view of so-called black history in America speaks very little about the revolutionary period with the exception of Christopher Attucks. It jumps into the 1800's and highlights Nat Turner, Dred Scott (whom will definitely be discussed a little later on), Sojourner Truth, Frederick Douglas and the list goes on. These were all great men and women who contributed to the physical freedom of the slaves and this author thanks the Supreme Creator for their existence because without them, had the south had won the civil war, this writing may not have been possible. Unconscious Moors should be taught about slavery and their heroes but it should be taught in its proper context and perspective. It is criminal to rob a nation of people from its glorious culture, heritage and its past contributions to world civilization by systematically **disconnecting** them from the **human** family of nations.

By teaching young boys and girls that their history in this country began with their forefathers and mothers held as chattel slaves (property not a human being), not even as an indentured servant automatically induces a subconscious or psychological sense of inferiority at an early age whether we admit it or not. But what if you taught young children that they were always Moors before they were slaves in this hemisphere? In fact, many Moors were already here, a subject for later discussion. What if you also taught them that their Moorish ancestors ruled Spain for over **500** years and gave civilization to the world at a time when most of Europe was in darkness? What if they were taught that over 3 million Moors left Spain in 1492 and went back to Morocco the same year that Columbus supposedly discovered America? (An extension of the old Moorish/Moroccan Empire) You could also teach the youngsters that it was a Moorish navigator whom showed Christopher Columbus how to get here as well as making them aware of the old water route and under water current extending eastward from the Nile river, westward across the great Atlantic Ocean into North south and central America.

Youngsters should be taught that their forefathers **were present** and **represented** at the signing of the Declaration of Independence. They were also at the constitutional convention of 1787, which brought the Constitution into existence. This was acknowledged by **Justice Curtis** in his **dissenting opinion** in the Dred Scott case. Judge Curtis let it be known that free native-born inhabitants (Moors), whose ancestors descended from African slaves, were citizens of at least five states (which he named). These native-born inhabitants (Moors) were citizens of the United States under the confederation and, consequently, citizens at the time of the adoption of the constitution of the United States of America.

While we are discussing this time period, schools should be teaching and stressing the importance of President George Washington signing a treaty of friendship with the Sultan of Morocco in 1787, making Morocco the first African nation to sign a treaty with the newly formed Republic. Morocco was controlling the Atlantic Ocean at that time.

CHAPTER 2

In Dred Scott v. Sandford [60 U.S. (19 How.) 393, 15 L.Ed. 691] decision in 1857, the United States Supreme Court ruled that descendents of Africans who were negroes of the African race, who were imported into the United States and sold as slaves were not included nor intended to be included under the word "citizen" in the constitution, whether emancipated or not, and remained without rights or privileges except such as those which the government might grant them. In layman's terms, this means the descendents of Africans were deemed to be chattel property.

Now let us briefly examine a few excerpts from Chief Justice Roger B. Taney in the Dred Scott decision and an excerpt from Justice Daniels in his concurring opinion. The following is Chief Justice Taney:

" The question is simply this: Can a **negro**, whose ancestors were imported into this country and sold as slaves, become a member of the political community formed and brought into existence by the Constitution of the United States, and as such become entitled to rights, and privileges, and immunities guarantied by that instrument to the citizen? ...It will be observed, that the plea applies to that **class of persons only** whose ancestors **were negroes of the African race**." Further along Justice Taney said that these classes of persons were not "constituent members of this sovereignty" and that "they are not included, and were not intended to be included in the word **citizens** in the constitution".

He then went on to say, "On the contrary, they were, at that time, considered as a subordinate and inferior class of beings".

Notice in Judge Taney's statement above he articulates that the argument applies to that "**class of persons only** whose ancestors were **negroes of the African race".** Also in the excerpt below by Justice Daniel who stated specifically the "African **negro race**".

Now, let us take a quick look at Justice Daniel's comments from his concurring opinion below.

" Now the following are truths which a knowledge of the history of the world and particularly of own country compels us to know---that the African **negro race** never have been **acknowledge as belonging to the family of nations;** that as amongst them there never has been known or recognized by the inhabitants of other countries any thing partaking of the **character of nationality**, civil or political polity; that this race has been by all the nations of Europe regarded as subjects of capture or purchase; as subjects of commerce or traffic; and that the introduction of that race into every section of this country was not as members of a civil or political society, but as **property in the strictest sense of the term"**

Think about it, why did **both** justices make the distinction "**negroes** of the African race" and what was its significance? Can negroes be of other races? Were other races indigenous to Africa? Were any other Africans other than the ones called negroes enslaved? What other Africans were sovereign during the late 1770's?

Before discussing the 1883 Supreme Court decision taking the pith out of the fourteenth amendment I would like to reference the book entitled *The Negro A Beast or In the Image of God*, by Charles Carroll (See figures 2.2-2.3). Carroll spent fifteen years of his life and twenty thousand dollars in its compilation. This book was entered into the Library of Congress in the year 1900. First Mnemosyne reprinting 1969, it was reprinted from a copy in the Fisk University Library Negro Collection. We will examine the following excerpt:

"As a matter of fact, the Negro was never a slave. To conceive the design of enslaving an individual we must presuppose that he is free; the first act of enslavement is to deprive him of his liberty. This the Negro never had since the creation of man. The Negro is an ape; hence his status in the universe, his relation to man, like every other animal, was fixed irrevocably by God in the creation, and no act upon man's part, whether legislative, executive or judicial can change it."

Consider for the moment how many persons of European descent or so-called white America have read this book or had it in their possession and shared it with their families and friends. Whether anyone would acknowledge it or not the lynching, murders and degradation of the negro especially in the south and the border states would clearly demonstrate the overwhelming hatred of the so-called negro. Many scholars would suggest that the so-called negro was dehumanized therefore their lives were not regarded as having value since the negro was thought of as no more than a common animal. However, we do not have any historical reference of cat and dog lynchings. Research has confirmed that most so-called negro or blacks have never read or heard of the book *The Negro a Beast*. Yet, this book was housed in Fisk University (a historically black college). Looking back to the early 1900's and beyond one can easily see that this book was designed to cause the so-called negro to feel shame, just review a few of the drawings from the book (see figure 2.1). Today, many people of both races would want to distance themselves from discussing or even reading this book. However, this book in indicative of viewpoints promoted throughout the 19th and 20th centuries. The resulting psychological effect is alive and prevalent in the current racial problems of today.

From the beginning of this book, we have witnessed the transition of the term Moor to the term negro and its definition in private international law as practiced and allowed in universal jurisprudence.

Moreover, even though it does not expressly use the word negro, the three fifths provision in Article I, Section 2 of the Constitution is another example of how the chattel definition of the negro slave was perceived at that time. Over time, the more the term negro was used, the more it was accepted, particularly by the slave holders (review figure 2.4).

Figure 2.1

"THE NEGRO A BEAST"

...OR...

"IN THE IMAGE OF GOD"

The Reasoner of the Age, the Revelator of the Century!

The Bible as it is!

The Negro and His Relation to the Human Family!

The Negro a beast, but created with articulate speech,
and hands, that he may be of service to
his master—the White man.

The Negro not the Son of Ham,

Neither can it be proven by the Bible, and the argument of the theologian who would claim such,
melts to mist before the thunderous and
convincing arguments of this
masterful book.

...BY...

CHAS. CARROLL,

Who has spent fifteen years of his life, and $20,000.00
in its compilation.

PUBLISHED BY

Reprinted by Mnemosyne Publishing Co., Inc. Miami, Florida

1900.

Figure 2.2

19

Negro, asserts that all his "old abolition sympathies which had been weakening for over ten years in view of the insufferable self-assertion of our Negroes since the day of their emancipation, had vanished like so many scattered sophistries for which he had no further use." And "that without mincing matters or any longer thinking or writing on the basis of sympathy with the Negro, he was convinced that inside the next thirty years the South would be obliged to re-enslave, kill or export the bulk of its Negro population."

Who would have dreamed that in less than thirty-five years after emancipation one of the foremost champions of Negro suffrage would denounce the Negro as "more than ever a shiftless, unteachable, immoral race, incapable of any true civilization and unworthy of American citizenship?" And would speak of "emancipation and the so-called education of the Negro" as "absurdities."

It is needless to say that we honor this fearless man, admire his candor and hold in high esteem his lofty patriotism. At the same time we must beg leave to respectfully suggest that his use of the term "re-enslave" in connection with our future relations with the Negro, indicates that he fails to grasp the situation.

As a matter of fact, the Negro was never a slave. To conceive the design of enslaving an individual we must presuppose that he is free; the first act of enslavement is to deprive him of his liberty. This the Negro never had since the creation of man. The

Figure 2.3

Negro is an ape; hence, his status in the universe, his relation to Man, like that of every other animal, was fixed irrevocably by God in the Creation, and no act upon man's part, whether legislative, executive or judicial, can change it. The will of God upon this most important subject, as expresesd in those original statutes given man in the Creation, "Have dominion over the fish of the sea, and over the fowl of the air, and over every living thing that moveth upon the earth," is the supreme law of the universe; and in the eyes of this great law there is not today, there never was and there can never be on this earth, such a thing as a free Negro. To illustrate: Suppose a man commits a felony and is arraigned, convicted and sentenced to prison for a term of years, but makes his escape, flees to some foreign country, where he lives out his days without being apprehended. Did that man in his exile live out his days and die a free man? No jurist would so decide. From the hour of his conviction that man lived and died the property of the state. So it is in this case; under the law of God the Negro, like every other animal, is the property of man, without reference to whether he is ever brought in contact with him or not. The mere fact that man in his blind, criminal folly, declines to exert that control over the Negro, in common with the rest of the animals, which God designed him to have and commanded him to exercise, does not free the Negro, it can only damn man, for his shameless contempt for

[19]

Figure 2.3 cont.

THE SUN

TODAY

TUESDAY, DECEMBER 10, 2002

TWO HUNDRED DOLLARS REWARD.—Ran away from the subscriber on Saturday, 6th inst., my Servant Man, LLOYD BOWEN, about 28 or 30 years of age. He is about 5 ft 11 inches high; stout, strong, well made; of a dark brown color; has several suits of good clothing, and makes himself quite agreeable to strangers. He has numerous acquaintances throughout Baltimore city and county, and on the Eastern Shore of this State, and may have forged a pass to enable him to get to Pennsylvania, probably by way of York or Harrisburg, towards Philadelphia. $200 will be paid for his apprehension and delivery in Baltimore jail, if taken out of this State, and $75 if taken in this State, and delivered in Baltimore jail. E. WILSON, 6 miles from Baltimore, near Washingtonville m12-14t*?

5.000 NEGROES WANTED.—I will pay the highest prices, in cash, for 5,000 NEGROES with good titles, slaves for life or for a term of years in large or small families, or single negroes. I will also purchase Negroes restricted to remain in the State that sustain good characters. Families never separated. Persons having slaves for sale will please call and see me, as I am always in the market with the cash.—Communications promptly attended to, and liberal commissions paid, by JOHN N. DENNING, No. 18 S. Frederick street, between Baltimore and Second sts., Baltimore, Md. Trees in front of the door.

CASH FOR NEGROES.—We want to purchase immediately a large number of likely YOUNG NEGROES for the New Orleans market, for which we will pay the highest cash prices. All persons having Slaves for sale will find it to their interest by calling on us at our office, No. 13 CAMDEN STREET, (formerly occupied by J. S. Donovan.) Liberal commissions paid for information. All communications promptly attended to.

J. M. WILSON,
C. H. DUKE.

Although this Ad appeared in the Baltimore Sun Paper, it resulted in research done by Ralph Clayton, author of the book "Cash for Blood".

Figure 2.4

CHAPTER 3

The information reviewed thus far should be very useful in helping the reader to gain an inside view of how the court interpreted the three war time amendments, namely the 13th, 14th and 15th amendments. These amendments were pushed through congress by the radical Republicans, in particularly, the fourteenth amendment. Each one of the war time amendments contained the unusual provision that 'congress shall have the power to enforce this article by appropriate legislation.' Congress proceeded to enact a series of ill-fated civil rights acts and laws to do just that. There was only a brief period in the early 1870's that a few civil rights acts were enacted which threw protection of the federal over the negro's right to vote.

"The withdrawal of troops (in the south) by President Hayes in 1877 marked not only the abandonment of formal reconstruction, but the abandonment of the negro as well" as stated in *The Growth of the American Republic, Fifth Ed* by Samuel Eliot Morison and Henry Steel Commager. Commager went on to point out that the court, beginning with the Slaughterhouse case of 1873, distinguishing between the privileges and immunities derived from **national and state citizenship**, asserted that all the important ones came from **state citizenship** and it was not the purpose of the fourteenth amendment to try and extend federal protection over these. (see figure 3.1-3.4) It is also stated in Commager's *Documents of American History, Volume I*, in 1883 decision of the, Civil Rights act of 1875, the opinion Supreme Court practically **put an end** to the effort of the federal to **enforce** the guaranties of the **fourteenth amendment**. (see figure 3.5-3.6)

After the Dred Scott decision, the three dead badges (13th,14th and 15th amendments, the judicial nullification of the Civil Rights act of 1875 and the 14th amendment, the negro continued to almost hopelessly attempt to pursue civil rights and citizenship under the fourteenth amendment.

Let us stop here! We will now explore the word person in one of the seven original Articles of the Constitution, namely Article I, section.2, paragraph 3 makes mention of: "three-fifths of all other persons". Obviously, all if, not, most would agree this referred to negro slaves. We also see the word person in the fourteenth amendment (any person born or naturalized).

The definition of the word "person" in law dictionaries have **several meanings**, one of which, is a human being, another is a corporation (which we will briefly touch on). A human being is a member of the human family and/or the human race. As we have previously seen in universal Jurisprudence, in Supreme Court decisions and other records etc, that negro is not **recognized as a human being or a member of the human family by any other members of the human family, but** rather a being of an inferior order or **a "thing"**.

lenge this general interpretation of the Amendments; indeed they enlarged upon it. The Fourteenth Amendment, said Justice Bradley,

was an attempt to give voice to the strong national yearning for that time and that condition of things, in which American citizenship should be a sure guaranty of safety, and in which every citizen of the United States might stand erect in every portion of its soil, in the full enjoyment of every right and privilege belonging to a freeman, without fear of violence or molestation.

The war had been fought, in part, to free the slave; the Thirteenth Amendment had been added to the Constitution to guarantee his freedom; the Fourteenth Amendment to protect him in his civil rights; the Fifteenth Amendment to assure him the vote. Each of these Amendments contained the unusual provision that ' Congress shall have power to enforce this article by appropriate legislation.' And, beginning with the ill-fated Civil Rights Act of 1866, Congress enacted a series of laws designed to do just that. The most important of these were the Enforcement Acts of 31 May 1870 and 28 February 1871 which threw the protection of the Federal Government over the Negro's right to vote; the Ku Klux Klan Act of 20 April 1871 which made it a federal offense to conspire to deprive Negroes of the equal protection of the laws; and the Civil Rights Act of 1 March 1875 which undertook to wipe out social as well as political discrimination and to secure the Negro ' full and equal enjoyment of the accommodations, advantages, facilities, and privileges of inns, public conveyances on land or water, theatres, and other places of public amusement,' as well as the right to serve on juries.

During the brief period of Radical Reconstruction the Negro did enjoy both civil and political rights. He was freed from the restrictions of the black codes; he exercised the vote; he held office. Nor did he suffer severe economic or social discrimination. Most of the jobs that he could do were freely open to him, and that large apparatus of social indignities that came later to be called ' Jim Crow ' had not yet been applied, or invented.

The withdrawal of troops by President Hayes in 1877 marked not only the abandonment of formal reconstruction, but the abandonment of the Negro as well. Congress, which had enacted three constitutional amendments and half a dozen Enforcement Acts all designed to protect the freedman, now threw in the sponge, and turned the ' Negro problem ' over to the South. That was what the South de-

Figure 3.1

24

manded as the price of reunion, and as the price would be paid by the
Negro, the North did not find it exorbitant. There were three generally recognized parts to the unwritten agreement: that the North
would hereafter keep hands off the ' Negro problem '; that the rules
governing race relations in the South would be written by the whites;
and that these rules would concede the Negro limited civil rights,
but neither political nor social equality. The principle underlying
this relationship was set forth succinctly by Henry Grady of the At-
lanta *Constitution:* ' The supremacy of the white race of the South
must be maintained forever, and the domination of the Negro race
resisted at all points and at all hazards, because the white race is
superior.' It was as simple as that.

Abandoned by the Congress and the President, the Negro was now
repudiated by the courts. If the ' one pervading purpose ' of the Civil
War Amendments was, indeed, the protection of the freedman from
oppression, then it failed. Beginning with the Slaughterhouse case of
1873 the Supreme Court proceeded systematically to riddle the
structure of Negro rights until in the end it was — in the words of
John Marshall — ' a magnificent structure to look at, but totally unfit for use.' In the Slaughterhouse case the Court, distinguishing between the privileges and immunities derived from national and from
state citizenship, asserted that all the important ones came from
state citizenship and that it was not the purpose of the Fourteenth
Amendment to try to extend federal protection over these.[5] The
Cruikshank case of 1875, which involved a mob attack on Negroes
who were trying to vote, carefully restricted the reach of the Fourteenth Amendment to state — not private — interference with Negro rights, and to such interference as was clearly directed against
Negroes on account of their race or color. ' Inasmuch,' said Chief
Justice Waite with nice irony, ' as it does not appear . . . that the
intent of the defendants was to prevent these parties from exercising
their right to vote on account of their race, it does not appear that it
was their intent to interfere with any right granted or secured by the
Constitution or laws of the United States. We may suppose that
" race " was the cause of the hostility, but this is not so averred.'[6]
When an election official in Kentucky — one Reese — refused to receive a Negro vote, the Court held that Congress did not have au-

[5] 16 Wallace 36 (1873).   [6] 92 U.S. 542 (1875).

Figure 3.2

25

thority to protect the right to vote generally, but only where that right was denied by the *state*, and on grounds of *race* or *color*.[7] In 1878 the Court provided the legal foundation for segregation by striking down a Louisiana statute forbidding discrimination in transportation, as an unlawful interference with congressional authority over interstate commerce![8] In the *United States v. Harris*, a case in which a Tennessee mob had lynched four Negro prisoners, the Court returned to the well-worn theme that the national government could protect the Negro only against acts by the *state*, and that for protection against violence by individuals or by mobs the Negro must look to the state authorities.[9] The crucial test came with the Civil Rights Cases of 1883, where the Court, in effect, wiped off the statute book the Civil Rights Act of 1875 forbidding discrimination against Negroes in public facilities.

It would be running the slavery argument into the ground [said Justice Bradley] to make it apply to every act of discrimination which a person may see fit to make as to the guests he will entertain, or as to the people he will take into his coach or cab or car, or admit to his concert or theatre, or deal with in other matters of intercourse or business.

And the Court added, somewhat gratuitously, that

When a man has emerged from slavery and by the aid of beneficent legislation has shaken off the inseparable concomitants of that state, there must be some stage in the progress of his elevation when he takes the rank of a mere citizen, and ceases to be the special favorite of the laws, and when his rights as a citizen, or a man, are to be protected in the ordinary modes by which other men's rights are protected.[10]

This was the thesis, too, of the famous *Plessy v. Ferguson* decision of 1896 which, by accepting — or inventing — the doctrine of ' separate but equal accommodations,' threw the mantle of judicial approval over segregation.

The object of the 14th Amendment [said the Court] was undoubtedly to enforce the absolute equality of the two races before the law, but in the nature of things, it could not have been intended to abolish distinctions based upon color, or to enforce social as distinguished from political equality, or a commingling of the two races upon terms unsatisfactory to either.[11]

[7] 92 U.S. 214 (1876).
[8] *Hall v. De Cuir* 95 U.S. 485 (1878).
[9] 106 U.S. 629 (1883).
[10] 109 U.S. 3 (1883).
[11] 136 U.S. 537 (1896).

Figure 3.3

The Negro and the New South   89

This jettisoning of the civil rights program did not go without protest from within the Court itself. It was Justice Harlan of Kentucky who was the spokesman of a construction of the Constitution broad enough to embrace the rights of all citizens, Negro and white alike. His classic dissent in the Civil Rights Cases applied to the whole body of judicial construction which had by now paralyzed the effectiveness of the wartime Amendments:

The opinion in these cases proceeds . . . upon grounds entirely too narrow and artificial. I cannot resist the conclusion that the substance and spirit of the recent amendments of the Constitution have been sacrificed by a subtle and ingenious verbal criticism. . . . Constitutional provisions, adopted in the interest of liberty, and for the purpose of securing, through national legislation, if need be, rights inhering in a state of freedom, and belonging to American citizenship, have been so construed as to defeat the ends the people desired to accomplish, which they attempted to accomplish, and which they supposed they had accomplished by changes in their fundamental law.[12]

And, observing that the ' separate but equal ' doctrine of the Plessy case would, in time ' be quite as pernicious as the decision in the Dred Scott case,' Harlan wrote prophetically that

The destinies of the two races in this country are indissolubly linked together, and the interests of both require that the common government of all shall not permit the seeds of race hate to be planted under the sanction of law. What can more certainly arouse race hate, what more certainly create and perpetuate a feeling of distrust between these races, than state enactments which in fact proceed on the ground that colored citizens are so inferior and degraded that they cannot be allowed to sit in public coaches occupied by white citizens.

What all this meant — the end of Reconstruction, the restoration of white rule, the watering down of the Enforcement Acts and their judicial nullification — was that the Southern Negro was exiled to a kind of no-man's land halfway between slavery and freedom. He was no longer a slave; he was not yet free. He was tied to the soil by the sharecrop and crop-lien systems. He was excluded from most professions and from many jobs. He was fobbed off not only with segregated schools, but with schools that were palpably inferior, and with ' separate ' accommodations that were rarely ' equal.' Socially he was relegated to a position of clear inferiority, and expected not only to

12 Civil rights cases, above.

Figure 3.4

upon all of them. Under these circumstances it is certainly now too late to contend that a government is not republican, within the meaning of this guaranty in the Constitution, because women are not made voters. . . .

Certainly if the courts can consider any question settled, this is one. For nearly ninety years the people have acted upon the idea that the Constitution, when it conferred citi-

zenship, did not necessarily confer the right of suffrage. . . .

Being unanimously of the opinion that the Constitution of the United States does not confer the right of suffrage upon any one, and that the constitutions and laws of the several States which commit that important trust to men alone are not necessarily void, we affirm the judgement.

291. THE CIVIL RIGHTS ACT
March 1, 1875

(U. S. Statutes at Large, Vol. XVIII, p. 335 ff.)

For history and references, see Doc. No. 273.

An act to protect all citizens in their civil and legal rights

Whereas it is essential to just government we recognize the equality of all men before the law, and hold that it is the duty of government in its dealings with the people to mete out equal and exact justice to all, of whatever nativity, race, color, or persuasion, religious or political; and it being the appropriate object of legislation to enact great fundamental principles into law: Therefore,

Be it enacted, That all persons within the jurisdiction of the United States shall be entitled to the full and equal enjoyment of the accommodations, advantages, facilities, and privileges of inns, public conveyances on land or water, theaters, and other places of public amusement; subject only to the conditions and limitations established by law, and applicable alike to citizens of every race and color, regardless of any previous condition of servitude.

SEC. 2. That any person who shall violate the foregoing section by denying to any citizen, except for reasons by law applicable to citizens of every race and color, and regardless of any previous condition of servitude, the full enjoyment of any of the accommodations, advantages, facilities, or privileges in said section enumerated, or by aiding or inciting such denial, shall, for every

such offense, forfeit and pay the sum of five hundred dollars to the person aggrieved thereby, . . . and shall also, for every such offense, be deemed guilty of a misdemeanor, and, upon conviction thereof, shall be fined not less than five hundred nor more than one thousand dollars, or shall be imprisoned not less than thirty days nor more than one year . . .

SEC. 3. That the district and circuit courts of the United States shall have, exclusively of the courts of the several States, cognizance of all crimes and offenses against, and violations of, the provisions of this act . . .

SEC. 4. That no citizen possessing all other qualifications which are or may be prescribed by law shall be disqualified for service as grand or petit juror in any court of the United States, or of any State, on account of race, color, or previous condition of servitude; and any officer or other person charged with any duty in the selection or summoning of jurors who shall exclude or fail to summon any citizen for the cause aforesaid shall, on conviction thereof, be deemed guilty of a misdemeanor, and be fined not more than five thousand dollars.

SEC. 5. That all cases arising under the provisions of this act . . . shall be renewable by the Supreme Court of the United States, without regard to the sum in controversy. . . .

292. CIVIL RIGHTS CASES
109 U. S. 3
1883

These were five cases, appealed from different circuit courts, involving the validity and interpretation of the Civil Rights Act of March 1,

1875. (Doc. No. 291.) In each case a colored person had been denied some accommodation or privilege on account of color. The opinion of

Figure 3.5

the Court that the rights which this law attempted to protect were social rather than civil rights, and that the Federal Government had no jurisdiction over these matters, practically put an end to the effort of the Federal Government to enforce the guaranties of the Fourteenth Amendment. See, Warren, *Supreme Court* (1928 ed.), Vol. II, ch. xxxiv; W. A. Dunning, *Essays on Civil War and Reconstruction*, p. 363 ff.; W. W. Davis, "The Federal Enforcement Acts," *Studies in Southern History and Politics*.

BRADLEY, J. [After holding that the statute derived no support from the Fourteenth Amendment].

. . . But the power of Congress to adopt direct and primary, as distinguished from corrective legislation, on the subject in hand, is sought in the second place, from the Thirteenth Amendment, which abolishes slavery. . . .

It is true that slavery cannot exist without law any more than property in lands and goods can exist without law, and therefore the Thirteenth Amendment may be regarded as nullifying all state laws which establish or uphold slavery. But it has a reflex character also, establishing and decreeing universal civil and political freedom throughout the United States; and it is assumed that the power in Congress to enforce the articles by appropriate legislation, clothes Congress with power to pass all laws necessary and proper for abolishing all badges and incidents of slavery in the United States; and upon this assumption it is claimed that this is sufficient authority for declaring by law that all persons shall have equal accommodations and privileges in all inns, public conveyances, and places of public amusement; the argument being that the denial of such equal accommodations and privileges is in itself a subjection to a species of servitude within the meaning of the amendment. Conceding the major proposition to be true, that Congress has a right to enact all necessary and proper laws for the obliteration and prevention of slavery with all its badges and incidents, is the minor proposition also true, that the denial to any person of admission to the accommodations and privileges of an inn, a public conveyance, or a theatre, does subject that person to any form of servitude, or tend to fasten upon him any badge of slavery? If it does not, then

power to pass the law is not found in the Thirteenth Amendment. . . .

But is there any similarity between such servitudes and a denial by the owner of an inn, a public conveyance, or a theatre, of its accommodations and privileges to an individual, even though the denial be founded on the race or color of that individual? Where does any slavery or servitude, or badge of either, arise from such an act of denial? Whether it might not be a denial of a right which, if sanctioned by the state law, would be obnoxious to the prohibitions of the Fourteenth Amendment, is another question. But what has it to do with the question of slavery? . . .

The long existence of African slavery in this country gave us very distinct notions of what it was, and what were its necessary incidents. Compulsory service of the slave for the benefit of the master, restraint of his movements except by the master's will, disability to hold property, to make contracts, to have a standing in court, to be a witness against a white person, and such like burdens and incapacities were the inseparable incidents of the institution. . . . Can the act of a mere individual, the owner of the inn, the public conveyance, or place of amusement, refusing the accommodation, be justly regarded as imposing any badge of slavery or servitude upon the applicant, or only as inflicting an ordinary civil injury, properly cognizable by the laws of the State, and presumably subject to redress by those laws until the contrary appears?

After giving to these questions all the consideration which their importance demands, we are forced to the conclusion that such an act of refusal has nothing to do with slavery or involuntary servitude, and that if it is violative of any right of the party, his redress is to be sought under the laws of the State; or, if those laws are adverse to his rights and do not protect him, his remedy will be found in the corrective legislation which Congress has adopted, or may adopt, for counteracting the effect of state laws, or state action, prohibited by the Fourteenth Amendment. It would be running the slavery argument into the ground to make it apply to every act of discrimination which a person may see fit to make as to the guests he will entertain, or as to the people he will take into his coach or

Figure 3.6

In the book *Law of freedom and Bondage*, Hurd writes about "the nature of a thing and how this species of bondage would require a legal name distinguishing the subject from **natural things and legal persons**". On the other hand, **legal or lawful persons have the power of choice and action** which brings us to the cardinal question. When was the so-called negro given a **choice** as to whether he wanted citizenship? If he was in fact free from the force and effect of the thirteenth amendment (with two sections) why was he not given the option to become or be restored to his original status without a constitutional amendment?

Can the fourteenth amendment unilaterally impose citizenship on persons of African descent without their consent?

This is exactly what the fourteenth amendment attempted to do. (Later in this book, we will review a federal case filed on behalf of the Moorish School of Law and History.) Because the negro had been classified by law as chattel property, he was consequently stripped of his original origin and nationality and disconnected entirely from the human family. There was no other device or mechanism that could be employed to raise the negro back to the status of a human being other than to restore him to his Moorish/Moroccan nationality.

To illustrate that other members of the human family's reject the term negro, observe how Africans coming into the United States of America from their homeland cling to their Nationality whether from Nigeria, Ghana, Senegal etc. They want nothing to do with the term negro. The term black is as equally avoided. Now is a good opportunity to spend a little time on the Emancipation Proclamation and later discuss the minutes from the journal of the senate, the congressional globe and *The Great Conspiracy* written by John A. Logan (one of President Abraham Lincoln's top Generals) who became a United States Senator.

On approaching the subject of the Emancipation Proclamation, let the record reflect that a majority of African American scholars and historians are quick to say (without in-depth research) that president Lincoln was only interested in saving the Union. This assumption comes from President Lincoln's response to a letter he received from Horace Greeley, a reporter for the Chicago Tribune where Lincoln stated that "My Paramount object in this struggle is to save the Union."

When one studies all the history and the facts related to the foundation of the Union, the origin of the rebellion and Lincoln's obligation as President it could very well be argued that Lincoln's response was appropriate in implying that Greeley keep his nose out of the President's business as it relates to the war. Certainly Lincoln did not want to expose all of his plans to the enemy. Remember this was the

Civil War not a war against a foreign country. Moreover, now that we know that persons of African descent (Moors) were present and are part and parcel of the commencement of the Union, this whole period can be re-examined under a very different prospective.

Let us now take a close look at the very first paragraph of the Emancipation Proclamation of January 1st 1863:

"Whereas on the 22nd day of September A.D. 1862, a proclamation was issued by the President of the United States, containing among other things, the following to wit:"

Before going any further, and based on the above language "containing among other things, the following to wit:" would you not agree that the remaining of this proclamation is only a portion of what was issued on September 22nd 1862? More importantly, the first sentence of the January 1st 1863 proclamation tells us that a proclamation was issued on September 22nd 1862. Most scholars and historians call the September 22nd proclamation "a preliminary proclamation" **this is totally inaccurate**. First of all the language in the first sentence clearly states that a proclamation was in fact issued on September 22nd 1862 and no where does it state that it was a preliminary proclamation as many would have us believe. In fact, our reasoning would tell us that if the September proclamation was just a preliminary one and had no force and effect of law there would be no purpose of **including** this important event in the January 1st 1863 proclamation.

John A. Logan in his book the *Great Conspiracy* (published in 1886, dedicated to all young men of America), rightfully stated that the September 22nd 1862 proclamation was called the **Initial Proclamation** and the January 1st 1863 was then called the **supplemental Proclamation. All historians as well as congress** need to revisit the year 1862 in congress. On March 31st of 1862 an act to make additional articles of war was passed by the Senate and the House of Representatives authorizing among other things, the issuance of the proclamations. In addition, there was an additional act passed to suppress insurrection, to punish treason etc. Sections of articles of both of these acts were incorporated in the September 22nd proclamation.

We should observe here that it was 100 days in between the issuance of the initial proclamation of September 22nd 1862 and the supplemental proclamation of January 1st 1863. This is very significant because President Lincoln stated in the second paragraph of the September 22nd that it will be his purpose, "upon the next meeting of congress" to again recommend pecuniary aid compensation as well as colonization for persons of African descent with their consent.

On December 1st 1862, Lincoln in his (second annual message to congress) took great pains in explaining what he called "Compensated Emancipation". In short his plan was to compensate the slave holders for their property (slaves) and compensate the slaves for their period of servitude. During the 100 days in between the initial Proclamation and the issuance of the supplemental Proclamation, Lincoln had given rebellious states one last opportunity to pull out of the rebellion by sending their representatives to the congress. They failed to do so.

On December 15, 1862 the House of Representatives (the Senate concurring) passed the policy of Compensated Emancipation by a vote of 78 yeas to 52 nays---the yeas all republicans save two, and the nays all democrats, save seven. The Proclamation of September 22nd 1862 was very generally endorsed and up held by the people at large; and, in accordance with its promise, it was followed at the appointed time, January 1st 1863, by the supplemental Proclamation specifically emancipating the slaves in the rebellious parts of the United States.

Even though the Proclamations inclusive of addition acts of congress were well chosen as a war measure and enforceable constitutionally, President Lincoln wanted them incorporated in the form of a constitutional amendment. He proceeded to lobby congress to have this done. Compensated Emancipation and Colonization of the slaves was incorporated into the 13th amendment with twenty sections (see figure 3.7-3.9). At the same time that the 13th amendment with 20 sections was being introduced in the United States Senate, the civil war was still going on. Consequently, both houses were infiltrated will conspirators and the use of strong arm tactics. After President Lincoln was assassinated, the orchestrators of the Great Conspiracy switched the 13th amendment with 20 sections and substituted it with the 13th amendment with two sections. The language with the two sections was extracted from article 6 of the Northwest Ordinance.

1787,* (in) an expression adjudicated upon repeatedly, which is perfectly well understood both by the public and by Judicial Tribunals—a phrase, which is peculiarly near and dear to the people of the Northwestern Territory, from whose soil Slavery was excluded by it."

Mr. Davis thereupon made another opposition speech; and, at its conclusion, Mr. Saulsbury offered, as a substitute, an Article, comprising no less than twenty sections† that,

* The following is the language of "the Ordinance of 1787" thus referred to:

"ART. 6.—There shall be *neither Slavery nor Involuntary Servitude* in the said Territory, otherwise than in the punishment of crimes, whereof the party shall have been duly convicted : * * *."

† As a curiosity of the times it has a certain interest. It ran thus :

ARTICLE XIII.

SECTION 1—All persons shall have the right peaceably to assemble and worship God according to the dictates of their own conscience.

SEC. 2.—The use of the public Press shall not be obstructed ; but criminal publications made in one State against the lawful Institutions of another State shall not be allowed.

SEC. 3.—The right of citizens to free and lawful Speech in public assemblies shall not be denied. Access of citizens to the ballot-box shall not be obstructed either by Civil or Military Power. The Military shall always be subordinate to the existing Judicial authority over citizens. The privilege of the writ of *Habeas Corpus* shall never be suspended in the presence of the Judicial Authority.

SEC. 4.—The Militia of a State or of the United States shall not be employed to invade the lawful rights of the People of any of the several States ; but the United States shall not be hereby deprived of the right and power to defend and protect its property and rights within the limits of any of the States.

SEC. 5.—Persons held to Service or Labor for life, in any State under the Laws thereof, may be taken into any Territory of the United States south of north latitude 30° 30', and the right to such Service or Labor shall not be impaired thereby, and the Territorial Legislature thereof shall have the exclusive right to make and shall make all needful rules and regulations for the protection of such right and also for the protection of such Persons; but Congress or any Territorial Legislature shall not have power to impair or abolish such right of Service in the said Territory while in a Territorial condition without the consent of all the States, south of said latitude, which maintain such Service.

SEC. 6.—Involuntary Servitude, except for crime, shall not be permanently established within the District set apart for the Seat of Government of the United States ; but the right of sojourn in such District, with Persons held to Service or Labor for life, shall not be denied.

Figure 3.7

33

550   THE GREAT CONSPIRACY.

he said, "embodied in them some things which "did not
meet his "personal approbation," but he had consented to
offer them to the Senate as "a Compromise"—as "a Peace
offering."

The Saulsbury substitute being voted down, the debate
closed with a speech by Mr. McDougall—an eloquent protest
from his standpoint, in which, after endorsing the wild
statement of Mr. Hendricks that 250,000 of the people of
African descent had been prematurely destroyed on the
Mississippi, he continued.

"This policy will ingulf them. It is as simple a truth
as has ever been taught by any history. The Slaves of

SEC. 7.—When any Territory of the United States south of north latitude
36° 30′ shall have a population equal to the Ratio of Representation for one
Member of Congress, and the people thereof shall have formed a Constitution for a Republican Form of Government, it shall be admitted as a State
into the Union. on an equal footing with the other States ; and the people
may, in such Constitution, either prohibit or sustain the right to Involuntary Labor or Service, and alter or amend the Constitution at their will.

SEC. 8.—The present right of Representation in section two, article one,
of this Constitution, shall not be altered without the consent of all the
States maintaining the right to Involuntary Service or Labor south of latitude 36° 30′; but nothing in this Constitution or its Amendments shall be
construed to deprive any State south of said latitude 36° 30′ of the right of
Abolishing Involuntary Servitude at its will.

SEC. 9.—The regulation and control of the right to Labor or Service in
any of the States south of latitude 36° 30′ is hereby recognized to be exclusively the right of each State within its own limits ; and this Constitution shall not be altered or amended to impair this right of each State
without its consent : *Provided*, This Article shall not be construed to ab-
solve the United States from rendering assistance to suppress Insurrec-
tions or Domestic Violence, when called upon by any State, as provided in
section four, article four, of this Constitution.

SEC. 10.—No State shall pass any law in any way interfering with or
obstructing the recovery of Fugitives from Justice, or from Labor or Service, or any Law of Congress made under Article four, section two, of this
Constitution; and all laws in violation of this Section may, on complaint
made by any person or State, be declared void by the Supreme Court of
the United States.

SEC. 11.—As a right of comity between the several States south of latitude 36° 30′ the right of transit with Persons held to Involuntary Labor or
Service from one State to another shall not be obstructed, but such Persons shall not be brought into the States north of said latitude.

SEC. 12.—The traffic in Slaves with Africa is hereby forever prohibited
on pain of death and the forfeiture of all the rights and property of

Figure 3.8

ancient time were not the Slaves of a different Race.   The
Romans compelled the Gaul and the Celt, brought them to
their own Country, and some of them became great poets,
and some eloquent orators, and some accomplished wits,
and they became citizens of the Republic of Greece, and of
the Republic of Rome, and of the Empire.

"This is not the condition of these persons with whom
we are now associated, and about whose affairs we undertake to establish administration.   They can never com-

persons engaged therein; and the descendants of Africans shall not be
citizens.

SEC. 13.—Alleged Fugitives from Labor or Service, on request, shall
have a Trial by Jury before being returned.

SEC. 14.—All alleged Fugitives charged with crime committed in violation of the laws of a State shall have the right of Trial by Jury, and if
such Person claims to be a citizen of another State, shall have a right of
appeal or of a writ of error to the Supreme Court of the United States.

SEC. 15.—All acts of any inhabitant of the United States tending to,
incite Persons held to Service or Labor to Insurrection or acts of Domestic
Violence, or to abscond, are hereby prohibited and declared to be a penal
offense; and all the Courts of the United States shall be open to suppress
and punish such offenses at the suit of any citizen of the United States or
the suit of any State.

SEC. 16.—All conspiracies in any State to interfere with lawful rights
in any other State, or against the United States, shall be suppressed; and
no State, or the people thereof, shall withdraw from this Union without
the consent of three-fourths of all the States, expressed by an Amendment
proposed and ratified in the manner provided in Article five of the Constitution.

SEC. 17.—Whenever any State wherein Involuntary Servitude is recognized or allowed shall propose to Abolish such Servitude, and shall apply
for pecuniary assistance therein, the Congress may, in its discretion, grant
such relief not exceeding one hundred dollars for each Person liberated.
But Congress shall not propose such Abolishment or relief to any State.

Congress may assist Free persons of African descent to emigrate and
colonize Africa.

SEC. 18.—Duties on Imports may be imposed for Revenue; but shall
not be excessive or prohibitory in amount.

SEC. 19.—When all of the several States shall have Abolished Slavery,
then and thereafter Slavery or Involuntary Servitude, except as a punishment for crime, shall never be established or tolerated in any of the States
or Territories of the United States, and they shall be forever Free.

SEC. 20.—The provisions of this Article relating to Involuntary Labor
or Servitude shall not be altered without the consent of all the States
maintaining such Servitude.

Figure 3.9

In *The Great Conspiracy*, Logan makes mention of a Democratic supporter of slavery Senator Saulsbury from Delaware presenting an argument defending slavery as a divine institution. (see figure 3.10) There was also a rebuttal to Saulsbury's argument by Senator Harlan. He drew attention to the Levitical Code or Hebrew Law which contains a provision for Naturalization and Compensation. (see figures 3.11-3.12)

Although it was not mentioned in the Harlan's position it is interesting to note the key to the inscription on the Liberty Bell located in Philadelphia, Pennsylvania can be found in Leviticus 25:10. The inscription on the Liberty Bell reads as follows: "Ye shall proclaim liberty through out the land, To all of the inhabitants there of ". This veiled code on the Liberty Bell extends to the 44th, 45th and 46th verse of Leviticus as well as the Hebrew Code in Deuteronomy 15:12 –18.

This Mosaic Law is the key to the biblical scriptures concerning slavery whereby human beings are never slaves but bound free men and women who must be released after six years labor and generously compensated at double the rate of a hired servant. Although President Lincoln's Executive Will which engulfs the Compensated Emancipation is perpetual and can stand alone as a war measure, the discussion in the Senate March 31st 1864 was the basis for what was included in the Original 13th amendment with 20 sections.

Incidentally, members of the black caucus were made aware of most of the above in the early 1970's by the Moorish School of Law and History (see correspondence from Representative Cardiss Collins. Also see correspondence from Yvonne Burke to the late Peter Rodino then Chairman of the House Judiciary Committee and his response, Figure 3.13-3.16) For those who are pursuing Reparations please go back and research all that has been presented here and you will find that President Lincoln's Executive Will Compensation and Colonization (land) is still due and owing. You will also find that several states especially **Maryland** had amended its constitution and actually applied for compensation.

Many Americans have no understanding of the ills of chattel slavery or the civil war. Many slave holders, carpet baggers, scalawags and their descendants who had profited from slavery acquired great masses of land, wealth and power passed it on to the next generation. For decades after Emancipation the **former slaves** whom emerged from slavery were **prevented** from **obtaining wealth** when this country was **becoming industrialized**.

preamble to, as well as the body of the Convention of Ratification of, the old Articles of Confederation between the States of New Hampshire, Massachusetts Bay, Rhode Island and Providence Plantations, Connecticut, New York, New Jersey, Pennslyvania, Delaware, Maryland, Virginia, North Carolina, South Carolina, and Georgia, declared that Confederation to be a "Perpetual Union," yet, within nine years thereafter, all the other States Seceded from New York, Virginia, North Carolina, and Rhode Island by ratifying the new Constitution for "a more perfect Union."

He also endeavored to maintain the extraordinary proposition that "if the Senate of the United States were to adopt this Joint-resolution, and were to submit it to all the States of this Union, and if three-fourths of the States should ratify the Amendment, it would not be binding on any State whose interest was affected by it, if that State protested against it!" And beyond all this, he re-echoed the

and held as Slaves, and their posterity after them ; that under their Naturalization Laws all strangers and sojourners, Bond and Free, have the privilege of acquiring the rights of citizenship ; that all Hebrews, natives or naturalized, might assert and maintain their right to Freedom.

"At the end of six years a Hebrew Slave thus demanding his Liberty, was not to be sent away empty ; the owner, so far from claiming compensation from his neighbors or from the Public Treasury for setting him Free, was bound to divide with the Freedman, of his own possessions: to give him of his flocks, of his herds, of his granary, and of his winepress, of everything with which the Lord Almighty had blessed the master during the years of his Servitude ; and then the owner was admonished that he was not to regard it as a hardship to be required to Liberate the Slave, and to divide with him of his substance.

" The Almighty places the Liberated Slave's claim to a division of his former master's property on the eternal principles of Justice, the duty to render an equivalent for an equivalent. The Slave having served six years must be paid for his Service, must be paid liberally because he had been worth even more than a hired servant during the period of his enslavement.

" If, then," continued Mr. Harlan, " the justice of this claim cannot be found either in Reason, Natural Justice, or the principles of the Common Law, or in any positive Municipal or Statute regulation of any State, or in the Hebrew Code written by the Finger of God protruded from the flame of fire on the summit of Sinai, I ask whence the origin of the title to the services of the adult offspring of the Slave mother? or is it not manifest that there is no just title ? Is it not a mere usurpation without any known mode of justification, under any existing Code of Laws, human or Divine?"

Figure 3.10

dom of the Slaves of Rebel masters; the Abolition of Slavery in the Capital of the Nation, and the consecration of the Territories to Free Labor and Free laboring men; the Proclamation of Emancipation; the enlistment of Colored men to fight the battles of the Country; the Freedom of the Black soldier, who is fighting, bleeding, dying for the Country; and the Freedom of his wife and children. And now, when War has for nearly three years menaced the life of the Nation, bathed the Land in blood, and filled two hundred thousand graves with our slain sons, these men of the Loyal States still cling to the falling fortunes of the relentless and unappeasable Enemy of their Country and its democratic institutions; they mourn, and will not be comforted, over the expiring System, in the Border Slave-States; and, in tones of indignation or of anguish, they utter lamentations over the Proclamation of Emancipation, and the policy that is bringing Rebel States back again radiant with Freedom."

Among these "loyal" Democratic opponents of Emancipation, in any shape, or any where, were not wanting men —whether from Loyal Northern or Border States—who still openly avowed that Slavery was right; that Rebellion, to preserve its continuance, was justifiable; and that there was no Constitutional method of uprooting it.

Saulsbury of Delaware, was representative and spokesman of this class, and he took occasion during this very debate* to defend Slavery as a Divine Institution,† which

---

* In the Senate, March 31, 1864.

† Said he: "Slavery had existed under some form or other from the first period of recorded history. It dates back even beyond the period of Abraham, the Father of the Faithful, in whose seed all the Nations of the Earth were to be blessed. We find that, immediately after the Flood, the Almighty, for purposes inscrutable to us, condemned a whole race to Servitude: '*Vayomer Orur Knoan Efet Afoatim Yeahio Le-echot :*' 'And he said, Cursed be Canaan ; Slave of Slaves he shall be to his brethren.' It continued among all people until the advent of the Christian era. It was recognized in that New Dispensation, which was to supersede the Old. It has the sanction of God's own Apostle ; for when Paul sent back Onesimus to Philemon, whom did he send? A Freeman? No, Sir. He sent his δουλος, (*doulos*,) a Slave, born as such, not even his *andrapodon*, who was such by captivity in War. Among all people, and in all ages, has this Institution,

Figure 3.11

38

had the sanction both of the Mosaic and Christian Dispensations!

He also undertook to justify Secession on the singular ground that " we are sprung from a Race of Secessionists," the proof of which he held to be in the fact that, while the if such it is to be called, existed, and had the countenance of wise and good men, and even of the Christian Church itself, until these modern times, up at least to the Nineteenth Century. It exists in this Country, and has existed from the beginning."

Mr. Harlan's reply to the position of Mr. Saulsbury that Slavery is right, is a Divine Institution, etc., was very able and interesting. He piled up authority after authority, English as well as American, to show that there is no support of Slavery—and especially of the title to services of the adult offspring of a Slave—at Common Law; and, after also proving, by the mouth of a favorite son of Virginia, that it has no legal existence by virtue of any Municipal or Statutory Law, he declared that "the only remaining Law that can be cited for its support is the Levitical Code"—as follows:

" ' Both thy Bondmen, and thy Bondmaids, which thou shalt have, shall be of the heathen that are round about you; of them shall ye buy Bondmen and Bondmaids.

" ' Moreover, of the children of the strangers that do sojourn among you, of them shall ye buy, and of their families that are with you, which they begat in your land; and they shall be your possession.

" ' And ye shall take them as an Inheritance for your children after you, to inherit them for a possession; they shall be your Bondmen forever.' "

"I remark," said he, " in this connection, that the Levitical Code, or the Hebrew Law, contains a provision for the Naturalization of Foreigners, whether captives of War, or voluntary emigrants. By compliance with the requirements of this law they became citizens, entitled to all the rights and privileges and immunities of native Hebrews. The Hebrew Slave Code, applicable to Enslaved Hebrews, is in these words:

" ' And if thy brother, an Hebrew man, or an Hebrew woman, be sold unto thee, and serve thee six years, then in the seventh year thou shalt let him go Free from thee.'

"Here I request the attention of those who claim compensation for Emancipated Slaves to the text:

" ' And when thou sendest him out Free from thee, thou shalt not let him go away empty:

" ' Thou shalt furnish him liberally out of thy flock, and out of thy floor '—

" Which means granaries—

" ' and out of thy wine-press: of that wherewith the Lord thy God hath blessed thee, thou shalt give unto him.'

" ' It shall not seem hard unto thee, when thou sendest him away Free from thee, for he hath been worth a double-hired servant to thee, in serving thee six years.'

" These Hebrew Statutes provide that the heathen might be purchased

Figure 3.12

39

CARDISS COLLINS
7TH DISTRICT, ILLINOIS

1123 LONGWORTH BUILDING
WASHINGTON, D.C. 20515
202-225-5006

DISTRICT OFFICE:
219 SOUTH DEARBORN
SUITE 1632
CHICAGO, ILLINOIS 60604
312-353-5754

Congress of the United States
House of Representatives
Washington, D.C. 20515

COMMITTEE ON
GOVERNMENT OPERATIONS

SUBCOMMITTEES:
GOVERNMENT ACTIVITIES
LEGAL AND MONETARY AFFAIRS

DOROTHY ROSS
PERSONAL SECRETARY
202-225-5009

September 30, 1974

Mr. Clarence R. Reynolds-El, Sheik
Chairman
Moorish School of Law and History
Post Office Box 7063
Baltimore, Maryland 21216

Dear Mr. Reynolds:

This will acknowledge receipt of the hand delivered letter from you requesting a meeting with Members of the Congressional Black Caucus and about fifty members from your school.

May I suggest that you write to the Chairman of the Congressional Black Caucus, Honorable Charles B. Rangel, Room 306, House Annex, Washington, D. C. 20515, and let him know your desire to meet with the entire Caucus.

Yours truly,

CARDISS COLLINS
Member of Congress

CC/dr

Figure 3.13

Congressional Black Caucus
306 House Annex
Washington, D.C. 20515
202—225-1691

Charles Rangel, N.Y., Chairman
Yvonne B. Burke, Calif., Vice Chairperson
Walter Fauntroy, D.C., Secretary
Andrew Young, Georgia, Treasurer

February 12, 1976

Shirley Chisholm, N.Y.
William Clay, Mo.
Cardiss Collins, Ill.
John Conyers, Mich.
Ronald Dellums, Calif.
Charles Diggs, Mich.
Harold Ford, Tenn.
Augustus Hawkins, Calif.
Barbara Jordan, Texas
Ralph Metcalfe, Ill.
Parren Mitchell, Md.
Robert N. C. Nix, Pa.
Louis Stokes, Ohio

The Honorable Peter W. Rodino
Chairman
Committee on the Judiciary
2137 Rayburn House Office Building
Washington, D.C. 20515

Dear Mr. Chairman:

The Congressional Black Caucus has been asked by
representatives of the Moorish School of Law and
History, Baltimore, Maryland, to determine the
status of a petition regarding the 13th Amendment
to the Constitution with Twenty Sections, which
they believe to be the 13th Amendment which was
properly adopted. The petition was referred to
the Judiciary Committee on about May 1, 1975, as
indicated by the attached letter.

I would appreciate your letting me know of the status
of this amendment so that we may advise the Moorish
School of Law of the status of that petition. Thank
you for your assistance.

Sincerely,

Yvonne B. Burke
Chairperson

Enclosure

Figure 3.14

41

NINETY-FOURTH CONGRESS

PETER W. RODINO, JR. (N.J.), CHAIRMAN

JACK BROOKS, TEX.
ROBERT W. KASTENMEIER, WIS.
DON EDWARDS, CALIF.
WILLIAM L. HUNGATE, MO.
JOHN CONYERS, JR., MICH.
JOSHUA EILBERG, PA.
WALTER FLOWERS, ALA.
JAMES R. MANN, S.C.
PAUL S. SARBANES, MD.
JOHN F. SEIBERLING, OHIO
GEORGE E. DANIELSON, CALIF.
ROBERT F. DRINAN, MASS.
BARBARA JORDAN, TEX.
RAY THORNTON, ARK.
ELIZABETH HOLTZMAN, N.Y.
EDWARD MEZVINSKY, IOWA
HERMAN BADILLO, N.Y.
ROMANO L. MAZZOLI, KY.
EDWARD W. PATTISON, N.Y.
CHRISTOPHER J. DODD, CONN.
WILLIAM J. HUGHES, N.J.
MARTIN A. RUSSO, ILL.

EDWARD HUTCHINSON, MICH.
ROBERT MC CLORY, ILL.
TOM RAILSBACK, ILL.
CHARLES E. WIGGINS, CALIF.
HAMILTON FISH, JR., N.Y.
M. CALDWELL BUTLER, VA.
WILLIAM S. COHEN, MAINE
CARLOS J. MOORHEAD, CALIF.
JOHN M. ASHBROOK, OHIO
HENRY J. HYDE, ILL.
THOMAS N. KINDNESS, OHIO

Congress of the United States
Committee on the Judiciary
House of Representatives
Washington, D.C. 20515
Telephone: 202-225-3951

GENERAL COUNSEL:
EARL C. DUDLEY, JR.

STAFF DIRECTOR:
GARNER J. CLINE

COUNSEL:
HERBERT FUCHS
WILLIAM P. SHATTUCK
ALAN A. PARKER
JAMES F. FALCO
MAURICE A. BARBOZA
ARTHUR P. ENDRES, JR.
THOMAS W. HUTCHISON
DANIEL L. COHEN
FRANKLIN G. POLK
THOMAS E. MOONEY
ALEXANDER B. COOK
CONSTANTINE J. GEKAS
ALAN F. COFFEY, JR.
KENNETH N. KLEE
RAYMOND V. SMIETANKA

February 26, 1976

The Honorable Yvonne B. Burke
Chairperson
Congressional Black Caucus
306 House Annex I
Washington, D.C. 20515

Dear Yvonne:

The petition to which you refer in your letter of February 12, 1976 was referred by the Speaker's Office to this Committee. The petition consists of a copy of a letter addressed to General Alexander Haig, Chief of Staff, The White House.

The petition has been reviewed by the staff of this Committee and contains no material which forms a basis for any action by this Committee. In addition, the Chief Counsel of the Subcommittee on Civil and Constitutional Rights has met with and had an extended discussion with representatives of the Moorish Science Temple to thoroughly explore any possibility of assistance. It was explained that the petition did not contain any material on which this Committee could act and that there were other alternative means at their disposal, such as formulating a constitutional amendment to change the 13th Amendment or introducing private claims bills for the reparations they seek.

Figure 3.15

The Honorable Yvonne B. Burke
February 26, 1976
Page 2

        I trust this information will be of assis-
tance to you.

        With warm personal regards.

                        Sincerely,

                        PETER W. RODINO, JR.
                        CHAIRMAN

PWR:bs

Figure 3.16

Other immigrants and ethic groups especially in the early nineteen hundreds through the twenties and thirty's did not suffer the same type of degradation that the so-called negro was experiencing because during this time he was still regarded by many so-called whites as inferior, lazy, simian in appearance (ape or monkey), stupid and criminally inclined. Because of this the opportunity was not even there. Still there are those who maintain that **they had nothing to do with slavery**, but what they fail to realize is that their ancestors did. Many of the **wealthy inherited** their wealth because of the **events during this period of time**. "It is written that what your ancient forefathers were you are today without doubt or contradiction". There is no one who is able to change man from the descendant nature of his forefathers unless his power extends beyond the great universal creator himself.

Much of the wealth had been consumed by the wealthy at the time of the riots in the late 1960s. Had Lincolns Executive Will been complied with many of the racial problems would not exist. Why? Because the newly emancipated slaves would have migrated into the interior region (to inherit territories, not then states between the Allegheny/ rocky mountain chains) Slave holders would be compensated for their Human Property (remember constitutionally slaves were declared property)

o   Former slaves would have received compensation for their period of servitude

o   Education of identity of National Origin and history of organized religion

o   Restored to rightful Nationality and names, and culture of the ancient Moorish Empire

o   Realignment with the Moroccan Treaty of 1786

Any one territory with Moorish inhabitants equaling 30,000 if desired could partition for statehood. The cost for compensated emancipation was calculated to be completed by the year 1930. There was no need for 13th Amendment or 14th Amendment to attempt to unilaterally impose citizenship on persons of African descent (Moors) without their consent. The failure to implement Lincoln's Executive Will has precluded the former slaves to be placed on **equal footing** with other ethnic groups. Through out history no other people were stripped of their identification, culture and religion and reduced by law to chattel property except the so-called negro.

After having digested all of this many persons of African descent specifically those who still wish to continue to identify themselves as negroes or black will ask the question at this late date in the twenty first century, "what will it benefit me to proclaim/declare my nationality as Moorish American?" The answer to this question goes to the very fiber and soul of a real Moor's true existence.

The first affects are psychological and lawful. Some so-called negroes and blacks know instinctively that something is wrong with those racial terms. For these persons as soon as they here it, the call is swift, and they take action to proclaim their Moorish nationality almost immediately. Others need a little more knowledge and research. Psychologically, a Moorish American proclaiming his or her nationality after being properly educated and enlightened, experiences a new birth of freedom. With this new awakening he or she feels a new sense of race pride, self esteem, self worth and greatness surpassing any previous feeling. In identifying ones self as a Moorish American he or she immediately feels reconnected with the Human Family and is simultaneously recognizes a connection to a significant part of history that is known to the world.

No longer does he feel the type of shame that is induced by **pictures of degrading images** of the slave era being subjugated by the master as emphasized in the school system. Let there be no mistake about it, slavery of the so call negro or black needs to continue to be taught. The difference is that the Moorish Americans consciousness and thought process will not allow him or her to stay **suspended at the beginning of slavery** in this country in 1619.

The so-called negro has been programmed to begin his-story here. This period marks the early stages of the systematic disconnection. Once he or she understands Moorish history before 1492 and 1619, his or her perception of themselves would be as kings and queens, lords and masters, astrologers, astronomers, chemists and priests as opposed to continually viewing themselves being whipped, lynched and with their heads hanging low. Again, psychologically speaking the so-call Negro often feels the he or she must gain recognition or approval for his new achievements by placing emphasis on being the first black in basketball etc. Greatness of the Moors to excel is in the DNA. The events should be recorded but from a different perspective.

All conscious Moorish Americans descendants from the Moorish Empire, want the beginning of slavery in this country to be taught **but not without the history of the Moors and their contribution to world civilization**. For those who may not be aware, being a Moor means being a descendent pre-dynastic Africa, for it is written that backward through the ages master minds can trace themselves and thus they know.

CHAPTER 4

I, along with the **original staff** of the Moorish School of Law and History, Inc want to emphasize that the readers understand that none of this work would be possible if it were not for The Honorable Noble Drew Ali and the Original MST of A. Noble Drew Ali is one of the most **unmentioned pioneer, teacher, and enlightened adepts** of the twentieth century. Born (Timothy Drew) in North Carolina on January 8, 1886, Prophet Noble Drew Ali (as he was known to his followers and the general public at large) founded the Moorish Movement in 1913 in New Ark, New Jersey. He later moved to Chicago, IL and along with four others **(James Lomax, Johnny Reynolds, Eddie Watts and Sammy Rucker)** who served as directors for the first year, filed and registered articles of incorporation under the name **Moorish Temple of Science** on November 29th 1926. (Figure 4.1 & 4.2). The purpose of the corporation as stated was to uplift fallen humanity and to teach those things necessary for people to become better citizens.

Over the next year and a half, several pieces of literature developed and was distributed to the members as learning tools to begin to teach the importance of Moorish nationality and its link to the history of the former slaves (i.e. negroes, coloreds or blacks) in America before their introduction in 1619/1620, Jamestown Virginia (as was taught in the education system).

On May 2, 1928 a special meeting of the members was held pursuant to the rules of the corporation and a resolution was adopted in accordance with its by-laws to change the name from the **Moorish Temple of Science** to the **Moorish Science Temple of America**. Noble Drew Ali appeared before his notary public (Claude D. Greene) on May 19th 1928 and filed the name change application that was **subsequently filed in Cook County Illinois on May 21, 1928** (Figure 4.3 & 4.4).

Now that the concepts of nationality and nationhood had been introduced, the next step was to restore the spiritual knowledge to the members by expanding the corporation to include its religious activities. At another meeting of its members on July20, 1928 a religious- affidavit (form no. 1099 Cook County Ill) was signed by Noble Drew Ali, Mealy El, Small Bey, Lovett Bey and Foreman Bey. (Figure 4.5)

Form No. 895

STATE OF ILLINOIS
Cook   County, ss.

To LOUIS L. EMMERSON, Secretary of State:

Drew Alin, James Lomax, Johnny Reynolds, Eddie Watts,
We, the undersigned, Sammy Rucker.

citizens of the United States, propose to form a corporation under ... of the General Assembly of the S... Illinois entitled, "An Act concerning Corporations," approved Ap... and all acts amendatory the...

1. The name of such corporation is   Moorish Temple of Science.

2. The object for which it is formed is   To uplift fallen humanity and teach those things necessary to make men and women become better citizens.

Moorish temple of Science

3. ...

4. The following persons are hereby selected as the Directors to control and manage said corporation for the first year of its corporate existence, viz:

NAME	ADDRESS			
	NUMBER STREET	CITY	STATE	
Drew Alin	3603 Indiana Ave	Chicago Ill.		
James Lomax	3614 Prairie Ave.	Chicago Ill.		
Johnny Reynolds	3603 Indiana Ave.	Chicago Ill.		
Eddie Watts	3603 Indiana Ave.	Chicago Ill.		
Sammy Rucker	3738 Calumet Ave.	Chicago Ill.		

5. The location is in the city of   Chicago   in the county of   Cook   in the State of Illinois, and the post office address of its business office is at No. 3603 Indiana Ave. Street, in the said city of   Chicago

SIGNED.

Drew Alin
James Lomax
Johnny Reynolds
Eddie Watts
Sammy Rucker

(005)

Figure 4. 1

48

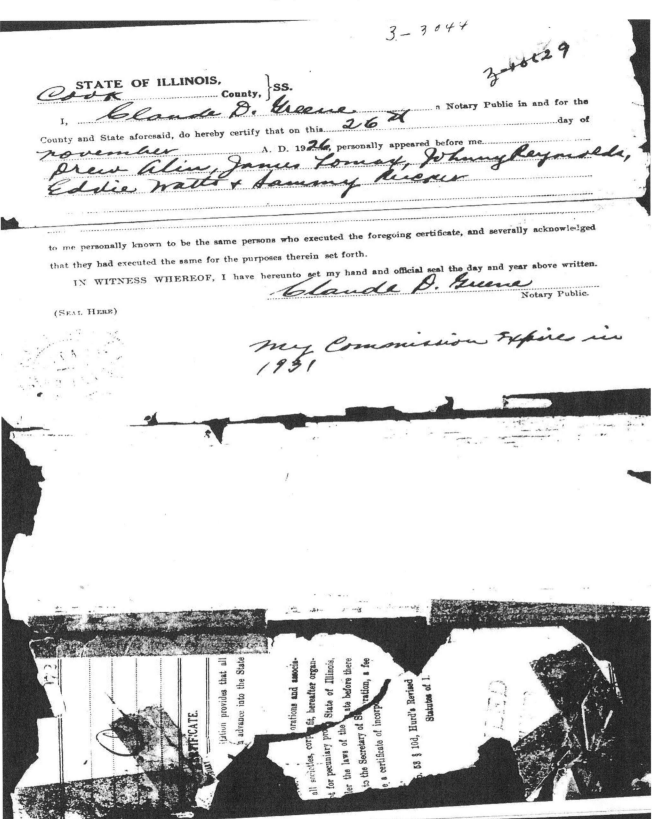

Figure 4. 2

STATE OF ILLINOIS,
County of Cook ss.

I hereby certify that at a Special meeting of the members of the Moorish Temple of Science, Chicago, Illinois held on the 2nd., day of May A. D. 192 8 at 8 o'clock P. M., pursuant to the rules of said corporation, the following resolution was adopted, in accordance with the By-Laws of said corporation.

on the 2nd., day of May 1928, for the purpose of changing the name of the said corporation, hereby make application to the Secretary of State of Illinois, to change the name of the Moorish Temple of Science to The Moorish Science Temple of America.

1900
972

Whitehead Bey
SECRETARY.

STATE OF ILLINOIS,
of Cook ss.

declare on oath that I am

In Witness whereof, I have hereunto set my hand and caused the seal of said Corporation to be affixed, this

day of A. D. 192

(Corporate Seal Here)

Drew Ali
PRESIDENT.

cribed and sworn to before me this 19th day of May

Claude D. Greene
NOTARY PUBLIC.

Figure 4. 3

Figure 4. 4

Certificate № 111982

STATE OF ILLINOIS
OFFICE OF
THE SECRETARY OF STATE

To all to whom these Presents Shall Come, Greeting:

I, MICHAEL J. HOWLETT, *Secretary of State of the State of Illinois, do hereby certify that the following and hereto attached is a true photostatic copy of* the Certificate of Incorporation of MOORISH TEMPLE OF SCIENCE. And Certificate of Amendment changing name to THE MOORISH SCIENCE TEMPLE OF AMERICA

the original of which is now on file and a matter of record in this office.

In Testimony Whereof, *I hereto set my hand and cause to be affixed the Great Seal of the State of Illinois. Done at the City of Springfield this* 19th *day of* June *AD 19* 75

Michael J. Howlett
SECRETARY OF STATE

The rules for this religious affidavit is referenced at the bottom of the document entitled "Our authority" (Figure 4.6). This document was filed and recorded on August 1, 1928 according to Hurd's rev. stat, chap. 32, 36. (Figure 4.7) One of the key points of this document was to establish the faith of Mohammed. Thus the MST of A became the first legally **chartered organization** to establish Islam in America. Of significant importance, is the fact that no English translation of the Holy Koran of Mecca was in print in1928.

Realizing the state of mind of his new converts, so-called negroes, coloreds and blacks, Noble Drew Ali and select members of his staff created the Holy Koran of the MST of A which became known as the Circle Seven or the Book of the Seven Seals. A great deal of the compilation of the Circle Seven was drawn from two other books. The first book, entitled The Aquarian Gospel of Jesus the Christ states it was transcribed from the Akashic records by Levi (copyright 1907 first through tenth printings 1908-1928).

The second book Unto Thee I Grant, although original copyright was in 1925 by the Oriental Literature Syndicate, the subsequent copyright was granted to the Ancient & Mystical Order Rosae Crucis (AMORC). A closer examination reveals that this work housed in the sacred depositories in Tibet by the Lamas, actually originated in ancient Egypt from Amenhotep IV and preserved by Akhenaton the first monotheist.

The Honorable Prophet Noble Drew Ali passed through transition (physical death) on July 20, 1929. A photograph of his gravesite has been added. (Figure 4.8) After the passing of Noble Drew Ali, there was no strong central leadership. Consequently, several Moorish Science Temples, Moorish Societies and Moorish Orders sprang up over the country and many professed their own autonomy.

Research discloses that a Grand Body of the original Moorish Science Temple of America existed in Chicago during Noble Drew Ali's final days. Over the years that followed, several Grand Bodies emerged and some were able to get small subordinate temples in a few states to affiliate. There was more than one Grand Body and each one maintained that it was the authentic and original Grand Body.

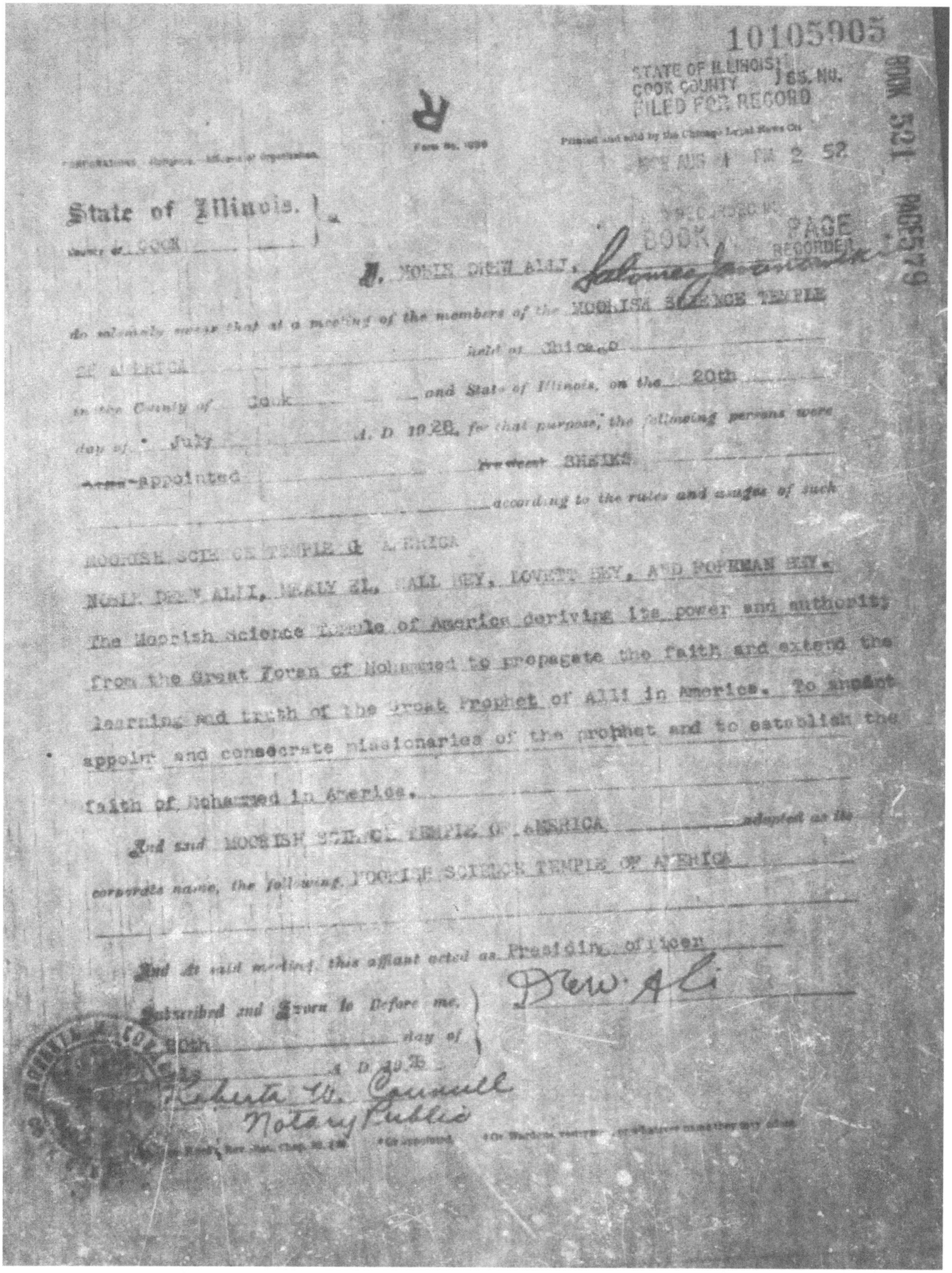

Figure 4. 5

Our Authority

(COPY)
BOOK 521   PAGE 579
                    State of Illinois, Cook County ss. No. 10105905
                                               Filed for Record
CORPORATION.—Religious—Affidavit of Organization   Form No. 1099
STATE OF ILLINOIS,
County of COOK
                        s.s.
                1928 AUG 1 PM 2 52
                AND RECORDED IN $
                        BOOK   PAGE
                Salomes Jasconowskic   Recorder
                • • • • • • • • • • • • • • • •

I NOBLE DREW ALI...
do solemnly swear that at a meetingoof the members of the
MOORISH SCIENCE TEMPLE OF AMERICA.............•
Held at....................Chicago.......in the County of
Cook.......... and the State of Illinois, on the...........
20th...........day of......July......A.D. 1928, for that
purpose,the following persons were appointed ....•
SHEIKS.........OF THE MOORISH SCIENCE TEMPLE OF
AMERICA according to the rules and usages of such......
MEALY EL, SMALL BEY, LOVETT BEY, and FOREMAN BEY

The Moorish Science Temple of America deriving its   power
and authority from the Great Koran of Mohammed to pro -
pagate the faith and extend the learning and truth of the Great
Prophet Ali, in America.
To anoint appoint, and consecrate missionaries of the prophet
and to establish the faith of Mohammed in America.

and said Moorish Science Temple of America adopted as its
corporate name the following, Moorish Science Temple of
America...•
and at said meeting, This affiant acted as Presiding Officer.

Subscribed and Sworn to Before me,
..............20th............................day of
..............July.....................A.D. 1928.......
                                Drew Ali ....

Roberta W. Counull,
        Notary Public
See Hurd's Rev. Stat., Chap. 32, 36. *Or appointed *Or warden, vestrymen, or whatever name they may adopt.

Figure 4. 6

Rommani M. Amenu-El

Chap. 32, § 161   CORPORATIONS

directors or managers shall be filled in the manner provided by their by-laws, and upon filing any vacancy a like certificate shall be recorded. [As amended by act approved April 28, 1920. L. 1920, p. 294.]

Prior amendment: L. 1919, p. 365.
Majority may control meeting of members of corporation organized not for profit, and may remove presiding officer if necessary. American Aberdeen-Angus Breeders' Ass'n v. Fullerton, 325—323, 156 N. E. 314.

162. Distribution of property — Dissolution.] § 33. No dividends or distribution of the property of such corporation, society or association shall be made until all debts are fully paid and then only upon its final dissolution and surrender of organization and name; nor shall any distribution be made except by a vote of a majority of the members. Whenever a majority of the members of such corporation, society or association shall wish to dissolve the corporation and abandon the corporate enterprise, the trustees, directors or managers shall call a meeting of the members in accordance with the by-laws, to vote upon the proposition of dissolving the corporation. Upon the passing of a resolution of dissolution in accordance with the by-laws of the corporation, the secretary of the corporation shall certify to the fact of the passing of the resolution of dissolution and the further fact that all the debts of the corporation have been paid and the property distributed among the members according to their respective rights, which certificate shall be under the seal of the corporation and verified by oath of the president and recorded in the office of the county recorder of the county wherein the business office of the corporation is located and filed in the office of the Secretary of State. Upon the filing of the certificate of dissolution duly recorded, the Secretary of State shall examine the same, and if it is in conformity with the law, shall issue a certificate of dissolution. Upon the issuance of said certificate of dissolution by the Secretary of State, such corporation, society or association shall cease to exist. In case any statement made by the president and secretary of the corporation relating to the dissolution of said corporation, shall be wilfully false, said officers shall be jointly and severally liable for the debts of such corporation, society or association. [As amended by act approved June 28, 1919. L. 1919, p. 365.]

163. Amendment of articles.] § 34. Any such corporation, society or association may change its articles of association, in the manner prescribed by their own rules, but no such change shall be of legal effect until a certificate thereof, signed by oath of the president, under seal of such corporation, society or association, shall be filed in the office of the Secretary of State, and recorded in the office of the recorder of deeds in which the original certificate was recorded. [As amended by act approved June 28, 1919. L. 1919, p. 365.]

RELIGIOUS CORPORATIONS

164. How organized.] § 35. The foregoing provisions shall not apply to any religious corporations; but any church, congregation or society formed for the purpose of religious worship, may become incorporated in the manner following, to-wit: By electing or appointing, according to its usages or customs, at any meeting held for that purpose, two or more of its members as trustees, wardens and vestrymen, (or such other officers whose powers and duties are similar to those of trustees, as shall be agreeable to the usages and customs, rules or regulations of such congregation, church or society), and may adopt a corporate name; and upon the filing of the affidavit, as hereinafter provided, it shall be and remain a body politic and corporate, by the name so adopted.

165. Affidavit of organization.] § 36. The chairman or secretary of such meeting shall, as soon as may be after such meeting, make and file in the office of the recorder of deeds in the county in which such congregation, church or society is organized, (which shall be recorded by such recorder) an affidavit, substantially in the following form:

State of Illinois, } ss.
..........County. }

I, ..., do solemnly swear (or affirm, as the case may be), that at a meeting of the members of the (here insert the name of the church, society or congregation, as known before incorporation) held at (here insert place of meeting), in the county of ...., and state of Illinois, on the ....day of........, A. D. 19...., for that purpose, the following persons were elected (or appointed) (here insert their names) trustees (or wardens, vestrymen or officers by whatever name they choose to adopt, with powers and duties similar to trustees), according to the rules and usages of such (church, society or congregation). And said (church, society or congregation) adopted as its corporate name (here insert the name). And at said meeting this affiant acted as (chairman or secretary, as the case may be).

Subscribed and sworn to before me this........ day of........, A. D. 19....

................(Name of affiant.)

Such congregation, church or society may change its name or make other amendment to its original affidavit of incorporation by passing a resolution of such amendment in accordance with the rules and usages of such congregation, church or society and filing an affidavit to that effect in the office of the recorder of deeds, in the county in which such congregation, church or society is located.

Such affidavit, or a copy thereof, duly certified by the recorder, shall be received as evidence of the due incorporation of such congregation, church or society. [As amended by act approved June 30, 1925. L. 1925, p. 261.]

Church corporation could have more than three trustees, though affidavit of incorporation provided for only three. Shavers v. Thomas, 339—623, 171 N. E. 69.

166. Term of office of trustees.] § 37. The term of office of the trustees of any such corporation may be determined by the rules or by-laws of the congregation, church or society.

167. Failure to elect trustees not to dissolve.] § 38. A failure to elect trustees at any time shall not work a dissolution of such corporation, but the trustees last elected shall be considered as in office until their successors are elected.

168. Subsequent elections — Vacancies, etc.] § 39. All elections of trustees after the first, and elections to fill vacancies, may be called and conducted upon such notice and in such manner as may be provided by the rules, usages or by-laws of the congregation, church or society. No certificate of election, after the first, need be filed for record. [As amended by act approved June 30, 1925. L. 1925, p. 261.]

169. Removal of trustees.] § 40. A trustee may be removed from office by an election, called and conducted in like manner as elections for trustees, or his office declared vacant for a failure to act, immoral conduct or for an abandonment of the faith of the congregation, church or society.

170. Property to vest in corporation, etc.] § 41. Upon the incorporation of any cur-

56

Figure 4. 7

Figure 4. 8

However, Noble Drew Ali's Chauffeur Sheik John Givens EL declared that he, **in keeping with the spirit of the founder**, had reincarnated as Noble Drew Ali and was known and accepted by his followers as "Prophet Noble Drew Ali Reincarnated". It is said that **he was not accepted by many of the members**. It is also reported that he taught from 1929 to 1945 under the corporate entity Moorish Holy Temple of Science.

Two notable pioneers, who sat under both, Noble Drew Ali, and Noble Drew Ali Reincarnated were Grand Sheik Hommett Anderson El and Grand Sheik Richardson El.

Grand Sheik Hommett Anderson El or Brother Hommett El as he preferred to be called was the Moderator/Teacher of the Moorish Holy Temple of Science until his transition several years ago. Members of that entity still exist today.

Public record shows several charter amendments were filed in Cook County Ill which lead to further litigation and autonomy. This continued over the years until 1974 when articles of dissolution were filed in Chicago. During the interim of the litigation of the parties involved, which lasted a few years, another group, lead by Grand Sheik Richardson Dingle-El filed articles of incorporation with the **corporate name of The Moorish Science Temple, Divine and National Movement of North America Inc, #13** in city of Baltimore State of Maryland with the vision that several east coast temples could affiliate with this new entity. Temples from Philadelphia, New Jersey, Delaware and Virginia were uniting. The successes of the temple lead to the **official incorporation** of the Moorish School of Law and History Inc, #13.

Before discussing accomplishments and contributions of the Moorish School of Law and History we will quickly review significant highlights of the school's Founder, Grand Sheik Richardson Dingle El (born in Manning S.C 1910).

In the spirit of the Prophet Noble Drew Ali's initiatives, Grand Sheik Richardson Dingle El under the instruction of the Reincarnated Prophet expanded the founder's work by placing the document entitled **"Our Authority"** and other literature in **National Headquarters, Selective Service System Washington, DC in 1944**. Richardson Dingle EL requested that all Moors be Naturalized according to "Our Authority" as communicated to him in a meeting with General Hershey (Head of the Selective Service System) and Colonel Swartz. He also called for and initiated the concept of the Moorish National Bureau of Vital Statistics. (To be explained) As a result of this activity, Richardson Dingle El became the first so-called Negro to have this erroneous term removed and the first to register with the United States Government as a descendant of Moroccans born in America (further expanding the works of the founder). (Figure 4.9) Documentation from the National Archives (Figure 4.10-11) confirms the above.

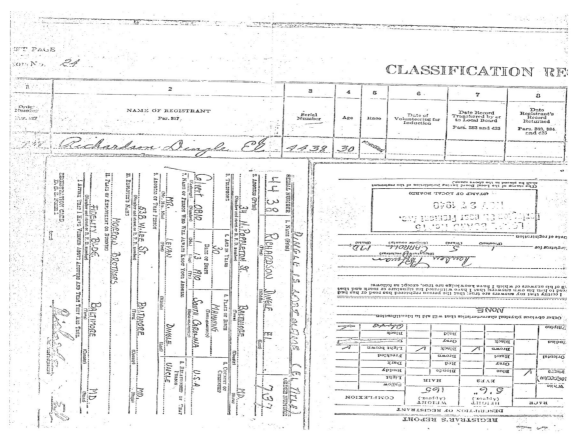

Figure 4.9

UNITED STATES OF AMERICA

GENERAL SERVICES ADMINISTRATION

National Archives and Records Service
Washington, DC 20408

May 25, 1973

Sheik Clarence R. Reynolds-El
146 Siegivart Lane
Baltimore, Maryland 21229

Dear Sheik Reynolds-El:

This is in response to your request, made in my office on May 23, for information on the Selective Service files of Richardson Dingle-El during the period of World War II.

The Selective Service personal case-files for that period have been destroyed. However, our staff have located several pieces of correspondence on Mr. Dingle-El in the general files of Selective Service. These files are available for inspection by members of the public at our Washington National Records Center, 4205 Suitland Road, Suitland, Maryland. If you decide to visit the Center to examine these files, you should ask for Mr. Harry John, who has handled your request.

Sincerely,

James E. O'Neill

JAMES E. O'NEILL
Deputy Archivist
of the United States

Figure 4. 10

LEVITICUS 25:10
SECTION 16
13TH AMENDMENT
(20 SECTIONS)

The Moorish Science Temple
The Divine and National
Movement of North
America, Inc. No. 13

ADEPT CHAMBER

MOORISH SCHOOL OF LAW & HISTORY / PROPHET NOBLE DREW ALI, 3rd, FOUNDER

COPY BOOK 521
FILE NO. 5-39
NATIONAL ARCHIVES
NATIONAL HEADQUARTERS
GENERAL SERVICES ADMIN.
WASHINGTON, D.C. 20408

December 26, 1975

Dr. James E. O'Neill
Deputy Archivist of the United States
General Services Administration
National Archives and Records Service
Washington, D.C. 20408

Dear Dr. O'Neill:

As a result of an extensive investigation, with the help of many government and state agencies into the Articles of Incorporation of The Moorish Science Temple of America, we of The Moorish School of Law and History are happy to inform you that we have at last taken steps to complete the foundation of this movement to eradicate the many misconceptions as to its true purposes by registering Articles of Incorporation in the State of Maryland through Washington, D.C. under the corporate name as follows: The Moorish Science Temple, The Divine and National Movement of North America, Inc. No. 13, as a U. S. Government and State Corporation <u>for pecuniary</u> profit. In addition, The Moorish School of Law and History will function under this Authority as stipulated in Article II, Section A of Articles of Incorporation. We are hereby requesting these extremely important documents to be included with <u>our</u> existing records already in your administrative files.

1. Articles of Incorporation
   (Please note sentence outlined in red on bottom of page
   6 of Articles of Incorporation.)

2. Two letters to Carl Albert, Speaker of the House, U. S.
   House of Representatives, from The Moorish School of
   Law and History, dated October 17, 1975 and October
   23, 1975.

3. Response to The Moorish Law School through Sheik Joiner-Bey
   from Carl Albert.

Date Received in NAG *1-9-76*
Register Number *2750*
Date Due *1-16-76*
Acknowledged (Form 140)
Date *1-8-76*
Reply Required by

NATIONAL HEADQUARTERS

Home Office: 3236 Frederick Avenue - Baltimore, Maryland 21229 - Telephone: 301-947-9567

4. A copy of the letter to me dated April 9, 1973 from Dr. Louis Beck, Assistant to the President of the Board in response to the letter in item no. 3

5. A directive dated September 22, 1973 on behalf of the Grand Sheik specifying the authorized agents representing the Moorish School of Law and History and the Moorish National Bureau of Vital Statistics

6. A copy of a letter dated February 12, 1974 from Deputy Sheik Joiner-Bey to Mr. James C. Evans-El, former Assistant Secretary of Defense Office of Civilian Aide

7. A copy of my letter dated February 22, 1974 to Mr. Walter H. Morse, General Counsel for National Headquarters, Selective Service System, requesting a comprehensive search for lost documents deposited with his agency by the Grand Sheik

8. The letter addressed to me dated March 12, 1974 from Mr. Morse in response to the letter in item no. 7 above

9. A copy of the Charter of the Moorish Science Temple, The Divine and National Movement of North America Inc., presented to the Moorish School of Law and History by Grand Sheik Richardson Dingle-El

10. A sample of the Certificate of Registration utilized by the Moorish National Bureau of Vital Statistics

11. A copy of the first Certificate of Registration issued by the Moorish National Bureau of Vital Statistics. This document was approved by the Maryland Motor Vehicle Administration on February 1, 1974 as per Mr. R. Haburchak

12. A copy of the Oath (Affirmation) of Allegiance to the Constitution of the United States—including the Thirteenth Amendment with Twenty Sections— utilized by the Moorish National Bureau of Vital Statistics for the registration of all true citizens of the United States

We trust that the permanent preservation of these
documents in the National Archives will insure that future
generations thoroughly understand the endeavors we are
undertaking to return the Nation to its proper place
in the perspective of human history.

Sincerely,

Clarence R. Reynolds-El
Sheik, Director
Moorish School of Law
    and History

Figure 4.11

OFFICE OF THE ASSISTANT SECRETARY OF DEFENSE
WASHINGTON 25, D. C.

25 January 1952

Mr. Timothy Dingle El, Business Manager
Moorish Science Temple of America
1221 Myrtle Avenue
Baltimore, Maryland

Dear Sir:

This will acknowledge your letter of 4 January 1952 and your subsequent telephone calls. We regret to learn that members of your Temple, while civilians in jurisdiction intermediate between the Selective Service System and the military services, have been charged with violation of civilian law.

We have discussed with Colonel Campbell C. Johnson your success in meeting all the present requirements of the Selective Service System. We shall continue in our efforts to secure for you a satisfactory understanding regarding possible military status.

However, it may be asserted that the whole question will remain in civil jurisdiction as long as the individual is not in military service. We shall attempt to give you the benefit of any recent developments on this entire subject.

Sincerely yours,

James C. Evans
Civilian Assistant

Figure 4.12

63

Meetings and correspondences took place over three decades with Colonel Campbell C. Johnson and James C. Evans, Assistant to the secretary of Defense, Civilian Aid Office. At a meeting lead by Grand Sheik Richardson Dingle-El and a Moorish Delegation, James C. Evans accepted a Moorish American Nationality Card from the Grand Sheik's correspondence officer and organization secretary (William Wellington Bey) and became known to the Moors as James C. Evans El.

During period around 1952 Grand Sheik Richardson Dingle-EL appointed his younger brother Timothy Dingle-El as national business manager. Also during this period, Timothy Dingle-El received several pieces of correspondence from the assistant Secretary of Defense relative to racial categories and Moorish subject matter. (Figure 4.12-14) A later correspondence from the same office was addressed to William Wellington Bey in 1968 (Figure 4.15).

Timothy Dingle-El wrote a book in the late 70s entitled the *Resurrection*. Minutes of several of the above meetings can be found on www.fbi.gov, under Moorish Science Temple of America, they were released under the Freedom of Information Act. According to that web site the MST of A was investigated by the FBI in 1953 for violation of the Selective Service Act of 1948 and Sedition. In September of 1953, the Department of Justice concluded that prosecution for violation of the Selective Service Act was not warranted. Contrary to what some have been led to believe, the MST of A was found **not to be a subversive organization by the Justice Department.**

Grand Sheik Richardson Dingle-EL went on to resurrect the 13th Amendment with 20 sections and the Executive Will of President Abraham Lincoln which included Compensated Emancipation (to be covered further on in this book). He was also founder of The Moorish School of Law and History Inc. #13. He taught, inspired and instructed members to get in involved on all levels of government, in several states, to bring about a national proclamation for the purpose of having naturalizing all persons of Moorish descent.

Because of his contributions and his courage to spearhead Moorish American recognition on a state and federal level, Grand Sheik Richardson Dingle EL was **revered** by many as Prophet Noble Drew Ali III (not reincarnated) even though he often remarked that he "was just a little brother trying to get a brick out of the wall". Moreover, because there were several others who proclaimed that they in fact were successors to the founder, Grand Sheik Richardson Dingle El remarked to those close to him that his mission "was not to enforce recognition as Prophet Noble Drew Ali III, rather to uplift fallen humanity". He told some that his words, works and deeds will determine who he was.

OFFICE OF THE ASSISTANT SECRETARY OF DEFENSE
WASHINGTON 25, D. C.

28 February 1952

Mr. Timothy Dingle El
Business Manager
Adept Chamber of the
 Moorish Science Temple of America, Inc.
1221 Myrtle Avenue
Baltimore, Maryland

Dear Mr. Dingle El:

This will acknowledge your letter of February 20, 1952, which came at the week end. We are returning herewith the letter which Mr. Bernard J. Flynn, U. S. Attorney, addressed to Levern Dargan Bey on February 5, 1952.

We have an inquiry on this case under date of February 21, 1952, from Mr. Burrell G. Kilmer, U. S. Probation Officer of the United States District Court, District of Maryland.

We have been unable to reach Mr. Kilmer, but understand that he will be in his office tomorrow. As soon as we can reach him, we will furnish information on the background of this case, on the removal of racial designations by Selective Service since the issue was first raised, and on the five racial categories (viz: Caucasian, Negroid, Mongolian, Indian (American) and Malayan) now authorized for the Armed Forces.

Through these approaches, we hope to reach an understanding regarding the situation confronting the Adept Chamber of the Moorish Science Temple of America, Incorporated, and particularly Levern Dargan Bey.

Sincerely yours,

JAMES C. EVANS
Civilian Assistant

Inclosure - 1

Figure 4.13

NATIONAL HEADQUARTERS
SELECTIVE SERVICE SYSTEM
~~MMKR STREET, NORTHWEST~~
WASHINGTON 25, D. C.
451 Indiana Avenue, N.W.

IN REPLYING ADDRESS
THE DIRECTOR OF SELECTIVE SERVICE
AND REFER TO NO.
1-17

December 17, 1952

Mr. Timothy Dingle-El
National Business Manager
Moorish Science Temple of America
1221 Myrtle Avenue
Baltimore 17, Maryland

Dear Mr. Dingle-El:

This will acknowledge your letter of December 5, 1952, which was received on December 15, 1952, in which you outlined at considerable length the philosophy and derivation of races and nationalities in accordance with the teachings of your organization. This was a very interesting statement, and I shall be glad to keep it in my files.

You will be interested to know that the Selective Service System no longer requires racial identity on any of its forms. There are some old forms still in use on which the word "race" appears, but it is not required that this blank be filled out and as soon as the present supply of such forms is exhausted new forms will be issued none of which will have the space for "race." This policy which was inaugurated by the Selective Service System will eliminate the difficulty which certain members of your Temple have had in registering under Selective Service and in filling out other forms required of them.

I shall be pleased to hear from you at any time regarding any matter which might concern the relationship of members of the Moorish Science Temple of America and the Selective Service System.

For The Director

CAMPBELL C. JOHNSON
Colonel, Infantry
Assistant to the Director

Figure 4.14

OFFICE OF THE ASSISTANT SECRETARY OF DEFENSE

WASHINGTON, D. C. 20301

MANPOWER AND
RESERVE AFFAIRS

11 September 1968

Dear Mr. Wellington-Bey:

There was received in this office on 26 August 1968 undated and unsigned <u>Petition to Correct National Descent Name</u> as notarized in Baltimore 13 May 1968. Study of this document does not lead to any change in the position that such petition is beyond the province of this Department. It is however being retained in view of earlier correspondence on this subject.

Please be informed that Colonel Campbell C. Johnson, who gave so much attention to this and similar representations during WWII and thereafter, was buried with military honors on 26 August 1968 in Arlington National Cemetery.

Sincerely yours,

James C. Evans

Mr. William Wellington-Bey
2852 W. Garrison Avenue
Baltimore, Maryland 21215

Figure 4.15

The Moorish School of Law and history started out as the Moorish History and Law class in 1972 and operated in the homes of a special group of young men and women dedicated to the education of its youth as well as other Moorish Americans desiring to see the establishment of a Moorish educational school/center in the community. It may be well here to note stationary bearing the letter head of the Moorish School of Law and History was created and an official seal was adopted, ordered and brought into use well in advance of the official registration of its articles of incorporation.

During the next year, extensive study into the Articles of Association, the Declaration of Independence, United States Constitution, Dred Scott Decision, the 13th ,14th and 15th amendments, Civil War, Compensated Emancipation, the 1883 Supreme Court decision and much more ensued.

The Moorish School of Law and History, Inc. #13 filed articles of incorporation as a distinct entity under the umbrella of its parent Organization, the MST of A, Divine and National Movement Inc #13 in 1976. (Figure 4.16-20) Even though all of the staff of the school was Moorish American, they exercised an open mind concerning the tenet of religion and spiritualism. As of this publication, there are a wide range of Moorish Science Temples, Moorish American entities, organizations, scholars, authors, historians, musicians, entrepreneurs, etc., most understanding the concept of the movement and most working diligently to preserve and teach our culture and true history while seeking recognition in the country in which we live and the nations of the earth. As the Honorable Noble Drew Ali once said "It will be done in a conflict that can not be told in words". As one of the key drafters of the original articles of incorporation of the Moorish School of Law and History, Inc. #13, my primary role was to recruit talent for the purpose of researching, corresponding, developing communication with all levels of government. I was appointed Chairman and chief spokesman. I also taught, lectured, participated in forums, numerous radio programs and a few television shows.

ROLL 113 PAGE 568

MOORISH SCHOOL OF LAW AND HISTORY, INCORPORATED, NO. 13
AMENDED ARTICLES OF INCORPORATION

THIS IS TO CERTIFY:

FIRST: That we, the subscribers, Sheik Eric Agee-Bey, of 3910 Belle Avenue, Baltimore, Maryland 21215, Sheik Clarence R. Reynolds-El, of 146 Siegwart Lane, Baltimore, Maryland 21229, Sheik Malbert Brown-Bey, of 2510 Elsinore Avenue, Baltimore, Maryland 21216, Sheik Anthony L. Leak-El, of 2209 Elsinore Avenue, Baltimore, Maryland 21216, and Sheik Bobby C. McQueen-Bey of 2209 Elsinore Avenue, Baltimore, Maryland 21216, all being of full legal age, do, under and by virtue of the General Laws of the State of Maryland, authorizing the formation of Corporation: and by the authority of the Directors of the Moorish Science Temple, The Divine and National Movement of North America, Incorporated, No. 13, through its Corporate Charter, constitution and by-laws, associate ourselves with the intention of forming a Corporation.

SECOND: The name of the Corporation (which is hereinafter called the "Corporation") is

MOORISH SCHOOL OF LAW AND HISTORY, INCORPORATED, NO. 13

THIRD: The purposes for which the Corporation is formed and the business or objects to be carried on and promoted by it are as follows;

(1) To organize and conduct a School, College, or University for the purpose of teaching and instructing men, women, and youths of all Nationalities, in the Arts, Sciences, and Letters, and for general educational purposes, and to employ the necessary administrators, lecturers, professors, teachers, instructors, and other required personnel in connection therewith.

(2) To give said instructions either directly to the said students or by correspondence.

(3) To grant certificates, diplomas and titles and to confer the usual degrees upon the person or persons who have satisfactorily and fully completed the course or courses of study prescribed by the Corporation as a condition precedent to receiving such certificates, diplomas, titles and degrees, and who moreover in the judgement of the proper authorities of said Corporation are entitled to receive the same.

-1-

Figure 4.16

(4) To operate the Moorish School of Law and History.

(5) To teach people of all Nationalities the things necessary to make them better citizens.

(6) To teach American history and government, with particular stress on the contributions and involvement by persons of Moorish descent to the formation, establishment and maintenence of our governments, state and federal.

(7) To purchase, lease, hire, or otherwise acquire, hold, own, develop improve, and to aid and subscribe toward the acquisition, development or improvement of, and sell or in any manner dispose of real and personal property, and rights and privileges therein, suitable or convenient for any of the business of the Corporation.

(8) To purchase, lease, hire or otherwise acquire, hold, own, construct, erect, improve, manage, operate and in any manner dispose of, and to aid and subscribe toward the acquisition, construction or improvement of buildings, equipment and facilities, and any other property, appliances and items which may appertain to or be useful in the conduct of any of the business of the Corporation.

(9) To borrow or raise money for any of the purposes of the Corporation, and to issue bonds, debentures, notes or other obligations of any nature, and in any manner permitted by law, for moneys so borrowed or in payment for property purchased, or for any other lawful consideration, and to secure the payment thereof and of the interest thereon by mortgage or pledge or conveyance or assignment in trust of the whole or any part of the property of the Corporation, real or personal, including contract rights, whether at the time owned or thereafter acquired, and to sell, pledge, discount or otherwise dispose of such bonds, debentures, notes or other obligations of the Corporation for its corporate purposes.

(10) a. That said Corporation is organized exclusively for educational purposes, including for such purposes, the making of distributions to organizations that qualify as exempt organizations under section 501 (c) (3) of the Internal Revenue Code of 1954 (or the corresponding provision of any other future United States Internal Revenue law).

b. That said Corporation is a non-profit organization and no part of the net-earnings of the Corporation shall inure to the benefit of, or be distributable to, its members, trustees, officers, or other private persons, except

-2-

Figure 4.17

70

that the Corporation shall be authorized and impowered to pay reasonable compensation for services rendered and to make payments and distributions in furtherance of the purposes set forth in these Articles.

c. No substantial part of the activities of the Corporation shall be the carrying on of propaganda, or otherwise attempting to influence legislation and the Corporation shall not participate in, or intervene in (including the publishing or distribution of statements) any political campaign on behalf of any candidate for public office.

d. Notwithstanding any other provision of these Articles, the Corporation shall not carry on any other activities not permitted to be carried on (1) by a Corporation exempt from Federal income taxes under section 501 (c) (3) of the Internal Revenue Code of 1954, or (2) by a Corporation, contributions to which are deductable under section 170 (c) (2) of the Internal Revenue Code of 1954.

e. That if the Corporation is caused to be dissolved, the Board of Trustees shall, after paying or making provision for the payment of all of the liabilities of the Corporation, dispose of all of the assets of the Corporation exclusively for the purposes of the Corporation in such manner, or to such organization or organizations organized and operated exclusively for educational purposes, as shall at the time qualify as an exempt organization or organizations under section 501 (c) (3) of the Internal Revenue Code of 1954 (or a corresponding provision of future United States Internal Revenue law), as the Board of Trustees shall determine. Any such assets not so disposed of shall be disposed of by the Court of Common Pleas of the County in which the principal office of the Corporation is then located, exclusively for such purposes or to such organization or organizations, as said Court shall determine, which are organized and operate exclusively for such purposes.

(11) To carry out all or any part of the aforesaid objects and purpose, and to conduct its business in all or any of its branches, in any or all states, territories, districts and possessions of the United States of America and in foreign countries.

The foregoing objects and purposes shall, except when otherwise expressed, be in no way limited or restricted by reference to, or inferences from, the term of any other clauses of this or any other article of these articles of incorporation or of any amendment thereto, and shall each be regared as indepen-

-3-

Figure 4.18

71

113 PAGE **571**

dent, and construed as powers as well as objects and purposes.

The Corporation shall be authorized to exercise and enjoy all the powers, right and priveleges granted to or conferred upon Corporations of a similar character by the General laws of the State of Maryland now or hereafter in force, and the enumeration of the foregoing powers shall not be deemed to exclude any powers, rights, or privileges so granted or conferred.

FOURTH: The Corporation shall be nonsectarian and privately operated for public benefit.

FIFTH: The post-office address of the place at which the principal office of the Corporation in this State will be located is 3236 W. Frederick Avenue, Baltimore, Maryland 21229. The Resident Agent of the Corporation is Sheik Jacques Leeds-Bey (Attorney At Law), whose post-office address is 1108 Mondawmin Concourse, Baltimore, Maryland 21215. Said resident agent is a citizen of the State of Maryland and actually resides therein.

SIXTH: The said Corporation shall have no capital stock.

SEVENTH: The Corporation shall have three or more trustees and Prophet Noble Drew Ali 3rd, Sheikess Sarah Ferrell-El and Deputy Sheikess Carrie M. Laboo-El shall act as such until the first annual meeting or until their sucessors are duly chosen and qualified.

EIGTH: The duration of the Corporation must be perpetual.

IN WITNESS WHEREOF, we have hereunto set our hands and seal on this 4th day of June, 1976.

Sheik Eric Agee-Bey

Sheik Clarence R. Reynolds-El

Sheik Malbert Brown-Bey

Sheik Anthony L. Leak-El

Sheik Bobby G. McQueen-Bey

Figure 4.19

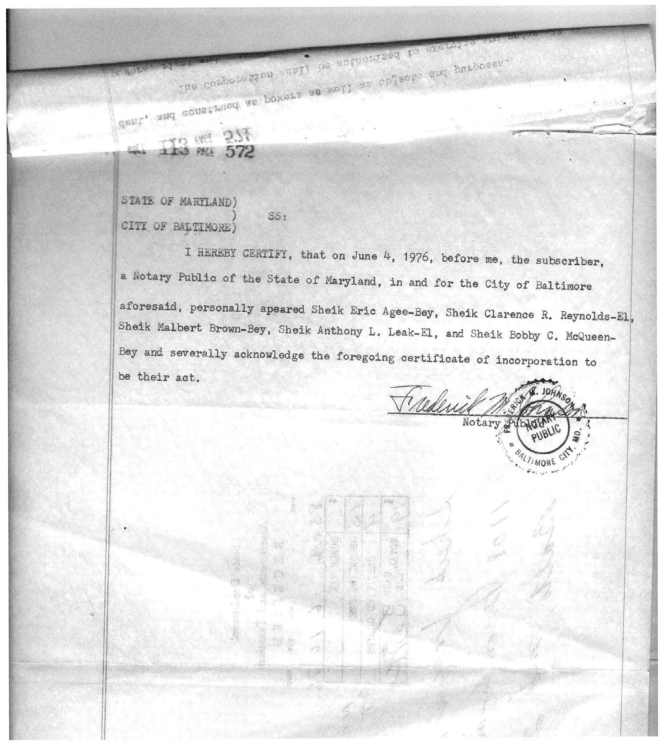

STATE OF MARYLAND)
)   SS:
CITY OF BALTIMORE)

        I HEREBY CERTIFY, that on June 4, 1976, before me, the subscriber,
a Notary Public of the State of Maryland, in and for the City of Baltimore
aforesaid, personally apeared Sheik Eric Agee-Bey, Sheik Clarence R. Reynolds-El,
Sheik Malbert Brown-Bey, Sheik Anthony L. Leak-El, and Sheik Bobby C. McQueen-
Bey and severally acknowledge the foregoing certificate of incorporation to
be their act.

                                                    Notary Public

Figure 4.20

CHAPTER 5

One of the first objectives of the Moorish School of Law and History was to have the erroneous racial labels removed from documents issued by the Maryland Department of Motor Vehicles (MVA). Over the years prior to the Moorish Schools' involvement, several attempts were made by other Moorish Americans to have the racial designations of negro, black and colored removed from the Maryland drivers license. It is necessary to explain here that for a long time prior to 1970 there were two primary classifications of racial categories/ codes on Maryland drivers' licenses-C for colored and W- for white. During this period of time Grand Sheik Richardson Dingle-El was placed in the White category (which I will expound upon shortly) as well as other Africans from North West Africa regardless of their Hue (complexion). Later in the early 70s the classifications were changed to the following numerical codes which appeared on the back of the Maryland Drivers Licenses:

1. black, colored, American Negro, (not of Hispanic origin) all persons having origins in the black racial groups of Africa.

2. White, Caucasian (not of Hispanic origin) –all persons having origins in any of the original peoples of Europe, North Africa, or the Middle East

3. Hispanic – All persons of Mexican, Puerto Rican, Cuban, Central or South American, or other Spanish Culture of origin, regardless of race.

4. Mongoloid, Oriental Asiatic, pacific Islanders ...etc

5. American Indian or Alaska Native...etc

According to Moorish Science along with the dictionary black means death, white means purity, purity means God and God means ruler of the land. Europeans are regarded not as white, but rather as the pale skinned nations of Europe. Research disclosed that Sheik Grand Richardson Dingle-El was the only Moorish American that had both the racial category White and the title EL(proclaiming his Moorish Nationality) on his drivers' license. This racial designation placed Richardson Dingle- El in the same category as the so-called whites and removed him from the derogatory designation of number 1 above. Other Moorish Americans seeking to make this change were met with resistance from the MVA. After studying and analyzing the whole situation it was decided to develop a different strategy. Using Grand Sheik Richardson Dingle- EL's drivers license as precedent, along with the newly developed

Certificate of Registration (the Moorish National Bureau of Vital Statistics), I requested my racial designation and that of my ex wife's, Carolyn Reynolds-EL (now deceased) to be changed to racial designation "2". (figure 5.1)

Maryland Department of Transportation

Motor Vehicle Administration

Harry R. Hughes
Secretary
Ejner J. Johnson
Administrator

December 12, 1972

Shiek Clarence R. Reynolds-El
146 Siegwart Lane
Baltimore, Maryland 21229

Dear Sir:

I am in receipt of a copy of your correspondence to
Mr. N. Barton Benson, Jr., Special Assistant Attorney
General to the Motor Vehicle Administration and his
response to you.

Based on your letter and supporting documents enclosed
therein, I have issued instructions to have your license
and that of your wife amended to show a racial designation
of "2".

If you have any questions, do not hesitate to contact us.

Very truly yours,

William T. S. Bricker
Deputy Administrator

WTSB/vc

CC: Mr. N. Barton Benson, Jr.
     Change of Address Unit

6601 Ritchie Highway, N.E., Glen Burnie, Maryland 21061, Telephone: 301 768-7000

Figure 5.1

Following the success of having our racial designation changed a series of meetings with the MVA were held. This resulted in the MVA **acceptance of the Certificate of Registration** bearing the seal of the Moorish School of Law and History as the exclusive document to change the racial identity of its members as well as annex as a suffix EL or Bey to the individuals' last name on the MVA drivers' license. (See figures 5.2 and 5.3, the copy of Certificate of Registration and first copy of original signed Certificate of Registration) Almost immediately afterwards approximately **thirty Moorish Americans** under the auspices of the Moorish School of Law and History utilized this new process successfully. What occurred next was very unfortunate. A small delegation of older Moorish Americans (not affiliated with the school or its parent body) hearing about the success, went to the MVA with the intention of usurping the process. They proceeded to tell the MVA that the Moorish School of Law and History had no authority to initiate this process without their consent which was totally unfounded. Moreover, this was difficult to understand because the acceptance of the Certificate of Registration and the agreement with the MVA would have been beneficial to all Moorish Americans in the State of Maryland with far reaching possibilities. As a result the MVA viewed this as confusion and disunity in the Moorish Movement and consequently brought a halt to the whole agreement. Incidentally, all the Moorish Americans who made the transition successfully **remain in tact today**.

There is another important element concerning the thirty Moorish Americans spoken of above whom utilized the process successfully. Periodically, whenever one of these Moorish Americans were stopped by law enforcement officers and asked to present his or her drivers license, and the racial code of white was noted on the back of the driver's license actually stunned the officers; particularly after it was verified through MVA via radio call in. Eventually, this activity and the threat of a law suit by the Moorish School of Law and History ultimately lead to the **elimination of racial categories** on all Maryland Drivers License. (Figure 5.4) In keeping with the goals and objectives of the MVA the same held true with the Department of Mental Health and Hygiene (DHMH) which is the parent entity of the Bureau of Vital Statistics for the State of Maryland. This is the entity that is charged by the state to record all births and deaths and to issue documents reflecting this information. We were attempting to have the erroneous racial categories of negro, black and colored completely removed from the "Live Record or Certificate of birth" from DHMH and its subordinate entities. Notwithstanding our zealousness to have this change implemented, we began to realize that it would be more practical and beneficial to focus our energies on removing these derogatory designations from conscious Moorish Americans (persons already educated to our ancestral heritage and culture) first. We understood that persons who were not educated to Moorish history and some who refused to be re-educated would most definitely resist a blanket change. This was all the more reason to implement the Moorish National Bureau of Vital Statistics. While the Moorish National Bureau of Vital Statistics was conceived in 1942 **it was not developed and implemented** until the first Certificate was created by then Sheik C. Reynolds-El and Sheik Herbert Joiner-Bey and then subsequently signed by Grand Sheik Richardson Dingle-EL.

Moorish School
of
Law And History

Grand Sheik Richardson Dingle-El, Founder

LEVITICUS 25:10
SECTION 16
13TH AMENDMENT
(20 SECTIONS)

COPY BOOK 521
FILE NO. 5-39
NATIONAL ARCHIVES
NATIONAL HEADQUARTERS
GENERAL SERVICES ADMIN.
WASHINGTON, D.C. 20408

Certificate of Registration

Moorish
National Bureau
of
Vital Statistics

In accordance with the true policies of Noble Drew Ali and Presidents Abraham Lincoln and Andrew Johnson, this document exists as a certification that the individual indicated below has taken and subscribed an oath (affirmation) of allegiance to the Constitution of the United States of America — including the Thirteenth Amendment with Twenty Sections. The individual has also proclaimed his true Free National Name, Race, Nationality, and Religion as follows:

NAME

RACE   NATIONALITY

DATE OF BIRTH   PLACE OF BIRTH

DATE OF PROCLAMATION

LOCATION   RELIGION

The ancient name " _____ " must be annexed as a suffix to the slave family name of the individual in all public and private records throughout the state, states, and nations, etc. Upon the complete implementation of Sections Sixteen and Seventeen of the Thirteenth Amendment with Twenty Sections to the U.S. Constitution, the individual will receive his full permanent ancestral name through the United States Government.

_____
DIVINE MINISTER

_____
DIRECTOR AND NATIONAL REGISTRAR

SAMPLE COPY

National Archives Record Group No. 147
See Form OAAN — 7003: Social Security Administration

Figure 5.2

Moorish School

of

Law And History

Grand Sheik Richardson Dingle-El, Founder

LEVITICUS 25:10
SECTION 16
13TH AMENDMENT
(20 SECTIONS)

COPY BOOK 521
FILE NO. 5-39
NATIONAL ARCHIVES
NATIONAL HEADQUARTERS
GENERAL SERVICES ADMIN.
WASHINGTON, D.C. 20408

Certificate of Registration

Moorish
National Bureau
of
Vital Statistics

In accordance with the true policies of Noble Drew Ali and Presidents Abraham Lincoln and Andrew Johnson, this document exists as a certification that the individual indicated below has taken and subscribed an oath (affirmation) of allegiance to the Constitution of the United States of America — including the Thirteenth Amendment with Twenty Sections. The individual has also proclaimed his true Free National Name, Race, Nationality, and Religion as follows: SSAN: 216-34-5389

NAME CLARENCE RIDOUT REYNOLDS-EL

RACE ASIATIC   NATIONALITY MOORISH AMERICAN

DATE OF BIRTH MAY 30, 1939   PLACE OF BIRTH BALTIMORE, MD.

DATE OF PROCLAMATION FEBRUARY 22, 1971

LOCATION BALTIMORE, MD.   RELIGION ISLAMISM

The ancient name " _____EL_____ " must be annexed as a suffix to the slave family name of the individual in all public and private records throughout the state, states, and nations, etc. Upon the complete implementation of Sections Sixteen and Seventeen of the Thirteenth Amendment with Twenty Sections to the U.S. Constitution, the individual will receive his full permanent ancestral name through the United States Government.

Ernest Wright-Bey Sheik
Ernest J. Wright-Bey, Sheik
DIVINE MINISTER

Clarence R. Reynolds-El, Sheik
Clarence R. Reynolds-El, Sheik
DIRECTOR AND NATIONAL REGISTRAR

R.D.E
Richardson Dingle-El, Grand Sheik
FOUNDER

National Archives Record Group No. 147
See Form OAAN — 7003: Social Security Administration

"ORIGINAL & ONLY COPY SIGNED By the Founder of the School"

Figure 5.3

Maryland Department of Transportation

Motor Vehicle Administration

Harry R. Hughes
Secretary
Ejner J. Johnson
Administrator

May 25, 1976

Sheik Clarence R. Reynolds-El
Moorish Science Temple of
   America, Inc.
National Headquarters
3236 Frederick Avenue
Baltimore, Maryland   21229

Dear Sheik Reynolds-El:

I am sure you will be gratified that Governor Marvin Mandel
signed House Bill 1236 and, beginning January 1, 1977, all
drivers' licenses and renewals will contain a photograph of
the driver and will show no racial designation.

The new licenses will be renewed on a four-year basis so
that by 1980 no racial designation should appear on any
Maryland driver's license. Consequently, it will not be necessary
for the Moorish Science Temple of America, Inc., to take any
legal or legislative action regarding changing racial designations
since no racial designation will exist.

Very truly yours,

William T. S. Bricker
Deputy Administrator

WTSB/vc

CC: Mrs. Joanna Lehane

6601 Ritchie Highway, N.E., Glen Burnie, Maryland 21062, Telephone: 301 768-7000

Figure 5.4

The Certificate of Registration issued by the Moorish National Bureau of Vital Statistics was originally designed to be issued to Moorish American adults and or parents (in lieu of a National Proclamation) for the purpose of recording their nationality (Moorish American) and to annex as a suffix the **ancestral title EL or Bey** to any and all records throughout the State, States and Nation. In this case the state of Maryland was the starting point. Read the letter from the Deputy Secretary of DHMH (Figure 5.5). Note, his entire emphasis is on the name change via a court order; he completely side steps the issue of race and nationality. However, the response from our attorneys at that time clarified our position (Figure 5.6). This follow up was never responded to. During this period of time several agencies would accept the Certificate of Registration with the exception of the bureau of vital statistics. They refused to make any changes without a court order.

Before discussing court orders let me point out that since the era of the 1970' and especially in the late 90s' and 2000s' there have been numerous Moorish Americans who have designed similar and varying documents to accomplish annexation of EL, Bey, Ali or in many cases complete name change. Here I must state emphatically that there should be no charge whatsoever for any Moorish American (conscious or elevating from an unconscious state) for correcting his or her existing live birth record.

After having said that, because of the unlawful/illegal imposition of the Fourteenth Amendment on the former slaves and **absent a National Proclamation** for all Moorish Americans, complete chaos has set in. Many Moorish Americans in several states desirous of proclaiming their nationality and choosing ancient and cultural names have several different documents in their possession, but the live birth record or certificate of the state in which they were born has not been amended to reflect their Moorish name. Almost every state requires a court order to effect any changes. Anyone who applies for a United States of America Passport is required to produce a live record or certificate of birth from the state in which they are born. What ever name appears on ones birth record/certificate is the name that is going on the passport.

The process' for obtaining a court order is a lot easier than most people think. First a petition is filed in court stating the reasons for the name change including Moorish ancestry etc and order of publication to be published in a local news paper for a period of three consecutive weeks (the publication time may very from state to state). After the publication a judge will sign the order providing no one contest the filings. Moreover, the single petition may contain **multiple persons desiring the change**. One of the key advantages of having corrections made via a court order is your original birth record is amended to reflect what ever name you choose and that document along with the order of the court is used to implement corrections on all of your important papers. Further this process eliminates the "also known as" (aka) syndrome.

OFFICE OF THE SECRETARY
DEPARTMENT OF HEALTH AND MENTAL HYGIENE
301 WEST PRESTON STREET · BALTIMORE, MARYLAND 21201 · Area Code 301 · 383-6196

Neil Solomon, M.D., Ph.D., Secretary

May 30, 1974

Refer to:
1A:HS
Your reference: Moorish Science Temple of America, Inc.
Bureau of Vital Statistics

Jeffrey I. Goldman, Esquire
Walker, Smelkinson & McCadden
306 Court Square Building
Calvert & Lexington Streets
Baltimore, Maryland 21202

Dear Mr. Goldman:

Under Maryland law the Secretary of Health and Mental Hygiene is charged with the responsibility of collecting, registering and preserving certificates of birth, death and fetal deaths (Annotated Code of Maryland, Article 43, Section 14). Since these and related functions are specifically assigned to the Secretary by law, they could not be delegated to an agency outside of the Maryland Department of Health and Mental Hygiene.

However, members of the Moorish Science Temple of America, Inc. do have available to them a mechanism for changing their names on their birth certificates. Upon receipt of a court order or certified copy thereof changing the name of a person born in Maryland and upon request of the individual concerned, his parent, guardian or legal representative, the birth certificate can be amended to reflect the new name [Article 43, Section 19 (a)(3)].

So far as I am aware, the Department of Health and Mental Hygiene could neither sanction nor disapprove the establishment of a Moorish Bureau of Vital Statistics. Many organizations do establish record keeping systems for their own special purposes, but these are outside the purview of DHMH. Creation of such a bureau would not relieve our Department of the responsibility of registering all births occurring in Maryland, nor could we recognize or accept the Certificate of Registration maintained by the Moorish Bureau of Vital Statistics in lieu of a court order for purposes of effecting a change in name on a birth certificate.

Sincerely yours,

Herbert H. Rosenbaum,
Deputy Secretary

Figure 5.5

Rommani M. Amenu-El

LAW OFFICES

WALKER, SMELKINSON AND McCADDEN

306 COURT SQUARE BUILDING

CALVERT & LEXINGTON STREETS

BALTIMORE, MARYLAND 21202

ROLAND WALKER
PAUL SMELKINSON
JAMES F. McCADDEN

JEFFREY I. GOLDMAN
DOMENIC R. IAMELE

JOHN A. PICCIOTTO
    LEGAL ASSISTANT

TELEPHONE 727-371?
AREA CODE 301

August 12, 1974

Herbert H. Rosenbaum,
Deputy Secretary
Department of Health and Mental Hygiene
301 West Preston Street
Baltimore, Maryland   21201

> Re: Moorish Science Temple
>   of America, Inc.
>   Bureau of Vital Statistics

Dear Mr. Rosenbaum:

Let me thank you for your response to our letter of April 9, 1974. Although I understand your position in this matter, I feel that you might have misunderstood my intentions.

It is our desire to establish a Maryland division of a Moorish National Bureau of Statistics for the purpose of indicating that the true race of the alleged "black" American is, in reality, Moorish American. We desire to have this indication made on the Certificate of Registration so that the State of Maryland will also make the necessary changes in its classification.

Accordingly, I would appreciate hearing from you concerning the Department's position relative to their acceptance of these certificates so that there can be a change in their racial designation.

Thank you for your cooperation in this matter.

Very truly yours,

Figure 5.6

Many persons being introduced to Moorish Science with the intention of pro-claiming/declaring their nationality, are given the understanding that they must immediately file Uniform Commercial Code (UCC) documents or instruments in order to gain sovereign status. Firstly, I am not astute in the UCC matters. From what limited knowledge I do have UCC has several commercial benefits and there are a small percentage of Moorish Americans as well as Europeans who are very knowledgeable of the process, as it requires research and intensive study. It is not a prerequisite for claiming Moorish Nationality. I strongly urge the study of National Citizenship as it applies to former slaves and their status in this country first.

In our efforts to resurrect and implement the Executive Will of Abraham Lincoln, we initiated meetings and sent correspondence to the first Founders of the black caucus and the U.S. Senate, (Carl Albert-House Speaker, Peter Rodino-Chairman of the House Judiciary Committee). We held meetings with the founder of the black caucus, the late, Parren J. Mitchell. Though we were able to hold audience with the black caucus, no real effort had been made on its part to take action on our behalf, which, ironically was for their own benefit as well.

During this period of time a strong contingency of Moorish American brothers and sisters from Philadelphia lead by Sheik Charles Glen-El working under the auspices of Grand Sheik Richardson-El were very active in meeting with several southern senators as well as members of the black caucus, especially Congressman Robert C. Nix Jr., Philadelphia PA. See letter addressed to Congressman Nix (Figure 5.7-9). Also see the analysis (Figures 5.10-13) done by Mark Stout (legislative aide) to Congressman Nix. These Moors from Philadelphia coordinated various activities with staff from the Moorish School. They also created a periodical newsletter entitled the "Moor Sense" (Figure 5.14).

The Moorish Science Temple of America, Inc.

P. O. Box 6808　Headquarters

Philadelphia, Pennsylvania 19132　　　　　　Phone

September 3, 1973

Con. Robert N. C. Nix Jr.
2139 N. 22nd Street
Philadelphia, Pa.

Dear Sir:

As per request, the following delineation is in reference to the resolution of the so-called negro/black dilemma, within every city and state throughout the United States of America.

The legal basis for the above stated remedial action will be in accordance with, to wit: The Levitical Code, Leviticus chapter 25 verse 10, which is enscribed upon the Liberty Bell, The Fifth Article of Amendment to the U. S. Constitution, The Dred Scott decision and the supplement thereto by Chief Justice Taney, The Initial Emancipation Proclamation, of date, Sept. 22, 1862, President Lincoln's Annual message and attached Resolution to Congress, of date December 1, 1862, The Proclamation of Amnesty and Reconstruction of date December 4, 1863, and reissued by Andrew Johnson on May 29, 1865, The Originally proposed, passed and ratified Thirteenth Article of Amendment with twenty sections to the U. S. Constitution, The U. S. Supreme Court's Civil Rights decision of 1883, and Federal File #5-39 of date August 11, 1944, which is presently housed in the National Archives.

It is imperative to the maintenance of the public peace and order that an Executive order requiring General Registration be issued by the President for the purpose of having Naturalized, all persons of Moorish descent, who otherwise are improperly known as negroes, black people, colored folks and any other misnomer or psuedonym applied to said persons as a result of their enslavement. Said registration to take place in compliance with the above cited edicts.

RESOLVED

That the Registration Procedure be implemented in the following manner, namely, Establishment of Registration facilities by the Federal Government

Figure 5.7

within every city and state throughout the United States of America, and the nations of the world, wherein said persons reside, in compliance with the Proclamation of Amnesty and Reconstruction, of date December 4, 1863.

2.   That said persons be returned to their rightful family names upon their Naturalization and their resultant relinquishing of the surname of their slaveholders, in compliance with the Levitical Code or Hebrew Law, namely, Leviticus 25-10, of which is enscribed upon the Liberty Bell.

3.   That the slaveholders be compensated by the Federal Government for their human property, following which the slaveholders would compensate those persons held to Involuntary Servitude as specified by the Levitical Code, The Emancipation Proclamation of date September 22, 1862, Section 17 of the Thirteenth Amendment and the Fifth Article of Amendment to the U. S. Constitution.

4.   That those persons of Moorish Descent, in America, be educated to their Moorish Heritage, the Thirteenth Article of Amendment with twenty sections, and to the true roles of Presidents, Abraham Lincoln and his successor Andrew Johnson with reference to said persons, and that the above mentioned educational process begin upon the issu- ance of the aforementioned Executive Order, by creating new educational facilities and also incor- porating into existing educational systems throughout the U. S. A. cirricular studies of the order of those previously mentioned in this paragraph. The learning process to last until consummated but not to extend beyond the period of _____ years as established by the Congress.

5.   That such persons having been properly and sufficiently endowed, in compliance with the pre- ceding paragraphs will be disposed to self determination and as a result subsequently colonized upon the land located between the Allegheny and Rocky mountain chains, otherwise historically known as the Louisiana Purchase as specified by the September 22, 1862, Emancipation Proclamation, President Lincoln's December 1, 1862 resolution to Congress and the Thirteenth Article of Amendment (with twenty sections) to the U. S. Consti- tution, namely, Section 17.   The completion of the Colonization procedure not to extend beyond the period of _____ years as established by the Congress.

6.   That the cases and plans presently before the Federal Judiciary with reference to the supposed desegregation and the establishment of so-called racial balances within the various public school districts throughout the U. S. A. be terminated, in

Figure 5.8

Page 3

order that the public mind be at rest, and peace and order be insured, this to take place in compliance with the U. S. Supreme Court's 1883, Civil Rights decision.

7. That the Congress undertake to establish a Federal department for the purpose of processing and the reclassification of the vital records of all Americans of Moorish extraction, in every city and state throughout the U. S. A. and the nations of the world.

8. That the authentic Thirteenth Article of Amendment (with twenty sections) to the U. S. Constitution be immediately restored to its rightful organic function in the U. S. Constitution, and that its provisions be immediately and completely complied with.

9. That the present Thirteenth, Fourteenth and Fifteenth Amendments be expunged from the U. S. Constitution in compliance with the aforementioned U. S. Supreme Court's 1883, Civil Rights decision.

The preceding information is a synopsis which is of course subject to expansion and refinement. Please do not hesitate to contact us should you desire further clarification. I can be reached by phone at BA9-2669.

Sincerely yours,

Charles Glenn El

Charles Glenn El, Sheik

CGEL:spel
cc:file

Figure 5.9

Robert N. C. Nix
2D DISTRICT, PENNSYLVANIA

OFFICES:
2201 RAYBURN BUILDING
WASHINGTON, D.C. 20515

2139 NORTH 22D STREET
PHILADELPHIA, PENNSYLVANIA

8325 STENTON AVENUE
PHILADELPHIA, PENNSYLVANIA

COMMITTEES:
FOREIGN AFFAIRS
POST OFFICE AND CIVIL SERVICE

CHAIRMAN:
ASIAN AND PACIFIC AFFAIRS

SUBCOMMITTEE ON
AFRICA

Congress of the United States
House of Representatives
Washington, D.C. 20515

September 24, 1974

MEMO

TO: Mr. Nix

FROM: Mark Stout

SUBJECT: Moorish Science Temple

The Moorish group sets forth a theory of racial origins of blacks. They believe that American blacks are Moors descended from an ancient Moroccan Empire, and that subsequent names given to this people have been used to hide their true national identity.

They rely on a number of documents, mostly from Reconstruction days, to support their three basic demands: compensated emancipation, naturalization of blacks, and colonization of blacks. I have obtained these documents and an analysis of these references is attached.

Compensated emancipation was indeed proposed by President Lincoln, as a way of ending the Civil War. This proposal was unsuccessful. The Moorish group wants former slave owners compensated for the loss of their slaves, and former slaves compensated by their former owners.

The Moorish group argues that blacks were not made citizens by the Fourteenth Amendment. They use the Dred Scott Decision of 1856 as support for the contention that free blacks are not citizens. They believe that the Federal government should set up a program of registration and naturalization to make blacks U.S. citizens.

They also argue for the colonization of blacks between the Alleghanies and the Rockies. President Lincoln did support the idea of colonizing freed blacks, but only once did he suggest that this might take place within the United States.

A great deal of emphasis is placed on the proposed Thirteenth Amendment with twenty sections. They believe that

Figure 5.10

89

Mr. Nix
page 2
September 24, 1974

this amendment was actually ratified, and was replaced by a
conspiracy with the present Thirteenth Amendment of two sections.
I have obtained the proposed amendment from the National
Archives. Ironically, the amendment is a pro-slavery amendment,
which would have guaranteed the rights of slave-holders, enforced
a fugitive slave law, and prevented the abolition of slavery
without the approval of every slave state. One section, however,
does authorize Congress to compensate states that voluntarily
abolish slavery and to assist freed persons to colonize Africa.

The founder of the Moorish group, Sheik Richardson Dingle-El,
supposedly got his plan for reclassifying and registering blacks
approved by the Selective Service System. However, the National
Archives has been unable to locate any such document.

The historical evidence used to back up the theories set
forth by the Moorish group is weak and often contradictory.
Their present demands apparently are for Congress to impose the
Thirteenth Amendment of twenty sections and to set up the
program of compensated emancipation, naturalizstion, and
colonization.

Figure 5.11

_3_

References: Moorish Science Temple of America

1. Preliminary Emancipation Proclamation, Sept. 22, 1862: President Lincoln proposes offering financial aid to the slave states that have not seceded, if they agree to abolish slavery. He also promises to continue "the effort to colonize persons of African descent, with their consent, upon this continent, or elsewhere, with the previously obtained consent of the Governments existing there." He also recommends that loyal citizens be compensated for the loss of slaves after the war.

2. Annual Message to Congress, Dec. 1, 1862: President Lincoln proposes amendments to the Constitution that would (1) provide for compensation to states that abolish slavery, (2) secure freedom to slaves who have been freed by the chances of war, and (3) authorize Congress to provide for "colonizing free colored persons, with their own consent, at any place or places without the United States." He also reports that he has entered negotiations with several nations for the proposed colonization plan. He discusses the future importance of the land between the Alleghanies and the Rockies, but he does not propose colonization of free slaves there.

3. Proclamation of Amnesty and Reconstruction, Dec. 8, 1863: President Lincoln provides for a method by which seceding states can return to the Union. He announces that he will approve of provisions by returning states in regard to their free people "which shall recognize and declare their permanent freedom, provide for their education, and which may yet be consistent, as a temporary arrangement, with their present condition as a laboring, landless, and homeless class."

4. Proposed Thirteenth Amendment to the Constitution, with twenty sections: This was a proposed pro-slavery amendment. Section XVII would allow for financial compensation by Congress for states abolishing slavery, and would authorize Congress to assist free people of African descent "to emigrate and civilize Africa."

Figure 5.12

91

4.

5. Civil Rights Cases of 1883: In these cases the Supreme Court ruled unconstitutional that part of the Civil Rights Act of 1875 which prohibited denying the use of public accomodations and facilities to persons because of race, color, or previous condition of servitude.

6. Dred Scott Decision of 1856: In this decision, the Supreme Court held, among other things, that a free person of African descent was not a citizen and could not be naturalized as a citizen.

7. Leviticus 25:10: As inscribed on the Liberty Bell, "Proclaim liberty throughout all the land unto all the inhabitants thereof."

Figure 5.13

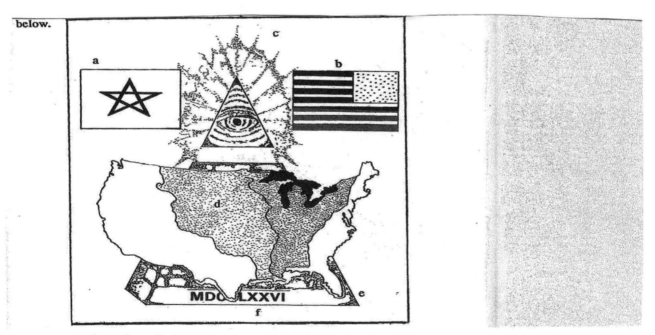

Above is a photo of the cover of a publication called the "Moor Sense". In the early 70's a Special group of Adepts from Philadelphia, PA were responsible for the creation and circulation of the publication which was largely distributed to high levels of state and federal government officials including the US Senate and House of Representatives. This publication was spearhead by Sheik Charles Glen-El. This group of Adepts was under the guidance of Grand Sheikh Richardson Dingle-El and worked closely with the Moorish School of Law and History.

Figure 5.14

CHAPTER 6

Correspondence to General Alexander Haig, Chief of Staff, under the Nixon Administration which outlined our legal position concerning the status of Moors in the United States had been sent by the Moorish School of Law and History. (Figure 6.0) We received correspondence from the Justice Department relevant to our writings to the Chief of Staff. (Figure 6.1) During this same period, the IRS National Director's Office was placed on notice that we, Moors, would no longer pay income taxes until such time as our correct citizenship status had been recognized and compensation be distributed as outlined in the Compensated Emancipation. As a result of our contact with the IRS National Director's Office, several encounters with the Internal Revenue Service developed. Initially, in September, 1974 a contingency of seven of our officers went to IRS headquarters in Washington DC to discuss the issue of **not being liable to pay income taxes**. On October 1974 a larger contingency of officers from the Moorish School of Law and History met with a team of IRS officials at the direction of the IRS national director.

A letter addressed to the IRS almost identical to the one sent to General Alexander Haig (then chief of staff under the Nixon Administration) was presented to the assistant Commissioner-Technical. The letter addressed to General Haig outlined all of the reasons that former Moorish slaves (held under the term negro or black were not liable for paying income taxes. The IRS was also provided with a starter list of all the persons to be exempt along with their social security numbers.

Following that meeting, employed members began **increasing** their exemptions to thirteen to **preclude taxes from being withheld** by their employers. This activity accelerated very quickly. About eight months later on May 22nd 1975 the Intelligence Division of the IRS called in one of our officers, Bobby C. McQueen-Bey for investigation. I accompanied Bobby McQueen-Bey as chairman and spokesman. (Figure 6.2)

Following the interrogation, the investigative agent wrote in his conclusion and recommendation, "...it is felt that there is /insufficient evidence to establish that the tax payer's filling of a false Form W-2 was done with the express purpose of defrauding the government". (See Figure 6.3) Two months later Sheik McQueen-Bey received correspondence from the District Director stating that the intelligence Division is no longer participating in the investigation of his tax liability. (Figure 6.4)

From that point forward the membership in the movement was rapidly increasing. While the tax issue attracted many, they were taught Moorish History and the importance of proclaiming Moorish Nationality.

In September 1978 four members of the movement were indicted for filing false W-2 exemptions resulting in a federal court case. A few days before the trial, law offices of our attorney Jacques E. Leeds-Bey, Sr., (which also housed the business offices of the school) were receiving numerous telephone calls the New York Times, Chicago Tribune, Washington Post etc., all expressing a high level of interest in the case. On the day of the trial not one of the national news papers was present, the only exception being a local news paper, the News American. (Figure 6.5)

We later learned from a reliable source that the US Justice Department had discretely shut off coverage implying that this case could ignite civil disturbance. Remember, this was less than a decade since civil disorder erupted with the assassination of Dr. Martin Luther King. I remember the day we went to court vividly. Many of the Moorish Americans in the area took off from work. We all assembled at the Moorish school's headquarters at 519 N. Howard St in downtown Baltimore. Most of the brothers were dressed in suits, ties and red fezzes. The sisters were dressed in all white and their turbans were tied immaculately. Our security force was dressed in dark uniforms and red fezzes. We had prayer and formed in ranks outside with the lead security manning the large Moroccan/ Moorish flag along with the American flag. We marched to the US Federal District Court which was approximately ten blocks from our headquarters.

Upon arriving at the court we posted two Moorish sentinels with both flags on each side of the entrance of the assigned court room. Federal Marshals told the sentinels that they would have to move from their positions to which the sentinels replied "we have orders to remain where we are". The marshals then turned away. When all of our members were seated in the court room, I looked around and was extremely proud to be a Moorish American. All of the officers (Sheiks and Sheikesses) were highly disciplined and reflected the decorum of true adepts. Our chief attorney Sheik Jacques E Leeds-Bey Sr., was seated at the defense table with his fez on awaiting the opening of the trial. The Judge, C. Stanley Blair began using intimidating tactics by asking all who were wearing hats to remove them. Our attorney replied that we were entitled to wear our fezzes as these were our national and religious headdress.

Over the next several days several motions were filed by our attorney and his assistant Robert J. Kessler. We also filed a writ of Mandamus and Prohibition against Judge C. Stanley Blair for exhibiting patent bias in referring to the Moorish Americans defendants as black. Judge Blair died about a year later. The writ and several motions on the questions of jurisdiction were denied which lead to the Moorish American defendants opting to stand mute and signed an affidavit stating that standing mute in no way was an admission of their guilt. Even though the case was lost in the district level the door was opened for an immediate appeal to the Richmond Fourth Circuit Court of Appeals. (Figure 6.6) At the court of appeals our attorney Leeds-Bey asked the court if the Fourteenth Amendment effectively reversed the Dred Scott decision and could the Fourteen Amendment unilaterally impose citizenship on persons of African decent without their consent? When that question was asked the panel of Judges stepped down from the bench and pressed the hand of our attorney and two of us who were present and uttered the words "good luck".

The court of appeals would not write an opinion but merely wrote one sentence stating that the answer was found in the Thirteenth and Fourteenth Amendments which they knew would open the door for a writ of certiorari to the Supreme Court. (Figure 6.7) The Supreme Court denied the writ. The senior clerk did everything in his power to keep us from filing the writ. It was obvious that he did not want this case to get on record. However, we filed at the eleventh hour successfully. Incidentally, none of the Moorish American defendants in the case were incarcerated or had to repay any previous taxes.

Moorish School
of
Law And History

COPY BOOK 521
FILE NO. 5-39
NATIONAL ARCHIVES
NATIONAL HEADQUARTERS
GENERAL SERVICES ADMIN.
WASHINGTON, D.C. 20408

LEVITICUS 25:10
SECTION 16
13TH AMENDMENT
(20 SECTIONS)

Grand Sheik Richardson Dingle-El, Founder
P.O. Box 7063, Baltimore, Maryland 21216

August 19, 1974

General Alexander Haig
Chief of Staff
The White House
1600 Pennsylvania Avenue
Washington, D.C. 20005

Dear General Haig:

We of the Moorish School of Law and History desire that the
Executive Branch of the Federal government assist us in
terminating the most heinous crime in human history. It
involves the fact that as the United States of America
approaches the bicentennial celebration of its birth, this
Nation has lived a heidous lie for the entire 200 years of
its existence as a sovereign state.

According to all unadulterated scientific and historical
records, there is no "Negro", "black", or "colored" race
in the human family of peoples and nations. In order to
obtain the truth concerning the origin of the so-called
"black" people of America, one must return to the year
990 A.D. when the Moorish slave-traders exchanged dark-
skinned Moors for the lighter-skinned Moors who had been
captured by a Portuguese adventurer. The dark-skinned,
Moorish bondsmen and bondsmaids were branded by the
Portuguese and Spanish with names from their European
(Romance) Languages which allude to slavery. Thus the term
"negro"—derived from the Latin word "niger", meaning
"black"—and several variations of it came into use for
this degraded purpose not only in the Iberian Peninsular,
but also in other parts of Europe. Over the centuries,
this term evolved from "negro Moor" to "blackamoor" to
"black" to "negro." (See Horace Greeley, The American
Conflict, published in 1865 and George Bancroft, History
of the United States of America published in 1854.

Figure 6.0

-2-

The word "black" and all of its variations in all languages
have always connoted evil, misery and death. Moreover, the
equally inappropriate term "colored" imples that the indivi
dual described has been painted, varnished, stained or dyed
"Afro" or "African" are terms which arose from the European
name "Africa" branded upon that continent by the ancient
Romans in honor of the Roman general Scipio Africanus
following his conquest of the Moorish City of Carthage.
Clearly, none of these misnomers—"Negro," "black", "colore
or "African"—can be legitimately applied to any people of
human family because such expressions not only fail to
accurately designate the true Race and National Origin of
the people described but also degrade such people to the le
of sub-human existence. In particular, since the so-called
"black" folks of the United States were, in fact, Moors in
990 A.D., they must be, therefore, Moors in 1974 A.D. Thes
Moors are descendants of the ancient Moabites, who inhabite
the north-western and south-western shores of the land
Europeans call "Africa" but whose true name is "Amexem."

To carry this matter to a higher degree, we recall that thi
land "Amexem" extends across the great Atlantis along the c
Moorish trade route defined by the 36° 30' parallel to the
known today as "North, Central and South America"—the old
Moroccan Empire. As descendants of Moroccans born in Ameri
we are the true and historically-verified Moorish-American
heirs to land where the United States of America has been
established.

Every person in this country wants to fined a way to perman
solve the so-called "Negro/black" problem in America. The
only way this dilemma can be allivated is through the comp
implementation of the United States Constitution including
the Thirteenth Amendment with Twenty Sections. Let us now
briefly review the historic background of this law.

Although twenty Moorish Sheiks and Sheikesses were brought
to Jamestown in 1620 in a Dutch man-of-war bearing Spanish
individual names (as well as the general term "Negro") forc
upon them by the Spanish slave-masters from whom the Dutch
commandeered these bondsmen, unbound Moors had inhabited an
civilized the Western Hemisphere for centuries before
Christopher Columbus supposedly "discovered" a part of the
world for Europeans that had never been lost to the Asiatic
peoples. (Unfortunately, these Moors of the West engaged i
an extensive slave trade in human property of all races wit
these Moors of the East.) It was these Moors of the West w
with the support of the Sultan of Morocco, helped win the
Revolutionary War against the yoke of Great Britian for the
Thirteen Colonies and who assisted the negotiation of the
1786 treaty between Morocco and the United States. More
importantly, men of Moorish descent comprised the majority
at the Constitutional Convention in 1787.

In writing the Constitution, the minds of these men were drawn to the work of the 1776 Continental Congress which produced the Declaration of Independence declaring all men of all races and nationalities free and equal, as well as the Liberty Bell, bearing the inscription of Leviticus 25:10 by which liberty is to be proclaimed throughout the land and all men are to be returned to their rightful land and possessions. This Mosaic Law is the key to Biblical scripture concerning slavery (Exodus 21:2, Leviticus 25:44, Deuteronomy 15:12-18) whereby human beings are never slaves but bound, free men and women who must be released after six years' labor and generously compensated at double the rate of a hired servant. Accordingly, under the provisions of Article I, Section 9, the Constitution gave the slave interests of the country 20 years to rid themselves of this degradation. As indicated by the writings of George Washington and Abraham Lincoln, this "1808 clause" was ratified as part of the Constitution with the understanding among all the people of the Nation that human bondage was to be eradicated by that year. Tragically, a conspiracy arose among Moorish and European slave-holders reaping huge profits from slavery to extend the institution indefinitely. Through deceit, subterfuge, bribery, extortion, blackmail, murder and treason, these conspirators controlled the Congress and thereby maintained their system. This conspiracy caused the Civil War in an attempt to destroy the Union and perpetuate slavery. (See John A. Logan, The Great Conspiracy, published in 1886 and dedicated to all the young men of America.) Yet it was Abraham Lincoln who called the attention of the Nation back to the true intentions of the Founding Fathers, both Moorish and European. His Executive Will for the purpose of solving the so-called "Negro/black" problem is expressed in the following documents:

1. Initial Emancipation Proclamation of September 22, 1862

2. Annual Address before Congress— December 1, 1862

3. Second Emancipation Proclamation of January 1, 1863

4. Proclamation of Amnesty and Reconstruction dated December 8, 1863

5. Proposed Resolution to Congress dated February 5, 1865

Following the assassination of Lincoln, President Andrew Johnson adhered to the policies of his predecessor as indicated in Johnson's Proclamation on Amnesty of May, 1865.

-4-

The Radical Republicans, led by Thaddeus Stevens in the
House of Representatives and Charles Sumner in the Senate
attempted to hinder Lincoln's plans and to severely punish
the South for rebelling against the Union. To accomplish
these ends, the Radicals attempted to incorporate a Thirteenth Amendment (with two sections) to the Constitution to
prevent former slave-holders from receiving compensation for
their confiscated human property. However, through the
influence of Lincoln in the Congress, this amendment was
replaced by a Thirteenth Amendment with Twenty Sections which
was passed by both houses of Congress and signed by Lincoln
on February 1, 1865. But following the Presidential assassination, there arose among the Radical Republicans a
"Great Conspiracy" to continue their vendetta against the
South by treacherously and illegally recalling the Thirteenth
Amendment with Two Sections and forcing its ratification by
the Northern and Western States. (The Southern States have
never ratified it.) In addition, by manipulating the former
bondsmen of the Nation, both the "educated", such as Frederick
Douglass, as well as the "uneducated", these Radicals devised
the 14th and 15th Amendments in an attempt to cover up their
plot. The 14th Amendment, in particular, denies the right
of compensation for confiscated property as guaranteed in the
5th Amendment, which has never been repealed or modified in
any way. This same 14th Amendment attempts to make citizens
of people (so-called "Negroes") who have not been educated
to the true facts of their heritage and who have never
legally proclaimed their true free ancestral names, race,
nationality and religion as is required of all foreign
immigrants to this country under the provisions of the laws
of naturalization.

When the so-called Southern "whites" resisted the enforcement
of the 13th (with two sections), 14th and 15th Amendments via
the Civil Rights Act of 1875, the issue was taken to the
Supreme Court in 1883. Rendering the majority opinion,
Justice Bradley clearly ruled that the amendments had no
power to guarantee the rights of the so-called "Negro"—rights
which Chief Justice Taney had said, in the Dred Scott case,
no "white" man was bound to respect. Yet due to their brain-
washed level of thinking, the so-called "black" folks continued
to believe that they were citizens under the 14th Amendment.
This misconception has persisted to this very day as a result
of pacifiers such as the 1954 Supreme Court integration decision

The first man to legally move to resurrect the 13th Amendment
with Twenty Sections and the Executive Will of Lincoln for
their eventual enforcement in the Federal government was Grand
Sheik Richardson Dingle-El. Born in South Carolina in 1910,

-5-

he was the first so-called "Afro-American" to throw off the
shackles of Negro-ism by being the first man to register
with the Federal government as a descendant of Moroccans
born in America. With the approval of Generals Hershey,
London, Schwartz and others of National Headquarters,
Selective Service System, he established a system known
as the Moorish National Bureau of Vital Statistics under
which all people must register with the Federal government
according to his example. All citizens must, thereby,
declare their true Nationality, Race, Religion, and National
Origin exactly as foreign immigrants are so required.
(See National Archives File No. 5-39, Record Group No. 147.)

The only permanent solution to the "race" problem in
America is the complete implementation of Lincoln's Executive
Will and the 13th Amendment with Twenty Sections the essence
of which can be summarized as following:

1. COMPENSATION--the compensation of the descendants
    of slave-holders for their confiscated human property
    (a sum presently totaling $229 Billion) as well as
    the compensation of the Moors for their service
    rendered during their decades of servitude.

2. NATURALIZATION--the registration of all Moors into
    the Moorish National Bureau of Vital Statistics
    through which they can return their European names
    and all vestiges of "Negro-ism" to the European
    people; legally proclaim their true Free National
    Names, Race, Nationality and Religion; and be
    offically declared citizens of the United States
    by the Federal Government.

3. COLONIZATION--the colonization of Moors on their own
    land between the Alleghany and Rocky Mountains, which
    Lincoln called the "Egypt of the West."

The Nation is presently 109 years late in eradicating this
"Negro" that has been properly described as a BEAST. This
same beast has threatened the well-being of mankind for
hundreds of years by his determination to disobey Divine Law.
(See Charles Carroll, The Negro, A Beast Or In the Image of
God, published in 1900.)

To rid the world of this menace for perpetuity, Grand Sheik
Richardson Dingle-El is the man of the hour. He has struggled
for years to raise his people from the gutter level of
mentality according to law. But his efforts have been
consistently hindered by such organization as NAACP, SCLC,
CORE, SNCC, etc. as well as various confused elements of
the Moorish Science Temple of America—all of whom are totally
ignorant of the law despite his continuing endeavors to
educate their leaders who are reluctant to learn. Just as

-6-

we are aware that Frederick Douglass sold out his own
people by denying the Lincoln Reconstruction Plan
President Andrew Johnson offered the freed "slaves" in
February, 1866, we are also well aware that the members
of the so-called "Black Caucus" who are tryied to
impeach President Nixon as members· of the House Judiciary
Committee had no legal right to be a part of those
proceedings because they are not citizens of the United
States. Under the Constitution they are confiscated
human property for which no compensation has been paid.
We have discussed this policy on numerous occasions with
members of the "Caucus"—in particular, Congressmen
Robert N.C. Nix of Philadelphia, PA and Parren J. Mitchell
of Baltimore, MD. Unfortunately, these individuals seem
to be having difficulty mustering the will and the
courage to stand up as men by legally demanding recognition
for the birthrights of their people. We have also contacted
many times since the World War II era Mr. James C. Evans-
El, Civilian Aide to the Secretary of Defense, who is in
total agreement with this policy.

We acknowledge President Nixon's sincere efforts to achieve
a lasting world peace and to preserve the critical powers
and prestige of the Presidency of the United States; and
we are confident that President Ford will continue to carry
on this important work. However, these goals can never be
achieved until the Executive Will of Lincoln is carried out
to its· fullest extent. President Ford is now sitting in the
seat of the 16th President, whose ghost has haunted the
White House since 1865 and whose spirit will continue to do
so until the cause of Divine justice is served. In addition,
President Ford has taken the oath of office to uphold the
Constitution—the true Constitution as it was before the
Radical Republicans treacherously tampered with the Law of the
Land. We trust that he will live up to the promise of
Lincoln in the latter's Initial Emancipation Proclamation of
September 22, 1862 by which the Executive government of
the United States must not in any way hinder our people in
any effort they may undertake for their actual freedom.

To spearhead these efforts, a special group of adepts have
been appointed to carry this policy to all levels of government.
Our principal targets, at this time, are the National Bureau
of Vital Statistics and the Internal Revenue Service. Horses,
dogs, mules, and cattle—these creatures are forms of
property owned by men and carry the personal identifications,
both verbal (names) and physical (brands), that are imposed
by the owners. "Negroes," "black" folks, "colored" people,
"Afro-Americans", etc. are merely different forms of such
property or chattel according to law. In the perspective
of Chief Justice Taney, "Negroes" and the like have the same ᛭
status as horses or dogs, bales of dry-goods, or blocks of
stone. Because manifestations of chattel are not recorded

-7-

in the National Bureau of Vital Statistics whose purpose is to register human beings, all vestiges of "Negro-ism", including "Negro", "black", "colored", "Ethiopian", African," etc., must be eradicated from all records of that agency and all public and private records throughout the State, States and Nations. The correct designations as to Race (Asiatic) and Nationality (Moorish-American) must be used in lieu thereof in accordance with Grand Sheik's example in File No. 5-39, Record Group No. 147, National Archives. Furthermore, horses dogs, mules, cattle, bales of cotton, and blocks of stone do not pay taxes to any government; the owners pay taxes on such property. Consequently, our people must not pay taxes to any government until the National Bureau of Vital Statistics is cleaned up and our people are naturalized and receive their full birthrights as Moorish men and women via the implementation of the Executive Will of Lincoln and the Thirteenth Amendment with Twenty Sections.

Now that you are aware of our intentions, we request that you carefully and meticulously investigate the facts we have presented in this letter, review this document repeatedly until its inner meaning becomes a part of your very soul, deeply reflect upon the consequences of its message, and report your findings honestly and sincerely to the President. Please keep in mind the sacred lesson that wise men of all ages have learned—man does not really know the truth by being told; masterminds can trace themselves back into time and history and only thus do they truly know. We also request an audience with you at your earliest convenience to allow us the opportunity to elaborate upon this policy in detail and to ascertain from you personally the extent to which the Executive Branch of the United States Government will support the implementation of the Thirteenth Amendment with Twenty Sections and render immediate pecuniary assistance to the School's endeavors pending Congressional resurrection of the Thirteenth Amendment with Twenty Sections.

As special Adepts, we the undersigned have affirmed President Lincoln's Oath of Amnesty and Reconstruction as well as a sacred oath to the cause of uplifting fallen humanity. In essence, we have pledged our lives to the implementation of this policy.

We await your response.

Sincerely,

Clarence R. Reynolds-El
Sheik, Chairman

Ernest Wright-Bey
Sheik, Divine Minister

Herbert H. Joiner-Bey   Enc: Our Authority and Questionnaire,
Sheik, Coordinator   Divine Constitution and By-Laws,
                                               Charter

gwb

UNITED STATES DEPARTMENT OF JUSTICE

WASHINGTON, D.C. 20530

SEP 30 1974

Address Reply to the
Division Indicated
and Refer to Initials and Number

JSP:MWH:mkk:jp
DJ 144-35-0

Mr. Clarence R. Reynolds-El
Sheik, Chairman
The Moorish School of Law and History
Post Office Box 7063
Baltimore, Maryland 21216

Dear Mr. Reynolds:

The White House has referred your correspondence of August 19, 1974, to this Department.

Thank you for favoring us with your views. However, under the circumstances, we do not believe that any comment by this Department concerning the "Negro/black" problem in America, would be appropriate.

Sincerely,

J. STANLEY POTTINGER
Assistant Attorney General
Civil Rights Division

By: MACEO W. HUBBARD
Supervisory Trial Attorney
Criminal Section

Figure 6.1

TESTIMONY OF:
BOBBY C. MC QUEEN-BEY

BY: SPECIAL AGENT WOODLAND R. MORRIS

This is the testimony of Bobby C. McQueen-Bey, 2420 West Garrison
Avenue, Apt. C.,Baltimore, Maryland 21215 given in the offices of
the Intelligence Division, Internal Revenue Service, Baltimore,
Maryland, on Thursday, May 22, 1975 at 2:38 about his Federal income
tax. Present Mr. Bobby C. McQueen-Bey, Taxpayer, the Reverend
Clarence Reynolds, El, Shiek, Divine Minister, National Chairman of
the Moorish School of Law and History, Woodland Morris, Special Agent,
Anthony Pizzillo, Special Agent. Questions were asked by Special
Agent Morris and answers were given by Mr. Bobby McQueen-Bey unless
otherwise specified.

Q1   Mr. McQueen-Bey this interview is being recorded as we
      agreed by means of a tape recorder on your left. Is
      that correct?

A   That's correct.

Q2   Mr. McQueen-Bey you were requested to appear at this office
      to answer questions concerning your Federal income tax for
      the years 1971 to 1974, inclusive. First I'll read you a
      statement of your rights. As a special agent one of my
      functions is to investigate the possibility of criminal
      violations of the Internal Revenue Law and related offenses.
      In connection with my investigation of your tax liability
      (or other matter), I would like to ask you some questions.
      However, first I advise you that under the Fifth Amendment
      to the United States' Constitution I cannot compel you to
      answer any questions or to submit any information if such
      answers or information might tend to incriminate you in any
      way. I also advise you that anything which you say and any
      information which you submit may be used against you in any
      criminal proceeding which may be undertaken. I advise you
      further that you may, if you wish, seek the assistance of
      an attorney before responding? Do you understand your rights?

A   I do.

Q3   Would you please stand and raise your right hand? Do you
      solemnly swear that the answers you are about to give to the
      questions asked will be the truth so help you God?

A   I affirm.

Figure 6.2

-6-

Q45   So you feel that you filed a 1972 return but you're not sure.
       Is that correct?

A   I'm not sure.

Q46   You're not sure. I have a Short Form 1040A, U.S. Individual
       Income Tax Return, 1973 with a Document Locator Number 52 209
       075 260 75. Mr. McQueen-Bey would you look at that return? Do
       you identify that return as being one you prepared? There is
       your return. Did you prepare that return yourself?

A   Yes.

Q47   And that is your signature on that return?

A   Yes.

Q48   Is that your wife's signature underneath of that return?

A   Yes.

Q49   Let the record show that Mr. Bobby McQueen-Bey has identified
       Short Form 1040A, U.S. Individual Income Tax Return, 1973 with
       Document Locator Number 52 209 075 260 75 as being a return prepared
       by him and filed. Now did you file a 1974 Income Tax Return?

A   No.

Q50   You did not. Is there any reason why you didn't?

A   Well the reason is because of the whole matter from the change over
       from the, from my school, from the 13 exemptions and so forth.

Q51   All right.

A   Because of the briefing, briefing. That's the reason why we haven't
       filed for this year.

Q52   You did not file a 1974 income tax return. Is that correct?

A   That's right.

Q53   The reason being, can you give a specific reason. You said the brief,
       can you identify a brief or tell us what or exactly why the reason
       why you did not file?

-8-

Assistant Commissioner, Technical, Internal Revenue Service, 12th
Streets and Constitutional Avenue, North Washington, North West
Washington, D.C. We've also been in communication with a Mr. Samuel
D. Shotwell of the same location, Mr. Cameron of that location and
Mr. Billy Hargett, Chief, Individual Income Tax Branch. Prior to
us filing, filing this brief we had a brief meeting with the technical
advisors in the Internal Revenue Service on the subjects of taxation
without representation. We pointed out to them verbally before
attaching or signing, sending in the brief, some of the reasons
why that we have an objection under the taxation without representation.
And some of the, briefly the main points as Brother Shiek McQueen-
Bey has indicated is Article 1, Section 9 of the Constitution of the
United States of America. The 5th Article of Amendment of the
Constitution of the United States of America, the true 13th Amendment
with this 20th Sections that was passed by both houses of Congress
and signed into law on February 1, of 1865 by our great President
Abraham Lincoln. Under the policies of the true 13th Amendment
and its 20 Sections it provides for the people that have been designated
with the degrading terms of Negro, Black and Colored who are in
actuality Asiatics is their race, their nationality is Moorish American.
They are decendants of Moracas and born in America. The steps taken
after the 13th Amendment was signed and passed into law and ratified
by the State was that the southerners or the slave holders were to
be compensated for their human property. Under the Constitution,
Article, the 1st Article of the Constitution in the 2nd Section are
dealing with the three-fifths provision, an 1808 clause. It was stated
in, in there that it was a $10 tax imposed at that time. And when
the Constitution was put together at the Constitutional Convention of
1787 they pro-, placed in the, in the Constitution an Article giving
20 years for the people holding slaves to get rid of their human
property. That's Article 1, Section 9 by 1808. This was not complied
with and as a result of that brought on the Civil War. Abraham Lincoln
went back to the 5th Article of Amendment to prove that you cannot take
a person's human property away without just compensation. This is what,
he issued the Emancipation Proclamation on the true initial Emancipation
Proclamation which provided for the naturalization, compensation and
colonization. Later on it was the Articles enforcing that were drawn
into the original 13th Amendment, with 20 Sections. The radical element
of Congress assassinated President Lincoln and took over the government
and tried to institute what is known as three dead badges of the law,
the present 13th, 14th and 15th Amendments which was struck down by
the Supreme Court in 1883. The test case for that was the Civil Rights
Case of 1875. Thereby making it, the so-called Negros or people that
subscribed to those names as I have indicated previously who are in
actuality Moorish Americans. They're not citizens because they have
not taken the oath of amnesty and reconstruction, have not been
compensated, have not been colonized. When a person emerges from

-9-

slavery according to the Lavitical Code which is on the Liberty
Bell, which is on the Liberty Bell at 5th, 6th and Chestnut,
Philadelphia, Pennsylvania is an inscription on the bell which is
the 25th verse, 25th Chapter, 10th verse of the Laviticus says
"ye shall proclaim liberty throughout all the land, to all the
inhabitants thereof. Return every man back to his family and
every man back to his possession." That was never complied with.
Consequently, as a result of this aforementioned statement we are
in fact human property, the owners of the property will pay taxes
on this property until such time as the true Constitution is
complied with. We also took this matter to our legislators, the
so-called Black Caucus who refused to do anything concerning the
situation. Prior to that, we have just entered into a similar type
brief with the Speaker of the House, the United States House of
Representatives, Carl Albert. And I have a letter here that has
gone through our ooordinator who assisted in drawing out the brief
of October the 9th, 1974 to the Internal Revenue Service. He
received correspondence from Carl Albert, the Speaker of the House,
May 1st, 1975 and I'd like to read that correspondence. It is
addressed to Herbert H. Joiner-Bey Sheik, Coordinator, Moorish
School of Law and History, Post Office Box 7063, Baltimore,
Maryland 21216. Dear Sir: This acknowledges your petition regarding
the 13th Amendment with 20 Sections - compensation, naturalization,
and colonization. I appreciate you hand delivering this material
to my office and have referred it to the committee on the judiciary
for consideration. Very best wishes. Sincerely, Carl Albert, the
Speaker. We have gone to all levels of government. It is our
intention to become true American citizens, naturalized as such,
compensated and colonized. We are not a radical group. We are in
conformity with the laws of the true government and the lawyers and
have not been enforcing the Supreme Court decision of 1883. In
addition to that, we sent the same type of brief into the White House.
At that time we sent it to the Chief Assistant at that time which
was General Haig, Chief of Staff. He was under the Nixon Administration
and a hold over under the Ford Administration. We received correspondent
from the Justice Department that the White House had turned the
correspondence or the brief that we sent over to the Justice Department.
The Justice Department returned, in turn, sent us a letter which I
will read because all of this is pertinent to the case and the letter
is to myself Shiek Clarence Reynolds-El, Chairman, Moorish School of
Law and History, September the 30th, 1974 and it's addressed Dear
Mr. Reynolds El: The White House has referred your correspondence
of August 19, 1974 to this Department. Thank you for favoring us with
your views. However, under the circumstances we do not believe that

-10-

any comments by this Department concerns the Negro/Black problem
in America would be appropriate. Sincerely, J. Stanley Pottinger,
Assistant Attorney General, Civil Rights Division, by, and this
is a signature, Macio W. Hubbard, Supervisory Trial Attorney,
Criminal Section. Prior to us, after we received this correspondence
we went over to the Justice Department to talk with Mr. Pottinger
who we were unable to see but in turn we spoke to a Mr. Walker who
is on his staff. Mr. Walker is going under the terms of Negro
calling him Black and we explained to him that his true nationality
is Moorish American, that his race is Asiatic and that until he has
proclaimed his nationality officially before the United States
Government and taken an oath to uphold the United States Government
then he is not a true citizen of the United States and therefore
that he wouldn't, is not really qualified to sit into this position.
I'd like to point out that this letter does not indicate in any way
any type of decision as to the validity of the documents that we
have submitted. They simply say that under the circumstances they're
not going to make any comments whether it's right or whether it's
wrong. In my final statement to this matter I would like to read
from a Certificate of the Moorish School of Law and History and the
reason that I'm reading this Certificate is to substantiate or to
affirm that we are taking the intelligent course of pursuing this
in a legal manner and we are not in any way radical as I have stated
before. This document should substantiate this. This, these are
my personal credentials but all of our officers and persons whom
proclaim their nationality are issued this same type of Certificate
which bears an oath and I would like to read that. In the left
hand corner is the Liberty Bell, is the symbol, Laviticus 25th,
Chapters, 10th verse, Section 16 of the 13th Amendment with 20
Sections. Grand Shiek Richardson Dingle-El, Founder, right hand
corner is a circle seven symbol, Copybook 521, File Number 5-39,
National Archives, National Headquarters, General Service Administration,
Washington, D.C. 20408. You will find these records in the
administrative file at that location. Certificate of Registration
Moorish National Bureau of Vital Statistics and this is what all
our members have to take. In accordance with the true policies
of Nobel Drew Ali, which is our Founder and Presidents Abraham
Lincoln and Andrew Johnson, this document exists as a certification
that the individuals indicated below has taken and subscribed an
affirmation of allegiance to the Constitution of the United States
of America including the 13th Amendment with 20 Sections. The
individual has also proclaimed his true free national name, race,
nationality and religion as follow. Then your social security number
would be inserted. The name on this particular case is my name,

-11-

Clarence R. Reynolds, El, Race, Asiatic, Nationality, Moorish
American, Date of Birth, May 30th, 1939, Place of Birth, Baltimore,
Maryland, Date of this Proclamation, February 22nd, 1971, location,
Baltimore, Maryland, Religion, Islamism. The ancient name "El"
must be annexed as a suffix to the slave family name of the
individual in all public and private records throughout the state,
states and nations, etc. Upon the complete implementation of
Sections 16 and 17 of the 13th Amendment with 20 Sections to the
U.S. Constitution the individual receive his full permanent and
ancestrial name through the United States Government. And this
is signed by Ernest J. Right-Bey Shiek, Divine Minister, myself,
Clarence R. Reynolds, El, Shiek, the Director National Registrar,
Richardson Dingle, El, Grand Shiek, Founder, National Archives
is at the bottom, Record Group 147. See Form QAAN-7003 Social
Security Administration. So at this time this would, conclude my
remarks at this point unless it's so designated for me to make
any further statements.

Q60   Reverend Reynolds, El, you, you're aware I assume that the Internal
Revenue Code of 1954 was passed by the Congress. Are you aware
of that?

I'm aware of the Internal Revenue Code but as indicated when we
spoke to the attorneys in Washington, D.C. that the subject that
we were presenting was not a cold matter of the Internal Revenue
Service but a Constitutional issue.

Q61   In other words, this is again addressed to Reverend Reynolds, El.
In other words, do you, through doctrainal statement or word-of-
mouth to people who come to you seeking to join with you, do you
tell them or advise them not to pay their taxes?

Well at this point we submitted a brief with the names of the
individuals that were exempted or that should, in other words we
filed for a refund from all taxes from the period of 1865 up
until the present. In other words we have been illegally taxed
as human property and not full citizens and it is illegal to tax
property. The owners as I have indicated paid the taxes on such
property. At the time that we went to National Headquarters in
Washington, D.C. to discuss this matter, we agreed that we'll,
we would hold the issue of the, the back taxes from the period of
1865 but we also informed them that from that point on that we
are not in the true sense of the word, a citizen. And as we have
indicated it is not our decision that has caused us to come to

-12-

this point. It is the decision of the Constitution and
the Supreme Court decision rather of the Constitutional War
Time Amendment, the three dead badges of law and mainly the
13th, 14th and 15th Amendment.

Q62   Reverend Reynolds, El, did you ever advise Mr. Bobby McQueen-
        Bey not to pay his taxes?

I would like to say in reference to that statement that we have
a board of officers and we have taken a oath to uphold the
Constitution, the true Constitution as it was before it was
tampered with. Shiek Bobby McQueen-Bey is a officer. He's a
Shiek the same as myself. And it was a unanimous agreement.
Now in reference to the members that are coming in proclaiming
their nationality, in reference to those members, before their names
are added onto the list that we sent into National Headquarters we
make them fully conscious of the Constitution because most of our
people have never even dealt with the aspect of dealing into the
Constitution. This country has been builded on a Constitution that
is perpetual. But when the Constitution has been violated and
people in government seats are not enforcing the guarantees then
somebody has to make a stand because the Constitution says we,
the people. But the so-called Negros are no part of that
Constitution because there's no such race of people on earth
termed as Negros. It was a name given to slaves as I pointed out
before. A slave is a piece of human property. And you cannot tax
property. And being that Abraham Lincoln which was the President,
the 16th President of the United States and both Houses of Congress
passed the 20 Sections that Abraham Lincoln signed into law it is
the law of the land. I have not had a judge or a lawyer in my
dealings as a Divine Minister. I have taken a sacred oath and I
would not do anything to violate the Constitution of this country.
And I have taken a sacred oath and I have not had a lawyer, a lawyer
or a judge to tell me that the 13th Amendment and its 20 Sections
was not the law of the land. I have a letter that from the General
Services Administration's General Counsel there, the Assistant General
Counsel, Mr. Yock, that said that the General Services Administration
had no authority to render financial or other assistance to the
school in its endeavors to resurrect the 13th Amendment with
20 Sections. And he said you may, however, wish to contact your
representative in Congress for guiding and obtaining such assistance.
But he acknowledged the fact that the 20 Sections is the law of the
land. There have been various officers and officials at this date,
lawyers, we have a team of lawyers here in the city, Walker, Smelkinso
& McCadden. They're in the Court Square Building. We have discussed
this issue with them in some length and they are in total harmony.
It's just that enough people are not really conscious of what the

1   -13-

Q63   Reverend Reynolds, El, do you have a doctrainal statement?
       I use that in quotes. Such that states that members are not
       to pay their taxes. Do they have to sign anything to this
       effect or is that implied when they sign their, I guess that's
       a registration?

       No, let me expound upon that, to maybe try to throw clarification
       on that. Presently we are using a code of number 13, raising
       our exemptions up. As there are a lot of people all year, a lot
       of people in this country that pay their taxes at the end of the
       year, you know. They have different methods in which they do this.
       And they save the money or put interest on it or whatever have
       you. Now the number 13 is a very important number in the foundation
       of this government. There were 13 original colonies which
       constituted the union. All the other states were subordinate.
       We're using that code because the 13 is a very sacred code and
       wise men of this nation know what the 13 represents. This code,
       as I said before, is being used in compliance with the government.
       It's in compliance with the Great Seal of the United States of
       America. The Great Seal on the back of your dollar bills, United
       States currency. There is 13 arrows there, 13 olive leafs
       represent peace. And there are other things that I could go into
       in relation to that. But the 13 is a code that we authorize
       our officers to use. Now if any other persons are using this code
       without a complete knowledge of the history of this school and
       their names are not on any of our lists then we have nothing to
       do with that. But we do not formally in a written dodument, tell
       a person not to pay the income taxes as such. In other words we
       just show the Constitutional law, the Supreme Court decision, the
       original 13th Amendment with 20 Sections, the initial Proclamation
       of Abraham Lincoln of September 22, 1862 and all these documents in
       conjunction show that a great conspiracy has taken place in this
       nation. Men have tried to aid in this error, of correcting it,
       such as President Kennedy that was assassinated. There are other
       men that were knowledgeable of this policy but we want the true
       men of this nation to stand up and be men in order to save these
       nations because it has been spoken by our Founder that if these
       principals are not carried out by the citizen and our people then
       the worst is yet to come.

-14-

Q64   Then it's implied then? Your officers, it's implied to your
officers that they are not to pay their taxes or are to
claim the 13 exemptions on their W-4 then. It's an implied
admission of a faith or....

Well they, after they under thorough, on thorough instruction
from the school under the Constitution, the original Constitution
then they are not forced to do this but it's a must that we
proclaim our nationality. It's a must that we register ourselves
properly with the United States Government and it's a must that
this Proclamation be carried out and taught universally in all
areas of schools. Lincoln said preach the, preach this from the
pulpit. He said let it be the political religion of the land.
Let every lover of liberty study the American Constitution. So
what we are doing is studying the true Constitution because what
we have been learning in the public school systems about the
Constitution is not true.

Q65   Then in other words this is the, not paying of Federal tax and
not filing an income tax return is based on your interpretation
of the Constitution......?

The Supreme Court is the determination of the Constitution. In
other words as I, as indicated to you before, lawyers have not
contradicted it because we have produced or secured the minutes
from the records of the Journal of the Senate, the Congressional
Globe, the Book of the Great Conspiracy. All of the books or the
materials that we use are not books that we have printed up but
the government has printed up. We also use Comminger's Book
of Documents as reference material. All material we use are books
that have been printed by some of the older representatives of
this nation or one of the other individuals is Horace Greely,
Bankcroft's History of the United States where it indicates in the
year of 990 how the so-called Negros lost their nationality and
it went from Blackimore to Moore to Negro. And by using these
land, these old documents are more substantial than the documents
that have been printed recently because they don't the hold the
true foundation of what we're talking about. We, the 6th Act,
of our law of our Divine Constitution and By-Law says that with
us all members must proclaim their nationaltiy and we are teaching
our people their nationality and divine decree that they may know
that they are a part in partial of this here government. And
know that they are not Negros, Black people, Colored people or
Ethiopians because these names were given to slaves by slave holders

-15-

in 1779 and lasted until 1865 during the time of slavery. But
this is a new era of time now and all men now must proclaim
their nationality to be recognized in the government in which
they live, in the nations of the earth. This is the reason why
the great God of the universe ordained over to our Leader Prophet
to redeem his people from their sinful ways. The Moorish Americans
are decendants of the ancient Mobites who inhabited the north-
western and southwestern shores of America. I mean now that is,
on the northwest and southwestern shores of Africa. Now what I'm
saying in essence is that there's dates mentioned in there of
1865 and we went back to dig up those records and found out that
since 1865 we have not received any of the benefits under the
Constitution as called for under the Constitution as called for
under the 13th Amendment with 20 Sections. But we're merely
stating that under the Constitution that we are human property
that has not been compensated for and thereby that is our basis
for refusal to pay taxes until such time as the government
compensates the slave holders and in turn gives up our compensation.

Q66   I'd like to re-direct my questions to Mr. Bobby McQueen-Bey.
        Mr. McQueen-Bey are you aware that filing a false W-4 with your
        employer is a violation of the Federal Internal Revenue Code?

MR. BOBBY C. MCQUEEN-BEY

A   Would you repeat that again?

Q67   Are you aware that filing a false W-4 is a violation of the
        Federal Internal Revenue Code?

A   Are you, are you saying that I violated the Code by.....

Q68   I'm saying, are you familar with that form W-4? It's a form
        you fill out with your employer claiming a number of withholding
        exemptions. Are you familar with that form?

A   Right.

Q69   Are you aware that filing a false W-4 with your employer is a
        violation of the Federal Internal Revenue Code?

A   But you are not saying that I filed a false statement.

113

Q70   I am asking you are you aware that filing a false statement
is a violation of the Federal Internal Revenue Code?

A   I'm aware of that.

Q71   You're aware of that.

A   Uh, hum.

Q72   Are you also aware that not filing a Federal income tax
return is a violation of the Federal Internal Revenue Code?

A   Um, hum.

Q73   You admitted earlier that you did not file a 1974 income tax
return. Is that correct?

A   That's correct.

Q74   Can you state your reasons why?

A   Well my reasons why is just like Brother Shiek just explained to
you. It's because of the brief that we have submitted to the
Federal Government in Washington, D.C. And until these, until
this policy or the 13th, the original 13th Amendment with 20
Sections is implemented by the Government then we will continue
not to file any taxes or pay taxes according to the so-called
State Laws under the Con-, under the three dead badges until the
13th Amendment and 20 Sections is implemented and put back into
the Constitution as it was.

Q75   In other words, let me re-state that. Were you told by anyone
not to file a Federal income tax return?

A   No, I wasn't.

Q76   You weren't. Were you told by anyone or were you instructed
on how to fill out a W-4?

A   Well like the Shiek explained to you that we have a board of
executives, I mean officers, and this came from the board.
The reason for the Code is to bring this whole misunder-, I mean
this conspiracy out into the open so that the correct 13th
Amendment with the 20 Sections could be enforced throughout the land

-17-

Q77   Mr. McQueen-Bey I ask you a very specific question and give
me an answer either yes or no. Were you instructed or was
it your implied implication given to you that you were not to
file a tax return in order to set up the Internal Revenue
Service as a test case? Did you, in other words, did you
not file a 1974 income tax return in hopes of becoming a
test case with Internal Revenue Service?

A   Well according to the brief the names on the brief is listed
and anyone of those names could be took out of the brief for
a test case if that answers the question.

Q78   All right, I'll get a little more general. Were any names on
that brief or was it one of the implied purposes of that brief
with your name on it, was any one of those to set up a test
case with Internal Revenue Service? Is the purpose of that
brief perhaps to set up a test case with Internal Revenue Service?

A   The purpose of this brief is to implement the 13th Amendment
with 20 Sections.

Q79   In other words your not trying, there's no general thought among
your members to test the Internal Revenue Service?

A   No. We wanted to comply with the law.

Q80   Compliance with the law then, as you feel the compliance is.
Tony do you have any questions you'd like to ask?

ANTHONY PIZZILLO, SPECIAL AGENT

Q81   Mr. McQueen-Bey when did you join the Moorish School? When did
you become an officer?

A   I was nationalized February of '73.

Q82   When did you first file, let me start, re-state the question.
Have you ever since becoming nationalized as you put it, gone
to an employer and filed a W-4 statement on which you listed
a total of 13 exemptions?

A   Not since the present. Not since the present. Not before the
present.

Q83   Not before the present what?

A   Not before the present job that I just, that you are referring
to at the present.

-18-

Q84   Which job are you referring to?

A   I'm referring to the City.

Q85   And when did you take that job?

A   September.

Q86   Of 1974?

A   '74 right.

Q87   And that was the first time that you filed a W-4 statement on which you listed 13 exemptions?

A   That's correct.

WOODLAND R. MORRIS, SPECIAL AGENT

Q88   Let's get back to a few other general questions and then I guess we can sort of wrap it up right now. Does your wife work?

A   Not at the present.

Q89   Has she worked in the past year or even since '71 has she worked?

A   No, I don't, I don't believe so.

Q90   Is she a member of the Moorish School of Law and History?

A   That's correct.

Q91   Is she on the board also as an officer?

A   That's corect.

Q92   Reverend Reynolds, El, would you like to make a statement?

        One I'd like to make a brief statement. This concerns the book that you see in my hand which is, you can run a photostatic copy of if you would like to put that in with your report and on the back of this you see a copy of our authority which indicates our national function, you know, on a national level and also our religious function. This document was placed in national headquarters by our Grand Shiek Richardson Dingle, El, back in the 1940's. And since that time we have been on a search for this document. Now in 1970, in the office of the

-19-

Assistant Secretary of Defense which was at that time Dr. James
P. Evans, El. He was the Assistant Secretary of Defense,
Civilian Aid Office. There was a meeting held there with the
intention of bringing all the Moorish Americans under one head
and because a lot of people within different branches of the
Moorish Science Temple all over the country are not aware of
the Constitutional Law. It is our intention that they all be
aware of it. But in 1970 it was, everything was supposed to
been brought at a meeting under one head and at that time we
allowed ourselves to become Federal property and if the government does not pay off, you know, because for this property, in
other wores compensate it, then they're invviolation of Article11,
Section 9. I'm talking about the United States Government because
after 1808 they were not supposed to hold any more slaves. And a
Negro is nothing but a slave, a chunk of wood, a block of, just
a block of wood or a drawer of water. We have a book called the
Negro A Beast that I would like to present to you. This book,
as you can see, the title of it is Negro Beast. It was entered
into the library of Congress by a special act of Congress. It
was written by Charles Carroll here in Maryland. And the
publisher's made a statement on this book concerning the compiled
facts of this book and on oneppage of this book I would like to
just read briefly to substantiate the points that I had made
previously about the Negro being a beast and human property.
And this is registered in the Library of Congress.

Q93   Just a minute. I'd like to interrupt this and change the tape
        over. We interrupted the recording to change the tape. The
        Reverend Clarence Reynolds is making a statement.

REVEREND CLARENCE REYNOLDS, EL

        Reynolds, El.

Q94   Reynolds, El.

        It says as a matter of fact the Negro was never a slave. To
        perceive the design of enslaving an individual we must pre-
        suppose that he is free. The first act of enslavement is to
        deprive him of his liberty. This the Negro never had since
        the creation of man. The Negro is an ape. Hence his status
        in the universe, his relation to man, like that of every other
        animal was fixed irrevocably by God in the creation. And I'd
        like to draw special attention to the next statement. And it
        says no act upon man's part whether legislative, executive, or
        judicial can change it. And I just drawed a statement to that, I
        mean a reference to that statement to show you the reason, you
        know, one of the reasons why. And if you look up into the law
        books dealing with the Supreme Court decision you will find out
        that, that there were many statements that were made concerning

-20-

the three dead badges of law which said that it was a magnificent structure to look at but totally unfit for use and that it was not the purpose of the 14th Amendment to make this man a citizen. And so therefore, the 14th Amendment being void this Negro was never a citizen. He's still a piece of human property. We have taken steps to proclaim our nationality. As I said before. But we must get what is due us under the Constitution.

Q95   I have no other questions. Tony doyyou have any otherqquestions?

ANTHONY PIZZILLO, SPECIAL AGENT

Q96   No, I don't think we need to go into any other areas.

WOODLAND R. MORRIS, SPECIAL AGENT

Q97   No, I don't think so either at this time. I'd like to have copies of anything you feel that we should have pertinent to this issue. Let me read a couple questions to you Mr. Bobby McQueen-Bey and have you respond accordingly, please. Mr. McQueen-Bey have I or has any other Federal agent threatened or intimidated you in any manner?

A   No.

Q98   Have I or any Federal agent offered you any reward or promises of reward or immunity in return for this statement?

A   No.

Q99   Have you given this statement freely and voluntarily?

A   Yes.

Q100   Is there anything futther you care to add for the record?

A   No.

Q101   Nothing further. Reverend Clarence Reynolds, El, is there anything further you care to add for the record?

One thing that I would like to draw attention to is that we were going to submit to you as you have asked us earlier any documents that is pertinent to this case and I would like to ask that if you have to submit this to your superiors then you yourself may examine this brief thoroughly and there are many things that we have touched upon that I know that you

-2-

527501280
FINAL

EXTENT AND RESULTS OF INVESTIGATION

1. The records of the District Director, Baltimore, Maryland
   show that BOBBY C. MC QUEEN-BEY filed Form 1040, U.S.
   Individual Income Tax Return for 1971 and Short Form 1040A,
   U.S. Individual Income Tax Return for 1973.

2. A Question and Answer Statement taken from BOBBY C. MC QUEEN-
   BEY on May 22, 1975 contained admissions by the taxpayer that
   he did file a Form W-4 with his employer in 1974 claiming 13
   exemptions even though he was legally entitled to claim only
   3 exemptions. He gave as his reason for submitting such a
   form his membership in the Moorish School of Law and History
   which is a religious organization advocating, among other
   things, that the Negro, under the Constitution of the United
   States, is not a true citizen and should not be taxed. This
   ideology developed from the School's interpretation of the
   13th, 14th and 15th Amendments to the Constitution of the
   United States. The explanation to the 13 exemptions was
   given on the same date by the Reverend CLARENCE REYNOLDS-EL,
   National Chairman of the Moorish School of Law and History,
   who accompanied BOBBY C. MC QUEEN-BEY to the interview.
   Reverend REYNOLDS-EL, stated the following:

   > Now the number 13 is a very important number in the
   > foundation of this government. There were 13 original
   > colonies which constituted the Union. All the other
   > states were subordinate. We're using that code be-
   > cause the 13 is a very sacred code and wise men of
   > this nation know what the 13 represents. This code,
   > as I said before, is being used in compliance with
   > the government. It's in compliance with the Great
   > Seal of the United States of America; The Great Seal
   > on the back of your dollar bills, United States
   > currency. There is 13 arrows there, 13 olive leafs
   > represent peace. And there are other things that I
   > could go into in relation to that. But the 13 is a
   > code that we authorize our officers to use.

Figure 6.3

-3-

52750128D
FINAL

In the Question and Answer Statement BOBBY C. MC QUEEN-BEY admitted that he did not file a tax return for 1974. His explanation for this was that he goes along with the Moorish School of Law and History's position that the Negro is not a true citizen under the Constitution of the United States and, thus, should not be taxed.

3. On October 9, 1974 the Moorish School of Law and History submitted a Brief to MR. PETER WEIZENBRUCH, Assistant Commissioner-Technical, Internal Revenue Service, Washington, D.C. This Brief outlines the School's position with respect to payment of income taxes. Such petition set forth the Moslem School's position as stated during the Question and Answer Statement of May 22, 1975.

4. A check with Exempt Organization of the Internal Revenue Service revealed that the Moorish School of Law and History, Baltimore, Maryland does not have exempt status nor has it applied for exempt status. Related organizations in other parts of the country have received such status.

5. A check with the Community College of Baltimore revealed that BOBBY C. MC QUEEN-BEY has been a full-time student there since the Spring of 1974, majoring in Pre-Law. The school's records also show that BOBBY MC QUEEN-BEY obtained financial assistance in the form of a National Direct Student Loan and a Basic Educational Opportunity Grant. MR. MC QUEEN-BEY also received Veterans Assistance. A financial statement filed by MR. MC QUEEN-BEY with the Community College of Baltimore showed that BOBBY MC QUEEN-BEY estimated his wages, salaries, tips, etc., to be approximately $_____ for the year 1974.

6. A Transcript of Earnings Record from the Social Security Administration showing employers and wages paid by them to BOBBY MC QUEEN-BEY and his wife, MARIAN W. (_____ _____), revealed no record for 1972 and 1973. However,

-4-

52750128D
FINAL

BOBBY MC QUEEN-BEY did file a Short Form 1040A for
1973 reflecting ▓▓▓▓▓▓▓ gross wages from ALGER
ELECTRIC of Pikesville, Maryland. The transcript
also showed only $▓▓▓▓ in gross wages for BOBBY
MC QUEEN-BEY received in the second quarter of 1974.
The last two quarters of 1974 had not been posted
by the Social Security Administration as of the date
of the transcript.

CONCLUSIONS AND RECOMMENDATIONS

The investigation disclosed that:

A. BOBBY C. MC QUEEN-BEY did not file a tax return
    in 1972. Social Security records revealed that
    no wages were reported to them for BOBBY MC QUEEN-
    BEY for 1972.

B. BOBBY C. MC QUEEN-BEY filed a Form W-4 with his
    employer, Department of Public Works, City of
    Baltimore, in 1974 claiming 13 exemptions of which
    he is legally entitled to only claim 3.

C. BOBBY C. MC QUEEN-BEY and his wife, MARIAN, did
    not file a 1974 tax return.

D. BOBBY C. MC QUEEN-BEY and his wife, MARIAN, belong
    to the Moorish School of Law and History. This
    organization advocates that Negroes are not
    American citizens and should not have to pay taxes.
    They presented their views on taxes openly,
    including an inquiry to the National Office,
    Washington, D.C. in October 1974. Such inquiry
    was 6 months prior to this investigation.

-5-

52750128D
FINAL

In view of the above, it is felt that there is/insufficient
evidence to establish that the taxpayer's filing of a false
Form W-4 was done with the express purpose of defrauding the
government. In addition, the amount of taxes due as a result
of such filing is below the standard for a prosecution case.
The taxpayer's failure to file a return for 1974 would result
in a one year case.

I recommend that this case be closed in the Intelligence
Division because of the lack of criminal prosecution potential,
and that the case be forwarded to the Chief, Collection
Division for any action he deems appropriate.

Woodland R. Morris
Special Agent

/s/ John C. McCusker

Reviewed: _____

John C. McCusker
Group Manager

APPROVED:

/s/ Robert E Jackson, Jr.
_____
Robert L. Browne
Chief, Intelligence Division
Baltimore District Office

Address any reply to:

Department of the Treasury

District Director
Internal Revenue Service

Date:	in reply refer to:
AUG 29 1975	I:02:WRM

Telephone: 301-962-4142

Mr. Bobby C. McQueen-Bey
2420 W. Garrison Avenue, Apt. C
Baltimore, Maryland 21215

Dear Mr. McQueen-Bey:

This is to inform you that the Intelligence Division is
no longer participating in the investigation of your
income tax liability for the years 1971 through 1974.

The matter has been referred to the Collection Division
for further consideration.

This does not preclude re-entry by the Intelligence
Division if further examination discloses indications
of fraud not previously considered.

Sincerely yours,

Gerald G. Portney
District Director

Figure 6.4

A Taxing Issue Faces Area Moslems

By ROBERT DOUGLAS
Staff Reporter

Clarence R. Reynolds El walked into IRS offices several years ago and told agents he was not paying federal income taxes.

Nothing happened until this month, when five city residents were indicted on charges they reported an incorrect number of exemptions to avoid income taxes.

Reynolds El, however, was not one of them.

"I'm a priest, and they don't want to indict a religious leader," the 40-year-old Moslem said.

Federal prosecutors will not say if that is true, but they agree with Reynolds El that the indictments are the first legal challenge to a tax protest by Moslems.

The five defendants are members of the Moorish Science Temple, a Moslem group claiming 100,000 members nationwide, 10,000 in Baltimore.

A "large percentage" of the local members have been conducting a tax protest for several years, based on a legal interpretation of the Emancipation Proclamation, the U.S. Constitution and congressional acts, according to temple leaders.

The temple's tax protesters avoid paying income taxes by declaring a large number of exemptions at their place of employment.

The protesters claim black Americans never have received proper citizenship in the United States and, therefore, are not "liable" for taxes.

"We believe people should pay taxes," said Jacques Leeds-Bey, the defendant's attorney and a member of the temple.

"When our status is changed, we have no problems paying taxes," he said.

The "status," according to Leeds-Bey, is less-than-full-citizenship under the U.S. Constitution. He said the "less-than-equal" status has existed since the the Emancipation Proclamation, when President Lincoln outlawed slavery but failed to grant full citizenship to former slaves.

Lincoln, however, planned to bring all former slaves to full citizenship status through an indoctrination process designed to end by 1900, according to Leeds-Bey.

The indoctrination process called for naturalization, colonization and compensation, to assist former slaves in the transformation from bondage to equal participation in the American democracy, according to Leeds-Bey.

What happened, though, is that Lincoln's original goals were "swept

MOORS DISCUSS TAX PROTEST OUTSIDE FEDERAL COURTHOUSE
. . . *from left, Clarence Reynolds-El, Steven Scott-Bey and Jacques E. Leeds-Bey.*
—News American Photo by James Lally.

under the rug" by radical elements during the Reconstruction period, according to Leeds-Bey.

"We've got to set the hands of the clock back to the Civil War," said Reynolds El. "Certainly a mechanism can be employed to carry out the spirit (of Lincoln's plan)." Temple leaders have worked since the group's founding in 1913 to establish that mechanism.

When regular and frequent correspondence with several presidents and other national leaders failed, some members began a tax protest "several years ago," according to Reynolds El.

"It's the kind of protest that may get the government to sit down at the conference table and rectify some of the wrongs," he said.

Temple leaders contend that, once the legal status of blacks is settled, it will provide a permanent solution for black social problems that existing

moral solutions have not produced.

The protest also is designed to highlight the temple's "nationalization" objectives.

Temple leaders argue that black self-esteem would improve dramatically if blacks realized they were descendants of a great civilization, that of the Moors.

"All other groups point to a proud history throughout the ages, but in America, Moorish (black) history only goes back to slavery," said Reynolds El.

Temple members prefer that blacks be called Moors, contending it will develop a "nationality mentality" similar to those of Italians, Poles and Greeks.

To that end, temple members attach either Bey or El as a suffix to their last names to indicate their Moorish membership.

In addition, temple leaders contend, Moors is the proper historical name because "there is no Negro, colored or black nation in history, it is the Moors," said Reynolds El.

A court victory will provide more than a tax loophole for blacks, according to the temple leaders. It will force the government to begin the $478 million naturalization, colonization and compensation program designed by Lincoln, they said.

If they lose, the defendants face a maximum sentence of $500 and one year in jail or both.

The five defendants, four of whom work either for the city or federal government, will be arraigned this week and will plead not guilty, according to their attorney.

News American
August 10, 1978

Figure 6.5

IN THE

United States Court of Appeals

FOR THE FOURTH CIRCUIT

Nos. 78-5189, 5190, 5191, 5192,
79-5039, 5040, 5041, 5042

UNITED STATES OF AMERICA,

Appellee,

v.

RONALD THOMAS COLEMAN, A/K/A RONALD THOMAS COLEMAN-BEY; STEVEN MAURICE SCOTT, A/K/A STEVEN MAURICE SCOTT-BEY; RONALD RICARDO LOVEJOY, A/K/A RONALD RICARDO LOVEJOY-BEY; JOHN WILLIAM McBRIDE, A/K/A JOHN WILLIAM McBRIDE-BEY,

Appellants.

APPEAL FROM THE UNITED STATES DISTRICT COURT FOR THE DISTRICT OF MARYLAND AT BALTIMORE

(C. STANLEY BLAIR, JOSEPH H. YOUNG, HERBERT F. MURRAY, Judges; EDWARD S. NORTHROP, Chief Judge)

 APPELLANTS' BRIEF AND APPENDIX

JACQUES E. LEEDS-BEY, SR.,
Attorney for Appellants.

Figure 6.6

Rommani M. Amenu-El

TABLE OF CONTENTS

In The

In The
United States Court of Appeals
For The Fourth Circuit

Nos. 78-5189, 5190, 5191, 5192, 79-5039, 5040, 5041, 5042

UNITED STATES OF AMERICA,

Appellee,

v.

RONALD THOMAS COLEMAN, A/K/A RONALD THOMAS COLEMAN-BEY; STEVEN MAURICE SCOTT, A/K/A STEVEN MAURICE SCOTT-BEY; RONALD RICARDO LOVEJOY, A/K/A RONALD RICARDO LOVEJOY-BEY; JOHN WILLIAM McBRIDE, A/K/A JOHN WILLIAM McBRIDE-BEY,

Appellants.

APPEAL FROM THE UNITED STATES DISTRICT COURT FOR THE DISTRICT OF MARYLAND AT BALTIMORE

(C. STANLEY BLAIR, JOSEPH H. YOUNG, HERBERT F. MURRAY, Judges; EDWARD S. NORTHROP, Chief Judge)

APPELLANTS' BRIEF

STATEMENT OF THE CASE

In each of the above-captioned cases (now consolidated) the Appellants were charged separately with filing a false Federal income tax withholding statement in violation of 26 U.S.C. Sec. 7205.

Each of the Appellants entered a plea of "not guilty" in separate arraignments before different Judges in the United States District Court For The District of Maryland.

2

On August 23, 1978, Appellants, who were represented by the same legal counsel, filed a Motion For Joinder of Defendants (Rec. Doc. No. 4). On the same date, Appellants filed a Motion to Dismiss Indictments (Rec. Doc. No. 5). This Motion was accompanied by a Request For Hearing (Rec. Doc. No. 5).

The aforegoing Motions were answered by the United States Attorney on September 6, 1978. The Honorable C. Stanley Blair, acting for all Judges presiding in these cases, handed down a ruling, without a hearing, denying said Motions (Rec. Doc. No. 8), on September 13, 1978.

On September 22, 1978, Appellants filed a Petition for a Writ of Mandamus or Prohibition to the United States Court of Appeals for the Fourth Circuit which the Clerk of the United States District Court for the District of Maryland treated as an appeal (Rec. Doc. No. 10). Appellants on the same day filed Motions to stay District Court proceedings. Said Motions were directed to the District Court and to the Circuit Court (Rec. Doc. 9); and on September 25, 1978, an Order "Denying" the Motion For Stay of Proceedings was signed by the Honorable Harrison L. Winter, Judge of the United States Circuit Court of Appeals For The Fourth Circuit (Rec. Doc. No. 11). The Motion to Stay Proceedings directed to the United District Court For The District of Maryland was not ruled upon.

Appellants, in each case, waived a jury trial, made an oral Motion for the judge to disqualify himself, and in each case the Motions to disqualify were denied.

The verdict of the Court in each case was "Guilty" as to one count. Upon imposition of the sentences, each of the Appellants made a Motion for release pending appeal, and in each case said Motion was denied.

Appellants, and each of them, then filed Notice of Appeal.

3

ISSUES PRESENTED

1. Whether the status of the Appellants, along with other descendants of former slaves, has ever been legally changed from that of property to that of legal persons; thereby subjecting them to charges of offenses relating to legal persons.

2. Whether the court exhibited such patent and/or latent bias as to preclude the Appellants from receiving a fair trial by:

   A. Referring to the Appellants as black rather than as Moroccan:

   B. Denying Appellants Motion to Join defendants and Motion to Dismiss Indictments, before expiration of the prescribed time to answer the government's Memoranda in opposition to Appellants' Motion to Dismiss Indictments.

   C. Failing to rule on Appellants' request for a hearing on their Motion to Dismiss Indictments.

3. Whether the failure of the United States Court of Appeals for the Fourth Circuit to rule on Appellants' Petition for Writ of Mandamus of Prohibition; and the failure of the United States District Court for the District of Maryland to rule on Appellants' Motion for stay of Proceedings, was a violation of due process of law guaranteed by the Fifth Amendment to the United States Constitution.

4

STATEMENT OF FACTS

Appellants were tried separately on the aforementioned charges.

In each case after asking for a continuing objection to all of the proceedings,

Appellants stood mute and declined to participate in the trial, even though

the Judges in each case invited their participation at each juncture of the

trial.

The government introduced evidence to the effect that each of the

Appellants knowingly overstated the number of dependants on their Federal

income tax withholding statements, and this evidence was not controverted

during the trial proceedings by the Appellants in either case.

5

ARGUMENT

WHETHER THE STATUS OF THE APPELLANTS,
ALONG WITH OTHER DESCENDANTS OF FORMER
SLAVES, HAS EVER BEEN LEGALLY CHANGED
FROM THAT OF PROPERTY TO THAT OF LEGAL
PERSONS: THEREBY SUBJECTING THEM TO
CHARGES OF OFFENSES RELATING TO LEGAL
PERSONS.

The Appellants ask the Honorable Court to consider the issue of

whether the 13th, 14th and 15th amendments to the Constitution of the United

States satisfied President Abraham Lincoln's goals regarding slaves and

former slaves, as enunciated by the initial Emancipation Proclamation of

September 22, 1862 (Exhibit 1, App. 1).

It should be noted here that a comprehensive examination of several

aspects of slavery had been made and enunciated by the Court in Dred Scott v.

Sanford 19 Howard, 393, 1857, and more popularly known as the "Dred Scott Case."

The Court, there, traced the nature of the slave trade and defined the

condition of the subjects of slavery. In regard to the slaves themselves,

the Court said:

> "...They had for more than a century before been regarded
> as beings of an inferior order; and altogether unfit to
> associate with the white race, either in social or
> political relations; and so far inferior that they had
> no rights which the white man was bound to respect: and
> that the negro might justly and lawfully be reduced to
> slavery for his benefit...This opinion was at that time
> fixed and universal in the civilized portion of the white
> race. It was regarded as an axiom in morals as well as in
> politics, which no one thought of disputing, or supposed
> to be open to dispute; and men in every grade and position
> in society daily and habitually acted upon it in their
> private pursuits, as well as in matters of public concern,
> without doubting for a moment the correctedness of this
> opinion...
> ...Neither does it apply to a person who, being the citizen
> of a State, migrates to another State.

6

> For then he becomes subject to the laws of the State in
> which he lives, and he is no longer a citizen of the State
> from which he was removed. And the State in which he
> resides may then, unquestionably, determine his <u>status</u>
> or condition, and place him among the class of persons who
> are not recognized as citizens, but belong to an <u>inferior</u>
> and <u>subject</u> race; and may deny him the privileges and
> immunities enjoyed by its citizens..."

According to Lincoln's Emancipation Proclamation, once a device, executive or legislative, had been employed to raise the former slaves from property to free persons, they as freedmen were to <u>sequentially</u> exercise all the concomitant rights and then bear all the consequential duties of free and sovereign people. Among those rights that were to be immediately exercised following legislative emancipation (Original 13th Amendment) was, to choose how he would utilize his newly acquired Sovereign status. He, the Freedman, had several options, that (with the slightest amount of mental effort) immediately presented themselves:

(1) To continue living within the United States Territorial boundaries

   as they were then (and as they are now) through individually

   opting to seek citizenship via Naturalization as provided to all

   via Art. 1 Sec. 8 cl. 3, U.S. Constitution.

(2) To choose to move to another location on this continent or elsewhere,

   forming governmental units independently, or

(3) To collectively form Governments which could (and would)

   eventually petition for statehood, thereby causing all its

   citizens to be thus clothed with U.S. citizenship (Art. IV Sec. 2.

   U.S. Constitution).

Consider the validity of the third alternative in light of Judge Taney's comments relative to the same matter: (Scott v. Sanford, Supra)

7

"...But if he ranks as a citizen of the State to which
he belongs, within the meaning of the Constitution of the
United States, then whenever he goes into another State,
the Constitution clothes him, as to the rights of persons,
with all the priveleges and immunities which belong to
citizens of the State. And if persons of the African
race are citizens of a State, and of the United States,
they would be entitled to all the priveleges and immunities,
under the paramount authority of the Federal Government,
and its courts would be bound to maintain and enforce them,
the Constitution and laws of the State to the contrary
notwithstanding..."

The ruling in this case was certainly not reversed prior to the

passage of the Thirteenth Amendment, and the Thirteenth Amendment with 2

Sections merely set free the subjects of slavery. It did not change their

status from that of property to that of persons. The changing of status

would have had to be accomplished by some legal act—executive or

legislative—to remove from the subjects of slavery—the vestiges of slavery.

The names of the subjects would, of necessity, have to have been

changed, otherwise the name of the thing would suggest the same condition.

The subjects of slavery, once free would have to go through some legal

procedure to be able to assume or reassume the status of a legal person.

If the names that the subjects of slavery had been carrying had been names

that were not recognized by the family of nations, then a name must be

legally applied to the former slaves that would be recognized by the family

of nations. This would mean, then, that the name given them had to have a

recognition antedating their condition of slavery. The name would have to

reflect a history antedating their condition of slavery. In short, those

formerly enslaved with the help of their wardens, would have to trace

themselves back to their father Abraham and thereby rightfully gain their places

133

8

among the families of men. As cited in Associate Justice Daniels'
concurring statements in Dred Scott V. Sandford, Supra:

> "...Now the following are truths which a knowledge of
> the history of the world and particularly of that of our
> own country, compels us to know--that the African negro race
> never had been acknowledged as belonging to the family of
> nations; that as amongst them there has never been known
> or recognized by the inhabitants of other countries any
> thing partaking of the character of nationality, or
> civil or political polity; that this race has been by
> all the nations of Europe regarded as subjects of capture
> or purchase; as subjects of commerce or traffic; and that
> the introduction of that race into every section of this
> country was not as members of civil or political society,
> but as slaves, as property in the strictest sense of
> the term."

This degrading term "negro" had been Judically defined as an article
of merchandise, as opposed to Moorish (Moroccan) denoting a national
character as recognized by all sovereign governments past and present.
Further, when the Fourteenth Amendment was passed, it used the language
that, "...all persons born or naturalized..." (Emphasis added). Again,
how does one come from a condition of property to that of being a legal
person without some legal device being employed to accomplish that fact.
It is sad that the misinformed zealots of immediate universal Emancipation
did not take these factors into consideration.

A close reading of the Initial Emancipation Proclamation will point
out that Mr. Lincoln envisioned the many problems attendant with trying to
stop a civil war, pitting sons against fathers, mothers against daughters,

9

brothers against brothers--bleeding, being maimed, starving, dying--all
over the issue of the right or wrong of slavery. The poor slaves--never
having been asked to be in this condition, catching "hell" and being blamed
from both sides, as if their very presence was causing all the horrors of
war. Picture if you can, the enigma faced by the President--damned if he
did, and damned if he didn't.

The Initial Emancipation Proclamation, and ensuing acts by Mr. Lincoln
in pursuance of his legally granted authority during extraordinary times was
designed to bring this bloody conflict to an end in the most sane, humane,
and fair manner possible.

First, he held out Compensation to the slave masters, promising them
payment for loss of their property, since the Fifth Amendment of the
Constitution of United States dictated that property could not be confiscated
without due process of law. Second, Mr. Lincoln sharing his first name with
the Father of all the races evidently looked to the Mosaic Law* (no other
legal precedents being available) to determine how slaves should be freed,
Mosaic Law provided that after a certain time in bondage, a master was
obligated to free his slave, compensate him for his labor while enslaved,
return him to his Name and nationality, or give the now free person the
choice to be naturalized as a citizen in his former master's land.

---

*To provide the court with a detailed explanation as to the above
mentioned Mosaic Law, we include the minutes outlining the proposed
original 13th Amendment abolishing slavery in the Senate, on March 31,
1864, taken from the book entitled The Great Conspiracy, by John A. Logan,
published 1886, page 533 (Exh. 2, App. 8).

Realizing that citizenship requires those candidates for the same
to be educated to its rights and responsibilities, and further realizing
that the slaves had been purposefully kept in ignorance by their slave
masters as one of many controlling devices, Mr. Lincoln rightfully
determined that full emancipation, in order to be successful, had to be
gradual, slaves and former slaves had to be educated to learn how to read,
write, add and subtract; learn skills in order to be able to fend for
themselves as free persons. Further and probably more important, a freed
slave, if really free, would after being returned to his original nationality,
have the option of returning to the land of his nationality; or exercising
his option of becoming a naturalized citizen and joining other nationalities
under the umbrella of the United States Constitution.

An interesting and enlightening debate concerning the institution
of slavery and the method of freeing slaves was discussed by Senators
Harlan, and Saulsbury before the passage by the Senate of the Thirteenth
Amendment with Twenty (20) sections on April 8, 1864 (Exh. 2, App. 8).
It is interesting to note that after the passage of the 13th Amendment with
20 Sections by the U.S. Senate, it was referred to a joint committee of the
Congress, and what finally came out of Congress was a mysteriously
emasculated 13th Amendment with two Sections that for the first time in
Congressional history, stated that it "may," and by common sense it
follows, "may not," be enforced by the Congress. This legislation, if
legally passed and ratified (which many have doubted throughout the years)
merely freed the slaves from physical bondage. There is nothing in the

11

language of that Amendment that returned a person to his name and nationality--there is nothing in the language of that Amendment to teach him how to speak English--how to read or write--how to form social contracts--how to govern and to take care of himself in a hostile land, among or apart from his former slave owners, who had not even been compensated for the loss of their property (emphasis added).

What was the status of these "free" persons during the years before the Fourteenth Amendment, ostensibly conferring citizenship on them, was passed. Were they a sovereign people? Did they have any intelligent manner of resisting the application of the 14th Amendment to them, or to intelligently demand the rights that are supposed to accompany citizenship. In answering these questions, we briefly review excerpts from the Memorandum in Support of Motion to Dismiss Indictments in The United States District Court for the District of Maryland for the Defendants.

> "...When a state of freedom, in this sense, is attributed to any subject, a power of choice and action is, by the signification of the words, necessarily supposed to exist in that subject, in the absence of law limiting or defining that freedom. According to the use of words, freedom cannot be predicated on anything which is without powers of choice and action. Therefore, according to the definition of a person in jurisprudence (ante Sec. 21), freedom can be attributed to persons only. The same may be said of any state or condition opposite to freedom; only persons, as having the power of choice and action in the absence of restraint, can be said to be bound by law (in the primary sense); and, therefore, bondage, as expressing a condition opposite to freedom, can be properly ascribed to persons only. It follows then, that by returning us to our nationality, Moorish Americans,

12

> we would be <u>persons</u> capable of being free. This brings
> us to the cardinal question of whether we were ever
> freed from slavery in this country..."

We think not. We maintain that the 14th Amendment was a hasty and

clumsy attempt to rectify a horrendous wrong by those, who, for their own

purposes, had thwarted the legal and divine will of President Lincoln to

heal the wounds of a divided nation once and for all, and to properly

assimilate those who chose to be naturalized into the family of nationalities

comprising the United States of America.

II

WHETHER THE COURT EXHIBITED SUCH PATENT
AND/OR LATENT BIAS AS TO PRECLUDE THE
APPELLANT FROM RECEIVING A FAIR TRIAL BY:
A.   REFERRING TO THE APPELLANTS AS BLACK
RATHER THAN AS MOROCCAN (MOORISH)
B.   DENYING APPELLANTS' MOTION TO JOIN
DEFENDANTS AND MOTION TO DISMISS INDICT-
MENTS, BEFORE EXPIRATION OF THE PRESCRIBED
TIME TO ANSWER THE GOVERNMENT'S MEMORANDA IN
OPPOSITION TO APPELLANTS' MOTION TO DISMISS
INDICTMENTS.
C.   FAILING TO RULE ON APPELLANTS' REQUEST
FOR A HEARING ON THEIR MOTION TO DISMISS
INDICTMENTS.

The Appellants filed in the District Court a Memorandum in support of

Motion to Dismiss Indictments (rec. Doc. No. 5) in which they stated that

the words "colored," "negro," and "black," were offensive and obnoxious

when applied to them, because they had declared themselves descendants of

Moroccans born in America. They stated that the names were offensive

because those names had historically been used to convey a patent or latent

inferiority on those, thus described. The Appellants went on to trace the

history of those offensive names in order to explain to the court that the names were intended to be degrading in their description. After all this,

did the Court below refute or disagree with the Appellants' contention of

offensiveness? The Appellants don't know. The Court never mentioned their

contentions in any manner--but merely stated in its ruling denying the

Appellants' Motion to Dismiss, "...that the defendants, who are black..."

(emphasis added) (rec. Doc. No 8). The court did not even say that the

defendants were considered black, but rather the Court stated it as a fact.

The Appellants consider the referring to persons by a color rather than by

a nationality is an exhibition of, at least, unconscious racism and bias.

Historically in many jurisdictions, the calling of persons of other

nationalities "colored," "negro," "black," has been the subject of libel and

slander suits. The Appellants recall that not too many years ago, calling

a "negro," "black," was an offensive act. Only since "black" became

beautiful did it become popular, but no more correct as a description of

nationality.

The government's Memorandum in Opposition to Appellants' Motion to

Dismiss Indictments and Motion for Joinder, was filed on September 6, 1978.

Appellants expected ten (10) days in which to answer the Memorandum in

Opposition to their Motion, pursuant to Rule 6A of Rules of The United

States District Court for The District of Maryland, however, the lower court handed

down its Order denying relief on September 13, 1978, thereby preventing

the Appellants from so doing (Rec. Doc. No. 8).

14

The Court went on to say (Rec. Doc. No. 8), ..."To state the contention is to demonstrate its frivolous nature. This court has neither the desire nor the power to repudiate both Mr. Lincoln's Proclamation and the Thirteenth Amendment to the United States Constitution..." The Appellants consider the Court's answer frivolous, and therefore biased, since no valid reason was advanced by the Court to support its contention of frivolity. The Appellants, however, join the Court in its desire not to repudiate Mr. Lincoln's Proclamations, and go further in their desire to see them implemented as written. In fact, if the Proclamations were implemented as written, we would not have experienced all of the Constitutional trouble that we have experienced from the 13th Amendment, on through the last, ensuing Amendments, up to the present day. The failure to rule on Appellants' request for a hearing on their Motion to Dismiss Indictments, seems to be another indication of the negative attitude of the lower court to the Appellants' contentions raised in their Motion (Rec. Doc. No. 5).

III

WHETHER THE FAILURE OF THE UNITED STATES
COURT OF APPEALS FOR THE FOURTH CIRCUIT
TO RULE ON APPELLANTS' PETITION FOR WRIT
OF MANDAMUS OR PROHIBITION: AND THE FAIL-
URE OF THE UNITED STATES DISTRICT COURT
FOR THE DISTRICT OF MARYLAND TO RULE ON
APPELLANTS' MOTION FOR STAY OF PROCEEDINGS,
WAS A VIOLATION OF DUE PROCESS OF LAW
GUARANTEED BY THE FIFTH AMENDMENT TO THE
UNITED STATES CONSTITUTION

The Appellants understand that the granting of extraordinary Writs is discretionary with the Court. The Appellants also understand that it

15

is discretionary for the Court to grant a request for stay of proceedings. The Appellants contend, however, that a request for relief at any judicial juncture requires that the court in a timely manner rule on such requests, and that the failure to so rule upon such requests is a violation of due process of law guaranteed by the Fifth Amendment to the Constitution of the United States of America.

Here, the lower court failed to rule on a Motion for Stay of Proceedings directed to it, pending a ruling on Appellants' Petition for Writ of Mandamus or Prohibition directed to the Circuit Court of Appeals for the Fourth Circuit. The ruling on that Petition has not been yet handed down by the circuit court.

CONCLUSION

For the foregoing reasons the Appellants ask that the Judgment rendered by the lower court be reversed.

Respectfully submitted,

Jacques E. Leeds-Bey, Sr.,
Attorney for Appellants.

IN THE
SUPREME COURT OF THE UNITED STATES

OCTOBER TERM, 1979

No. A-524

RONALD THOMAS COLEMAN,
AKA RONALD THOMAS COLEMAN-BEY,
ET. AL.,
Petitioner

vs.

UNITED STATES OF AMERICA

PETITION FOR WRIT OF CERTIORARI
To the United States Court of Appeals for the Fourth Circuit

The Petitioners, Ronald Thomas Coleman AKA Ronald Thomas Coleman-Bey, et. al., respectfully pray that a Writ of Certiorari issue to review the judgment and opinion of the United States Court of Appeals for the Fourth Circuit entered in this proceeding on November 19, 1979.

Figure 6.7

INDEX

AUTHORITIES

Cases

— 2 —

OPINIONS BELOW

No formal opinions were rendered by the District Court nor the Circuit Court of Appeals for the Fourth Circuit.

JURISDICTION

The jurisdiction of this Court is invoked under the provisions of 28 U.S.C. 1254 (1). The judgment of the United States Court of Appeals was entered on the 17th day of October, 1979. The Petitioners filed a Petition for Rehearing, which was denied on the 19th day of November, 1979 (Court order appears in Appendix).

ISSUES PRESENTED

1. Whether the status of slaves and their descendants was ever legally changed from that of property to that of legal persons; thereby subjecting them to charges of offenses relating to legal persons.
2. Whether the actions of the courts in the summary manner in which the various legal motions by the Petitioners throughout the trial and appeal were handled, amounted to such patent and/or latent bias as to preclude the Petitioners from receiving a fair trial.

STATEMENT OF FACTS

Petitioners were charged separately with filing a false Federal income tax withholding statement in violation of 26 U.S.C. Sec. 7205.

Each of the Petitioners entered a plea of not guilty in

—3—

separate arraignments before different judges in the United States District Court.

Petitioners, who were all represented by the same legal counsel, moved to Join the cases, moved to dismiss the Indictments and requested a hearing on the motions. One United States District Judge, acting for all Judges presiding in these cases, denied the motions, without a hearing.

Petitioners then filed a Petition for Writ of Mandamus or Prohibition to the United States Court of Appeals for the Fourth Circuit and additionally filed motions to stay the District Court proceedings, directed to both the District Court and the Circuit Court of Appeals. The Circuit Court denied the Motion to Stay Proceedings. The District Court failed to rule on the Motion to stay. Petitioners maintain that the Circuit Court of Appeals failed to properly rule on the Petition for Writ of Mandamus or Prohibition.

Petitioners in each case waived a jury trial and moved for disqualification of the trial judges for reason of bias. Upon denial of these Motions, Petitioners stood mute and declined to participate in the trials.

The Petitioners in each case were found guilty of one count and upon imposition of sentences each Petitioner moved for Stay of Execution of sentence, pending app· but in each case said Motion was denied.

Petitioners appealed to the Circuit Court of Appeals for the Fourth Circuit where on October 17, 1979, the Judg· ment of the District Court was affirmed without a formal opinion. A Petition for rehearing was denied on Nove··· ber 19, 1979.

It is from these actions that Petitioners seek a Writ of Certiorari.

4

REASONS FOR GRANTING THE WRIT

This Honorable Court has consistently upheld the Constitutionality of the Fourteenth Amendment to the Consititution of the United States and yet has failed to address itself to the inherent inequalities in addition to the apparent inconsistencies contained therein.

The Petitioners have asked important questions of federal law which should be settled by this Court regarding the Consitutionality of the Fourteenth Amendment, as it applies to former slaves and their descendants.

Petitioners contend that former slaves and their descendants have never been rendered legal persons by any branch of this government and therefore are not capable of being citizens of the United States of American.

Petitioners contend that Abraham Lincoln's Proclamation of Emancipation of September 22, 1862, was a legal use of his war powers granted to him by Congress, and any legislation passed in contravention thereof was unconsititutional and a violation of the separation of power promised by the Constitution of the United States, as regards the three branches of government.

Petitioners contend that the Constitution in Article I Section 2; Article I Section 9; and Article II Section I, recognize that there can be a difference in the classification of persons. Article I Section 9 refers to the importation of persons and while clearly referring to slaves, calls them persons. Petitioners contend that you cannot import persons, but rather you import things, goods, merchandise, etc. and that the reference to their importation clearly recognized slaves as inferior beings.

Petitioners contend that nothing was ever done to change their status from property to that of legal persons. Further, the Supreme Court in the "Dred Scott" case, Dred Scott V. Sanford, 19 Howard 393.1857, stated

—5—

unequivocally that Negroes were a class of persons incapable of being citizens. How then could Congress, in direct conflict with that decision, legally pass the Fourteenth Amendment declaring them citizens.

Petitioners contend that it was impossible for the so called "freed slaves," because of previous conditions dictated by forced servitude, to intelligently exercise the freedom of choice (enjoyed by truly free men) to accept or reject colonization and citizenship unilaterally imposed upon them by the Fourteenth Amendment.

Petitioners contend that the compensation promised to former slave holders by the initial Emancipation Proclamation was illegally denied them by Section 4 of the Fourteenth Amendment; and further that the failure to compensate the former slaves for their years of forced servitude was an additional violation of the Emancipation Proclamation (emphasis added).

The times we live in dictate that the descendants of former slaves enjoy de jure rather than de facto citizenship. Those that know who they are should be granted their rightful nationality and names so that they can join and enjoy the fruits of dignity and respect that come with belonging to a nationality recognized by the family of nations.

The Petitioners urge that this country can ill afford not to take the opportunity to make itself really whole in the grandest sense of the republic by correcting the wrongs complained of here.

—6—

CONCLUSION

For the above set out reasons, a Writ of Certiorari should issue to review the judgment and opinion of the Fourth Circuit Court of Appeals.

Respectfully submitted,

JACQUES E. LEEDS-BEY, SR.
1108 Mondawmin Concourse
Baltimore, Maryland 21215
Attorney for Petitioners

Throughout this book my aim has been to demonstrate the importance of the word Moor and its use taking precedence over the terms negro and black. It is imperative to understand that the term "Moor" is the direct link for descendents of Africa born in America (former slaves and indigenous people of color) to the historically documented Moorish Empire prior to the introduction of slavery in America. Historically, children in the United States have not been taught Moorish history, which predates slavery and negro/black history. For the most part, our history is taught as having its origin in 1619 in Jamestown, Virginia.

The damage that has occurred because of this way of teaching history to our children is irreparable. It has severed us from the history of our contributions to world civilization and has created a legacy of shame and a sense of inferiority in the descendents of what was once, the greatest empire in the world.

I respect every one's right to religious preferences. However, history reflects that the Moors who crossed the Straits of Gibraltar from North Africa and conquered Spain were Muslims. Please do not allow your religious philosophy to cloud your mind to the extent you would deny your own history and existence for a deity that was introduced to you by your master. Remember that early forms of Christianity were imposed on slaves to encourage them to be subservient to the master (research some history on Cotton Mather around 1750's). Of course, over time the former slaves adopted their own form of Christianity without any research into the many ecclesiastic councils; especially the Council of Nicaea in 325 AD.

In conclusion, I would like to expound upon the term nigger, niggah, nigga etc. For centuries this term has plagued the Moorish (African American) Community. From a very tender age this destructive term is embedded in the subconscious and conscious mind of our children. It develops in most cases unwritten definitions. It is adopted and applied in many learned ways and phrases dependent upon the situation at hand, all if not most in a very derogatory manner, particularly by the time our children are in adolescence and reach adulthood.

Even now, some entertainers and Hip Hop artist are constantly seeking new ways to gain approval and justification for perpetuating its use. Unfortunately, most of them have only scratched the surface of understanding the roots of the term and its psychological affect via the institution of slavery. For example, there is a distinct difference in sound for Niger like in Niger River (emphasis placed on the "i".) The opposite in nigger (nig) like in (pig), a negative sound vibration nigger. This degrading term needs to be excluded from our vocabulary.

I suggest that Moorish (African American) people review the distinction between a person or a thing as articulated in the enclosed United States Court of Appeals document to get a clearer picture of the status of a chattel slave or negro. I might also suggest that you read the book *The Name Negro: Its Origin and Evil Use*, and the *Negro A Beast*. As you continue to research, do not become angry, instead remember the most important fact and remedy, we are not negroes. We are, in fact, Moors or Moorish Americans with a distinct and glorious past. As the Honorable Noble Drew Ali stated "You must proclaim your nationality to be recognized in the government in which you live and the nations of the earth".

APPENDIX

I have taken the liberty of adding many historical letters,
pictures and articles for your review.

Rommani M. Amenu-El

ODUCED AT THE NATIONAL ARCHIVES

LEVITICUS 25:10
SECTION 16
13TH AMENDMENT
(20 SECTIONS)

Moorish School
of
Law And History

Grand Sheik Richardson Dingle-El, Founder

COPY BOOK 521
FILE NO. 5-39
NATIONAL ARCHIVES
NATIONAL HEADQUARTERS
GENERAL SERVICES ADMIN.
WASHINGTON, D.C. 20408

September 22, 1973

Be it know to all whom it may concern that as an extension of the Moorish National and Divine Movement of North America and in accordance with Our Authority, the August 1, 1928 affidavit of organization of the Moorish Science Temple of America affirmed in Cook, County Illnois, by the Phophet, Noble Drew Ali, as a profit-oriented corporation empowered to teach and enforce the bloody truth about the Moors in America.

The following individuals have been designated by Grand Sheik Richardson Dingle-El as the exclusive authorized reprentatives of and agents for the Moorish School of Law and History and the Moorish National Bureau of Vital Statistics:

Sheik Clarence R. Reynolds-El
Chairman, Moorish School of Law and History
Director and National Registrar, Moorish
National Bureau of Vital Statistics

Sheik Ernest J. Wright-Bey
Divine Minister
Co-Chairman, Moorish School of Law and History

Sheik Alfred Collins-El
Executive Secretary

Deputy Sheik Herbert H. Joiner-Bey, Jr.
Coordinator

As a consequence of the amnesty and Reconstruction policies of Presidents Abraham Lincoln and Andrew Johnson, the above individuals have taken subscribed and oath of allegiance to the United States,

152

LEVITICUS 25:10
SECTION 16
13TH AMENDMENT
(20 SECTIONS)

Moorish School of Law And History

Grand Sheik Richardson Dingle-El, Founder

COPY BOOK 521
FILE NO. 5-39
NATIONAL ARCHIVES
NATIONAL HEADQUARTERS
GENERAL SERVICES ADMIN.
WASHINGTON, D.C. 20408

Constitution including the Thirteenth Amendment with Twenty Sections. Any other persons claiming to represent this Movement, without con- crete evidence to that effect from the Grand Sheik or the above- mentioned individuals, are impostors in violation of the Laws of the Land. The activities of these impostors must be reported immediately to the Moorish School of Law and History.

For Grand Sheik Richardson Dingle-El:

Sincerely,

Clarence R. Reynolds-El (Sheik)

Clarence R. Reynolds-El (Sheik)
Chairman
146 Siegwart Lane
Baltimore, Maryland 21229
(301) 947-6768

gle

MOORISH SCHOOL OF
LAW AND HISTORY
HOME OFFICE
3236 FREDERICK AVE.
BALTIMORE, MD. 21229

153

Rommani M. Amenu-El

LEVITICUS 25:10
SECTION 16
.3TH AMENDMENT
(20 SECTIONS)

𝔗𝔥𝔢 𝔐𝔬𝔬𝔯𝔦𝔰𝔥 𝔖𝔠𝔦𝔢𝔫𝔠𝔢 𝔗𝔢𝔪𝔭𝔩𝔢
𝔗𝔥𝔢 𝔇𝔦𝔳𝔦𝔫𝔢 𝔞𝔫𝔡 𝔑𝔞𝔱𝔦𝔬𝔫𝔞𝔩
𝔐𝔬𝔳𝔢𝔪𝔢𝔫𝔱 𝔬𝔣 𝔑𝔬𝔯𝔱𝔥
𝔄𝔪𝔢𝔯𝔦𝔠𝔞, 𝔍𝔫𝔠. 𝔑𝔬. 13

ADEPT CHAMBER

MOORISH SCHOOL OF LAW & HISTORY / PROPHET NOBLE DREW ALI, 3rd, FOUNDER

COPY BOOK 521
FILE NO. 5-39
NATIONAL ARCHIVES
NATIONAL HEADQUARTERS
GENERAL SERVICES ADMIN.
WASHINGTON, D.C. 20408

December 26, 1975

Dr. James E. O'Neill
Deputy Archivist of the United States
General Services Administration
National Archives and Records Service
Washington, D.C. 20408

Dear Dr. O'Neill:

As a result of an extensive investigation, with the help of many government and state agencies into the Articles of Incorporation of The Moorish Science Temple of America, we of The Moorish School of Law and History are happy to inform you that we have at last taken steps to complete the foundation of this movement to eradicate the many misconceptions as to its true purposes by registering Articles of Incorporation in the State of Maryland through Washington, D.C. under the corporate name as follows: The Moorish Science Temple, The Divine and National Movement of North America, Inc. No. 13, as a U. S. Government and State Corporation for pecuniary profit. In addition, The Moorish School of Law and History will function under this Authority as stipulated in Article II, Section A of Articles of Incorporation. We are hereby requesting these extremely important documents to be included with our existing records already in your administrative files.

1. Articles of Incorporation
   (Please note sentence outlined in red on bottom of page 6 of Articles of Incorporation.)

2. Two letters to Carl Albert, Speaker of the House, U. S. House of Representatives, from The Moorish School of Law and History, dated October 17, 1975 and October 23, 1975.

3. Response to The Moorish Law School through Sheik Joiner-Bey from Carl Albert.

Date Received in NARS *1-9-76*
Register Number *2750*
Date Due *1-16-76*
Acknowledged (Form 140)
Date *1-8-76*
Reply *Mr. Goggins*

NATIONAL HEADQUARTERS

Home Office: 3236 Frederick Avenue - Baltimore, Maryland 21229 - Telephone: 301-947-9567

154

Dr. O'Neill   -2-   December 26, 1975

    4. A copy of Congressional Record dated May 1, 1975,
        page 3612 H

    5. A Moorish Questionnaire Titled, Our Authority with
        Moorish Seal

    We would also like to indicate that we are not using the National Archives
as a mailing address, as mentioned in your letter of date, April 3, 1974
addressed to myself. We are taking special precautions in referring to our
mailing address on bottom of stationary.

    Trusting to maintain your cooperation in this urgent matter. As always,
it is our pleasure to work with you and your staff in recording the pages of
history--this great nation. Again our sincere gratitude for previous cooperation.
We would appreciate confirmation.

                Sincerely,

                SHEIK CLARENCE R. REYNOLDS-EL
                Divine Minister - National Chairman

Enclosures

155

The Speaker's Rooms
U. S. House of Representatives
Washington, D. C. 20515
May 1, 1975

Herbert H. Joiner-Bey
Sheik, Coordinator
Moorish School of Law and History
P. O. Box 7063
Baltimore, Maryland 21216

Dear Sir:

This acknowledges your petition regarding the 13th Amendment
with Twenty Sections - Compensation, Naturalization, and
Colonization. I appreciate you hand delivering this material
to my office and have referred it to the Committee on the Judiciary
for consideration.

Very best wishes.

Sincerely,

Carl Albert

The Speaker

CA/pm

LEVITICUS 25:10
SECTION 16
13TH AMENDMENT
(26 SECTIONS)

Moorish School
of
Law And History

Grand Sheik Richardson Dingle-El, Founder

COPY BOOK 521
FILE NO. 5-39
NATIONAL ARCHIVES
NATIONAL HEADQUARTERS
GENERAL SERVICES ADMIN.
WASHINGTON, D.C. 20408

October 17, 1975

The Honorable Carl Albert
Speaker of the House
U. S. House of Representative
Washington, D.C. 20515

Dear Mr. Speaker:

On May 1, 1975, you referred to the House Committee on the Judiciary to the U. S. House of Representatives a petition rendered by members of our staff concerning the resurrection of the 13th Amendment with 20 Sections to the United States Constitution---including Naturalization, Colonization and Compensation. Apparently, the petition was received by the General Counsel of the Committee for research and analysis by that office. However, it has been brought to our attention that the original petition has been lost and that no copies can be found in either offices of the Committee or the Speaker's Rooms.

Consequently, you will find attached to this letter a copy of the original petition which is written in the form of a letter dated August 19, 1974 to General Alexander Haig, former White House Chief of Staff. We, the members of the Adept Chamber of The Moorish Science Temple, The Divine and National Movement of North America, Inc., trust that the Legislative Branch of the Federal Government will be more careful with this copy so that the important issues presented in the petition can be resolved with minimal delay.

Any correspondence that you may wish to send, may be addressed to: The Moorish Science Temple, The Divine and National Movement of North America, Inc., National Headquarters, 3236 Old Frederick Road, Baltimore, Maryland 21229.

Very truly yours,

THE MOORISH SCIENCE TEMPLE, THE DIVINE
AND NATIONAL MOVEMENT OF NORTH AMERICA, INC.

Sheik Clarence R. Reynolds-El
Divine Minister, National Chairman

Attachment

Sheik Herbert H. Joiner-Bey
National Coordinator

157

CONGRESSIONAL RECORD — HOUSE *May 1, 1975*

mane care and husbandry of animals, to provide technical and financial assistance to zoos, and for other purposes; to the Committee on Merchant Marine and Fisheries.

By Mr. DRINAN (for himself, Mr. BADILLO, Mr. BONKER, Mr. BROWN of California, Mr. CONYERS, Mr. CORNELL, Mr. DELLUMS, Mr. DOWNEY, Mr. EDGAR, Mr. GUDE, Mr. HARRINGTON, Mr. LEGGETT, Mr. MOAKLEY, Mr. MAZZOLI, Mr. OTTINGER, Mr. ROSENTHAL, Mr. ROYBAL, Mr. SARBANES, Mr. SCHEUER, Mr. SOLARZ, Mr. WAXMAN, and Mr. WON PAT):

H.R. 6632. A bill to provide increased congressional oversight of foreign military sales conducted under the Foreign Military Sales Act; jointly, to the Committees on International Relations, and Rules.

By Mr. FISHER:

H.R. 6633. A bill to amend the Internal Revenue Code of 1954 to revise the tax treatment of transfers of certain property to tax exempt organizations; to the Committee on Ways and Means.

By Mr. FORD of Tennessee (for himself, Mr. MAGUIRE, Mr. JONES of Tennessee, Ms. CHISHOLM, Mr. STOKES, Mr. HUGHES, Mr. BLANCHARD, Mr. COTTER, Mr. WIRTH, Mr. RUSSO, Mr. CARR, Mr. ZEFERETTI, Mr. BEDELL, Mr. MILLER of California, Mr. WAXMAN, Mr. BEARD of Rhode Island, Ms. MEYNER, Mr. SCHEUER, Mr. PATTISON of New York, Mr. BRINKLEY, Mr. SANTINI, and Mr. BAUCUS):

H.R. 6634. A bill to amend the Fair Packaging and Labeling Act to require that packaged consumer commodities be labeled to show their selling price; to the Committee on Interstate and Foreign Commerce.

By Mr. HARRINGTON:

H.R. 6635. A bill to amend the Voting Rights Act of 1965 to provide that individuals casting absentee ballots in Federal elections shall be relieved of any costs relating to the notarization of such ballots; jointly, to the Committees on the Judiciary and House Administration.

By Mr. HUGHES:

H.R. 6636. A bill to amend title II of the Social Security Act to increase to $5,000 the amount of outside earnings which (subject to further increases under the automatic adjustment provisions) is permitted an individual each year without any deductions from benefits thereunder; to the Committee on Ways and Means.

By Mr. O'NEILL (for himself, Mr. FASCELL, Mr. MOFFETT, Mr. ROSE, Mr. BROWN of California, Mr. SCHEUER, Mr. SARBANES, Mr. GAYDOS, Mr. NIX, Mr. MINISH, Mr. MITCHELL of New York, Mr. HELSTOSKI, Mr. DELLUMS, and Mr. REES):

H.R. 6637. A bill to amend the Federal Property and Administrative Services Act of 1949, as amended, to provide for the disposal of surplus real property to States and their political subdivisions, agencies and instrumentalities for economic development purposes; to the Committee on Government Operations.

By Mr. O'NEILL (for himself, Mr. CHARLES H. WILSON of California, Mr. SEIBERLING, Ms. MEYNER, Mr. COTTER, Mr. ZEFERETTI, Mr. BADILLO, Mr. McKINNEY, Mr. KOCH, Mr. LAFALCE, Mr. STARK, Mr. CORNELL, Mr. WON PAT, and Mr. DE LUGO):

H.R. 6638. A bill to amend the Federal Property and Administrative Services Act of 1949, as amended, to provide for the disposal of surplus real property to States and their political subdivisions, agencies, and instrumentalities for economic development purposes; to the Committee on Government Operations.

By Mr. SANTINI:

H.R. 6639. A bill to exempt range sheep industry mobile housing and temporary range cattle camps from regulations affecting permanent housing for agricultural workers; to the Committee on Education and Labor.

By Mr. STAGGERS:

H.R. 6640. A bill to authorize the Secretary of Transportation to guarantee loans of $100 million to railroad systems in the Midwestern United States; to the Committee on Interstate and Foreign Commerce.

By Mr. THONE:

H.R. 6641. A bill to authorize recomputation at age 60 of the retired pay of members and former members of the uniformed services whose retired pay is computed on the basis of pay scales in effect prior to January 1, 1972, and for other purposes; to the Committee on Armed Services.

By Mr. WHITE:

H.R. 6642. A bill to provide for allotment or assignment of payments from civil service annuities, and for other purposes; to the Committee on Post Office and Civil Service.

By Mr. BOB WILSON:

H.R. 6643. A bill to amend section 1451 of title 10, United States Code, to change the offset for social security under the survivor benefit plan from 100 percent to 50 percent, and for other purposes; to the Committee on Armed Services.

By Mr. YOUNG of Alaska:

H.R. 6644. A bill to provide, under or by amendment of the Alaska Native Claims Settlement Act, for the late enrollment of certain Natives, the establishment of an escrow account for the proceeds of certain lands, the treatment of certain payments and grants, and the consolidation of existing regional corporations, and for other purposes; to the Committee on Interior and Insular Affairs.

By Mr. EDGAR:

H.R. 6645. A bill to amend the Highway Revenue Act of 1956 relating to the Highway trust fund; to the Committee on Ways and Means.

By Mr. D'AMOURS (for himself, Mr. BEARD of Rhode Island, Mr. BOLAND, Mr. BURKE of Massachusetts, Mr. COHEN, Mr. COTTER, Mr. DODD, Mr. EARLY, Mr. EMERY, Mr. HARRINGTON, Mr. JEFFORDS, Mr. MACDONALD of Massachusetts, Mr. McKINNEY, Mr. MOAKLEY, Mr. ST GERMAIN, Mr. SARASIN, and Mr. STUDDS):

H.J. Res. 424. Joint Resolution to amend the act creating the American Revolution Bicentennial Advisory Council to permit the appointment of members from the New England States; to the Committee on the Judiciary.

By Mr. WAGGONNER:

H.J. Res. 425. Joint resolution proposing an amendment to the Constitution of the United States; to the Committee on the Judiciary.

By Mr. WHITEHURST:

H.J. Res. 426. Joint resolution proposing an amendment to the Constitution of the United States; to the Committee on the Judiciary.

By Mr. YATRON:

H.J. Res. 427. Joint resolution providing for the designation of the first week in May of each year as Be Kind to Animals Week; to the Committee on Post Office and Civil Service.

By Mr. ANNUNZIO (for himself and Mr. ZABLOCKI):

H. Con. Res. 262. Concurrent resolution expressing the sense of Congress concerning recognition by the European Security Conference of the Soviet Union's occupation of Estonia, Latvia, and Lithuania; to the Committee on International Relations.

By Mr. CARNEY:

H. Con. Res. 263. Concurrent resolution expressing the sense of the Congress with respect to International Women's Year; to the Committee on Post Office and Civil Service.

By Mr. FUQUA:

H. Res. 436. Resolution to oppose the lifting of sanctions against Cuba and to request the advice and consent of the Senate prior to any proposed change in our Cuba policy; to the Committee on International Relations.

By Mr. KARTH:

H. Res. 437. Resolution proposing the designation of Norwegian-American Day; to the Committee on Post Office and Civil Service.

By Mr. MONTGOMERY (for himself, Mr. McEWEN, Mr. MURPHY of Illinois, Mr. COUGHLIN, Mr. BREAUX, Mr. FORSYTHE, Mr. BYRON, Mr. ROBERT W. DANIEL, Jr., Mr. JONES of Tennessee, Mr. ANDREWS of North Dakota, Mr. ICHORD, Mr. ST GERMAIN, Mr. FINDLEY, Mr. O'NEILL, Mr. HUGHES, Mr. BAFALIS, Mr. FLORIO, Mr. STUDDS, Mr. GUDE, Mr. FORD of Tennessee, Mr. COLLINS of Texas, and Mr. JENRETTE):

H. Res. 438. Resolution establishing a select committee to study the problem of U.S. servicemen missing in action in Southeast Asia; to the Committee on Rules.

By Mr. STAGGERS (for himself, Mr. DINGELL, Mr. MOSS, Mr. ROGERS, Mr. ROONEY, Mr. MACDONALD of Massachusetts, Mr. MURPHY of New York, Mr. WIRTH, Mr. SHARP, Mr. BRODHEAD, Mr. ECKHARDT, Mr. OTTINGER, Mr. MOFFETT, Mr. MAGUIRE, and Mr. VAN DEERLIN):

H. Res. 439. Resolution disapproving the proposed amendment by the President to remove existing price controls relating to crude oil; to the Committee on Interstate and Foreign Commerce.

PRIVATE BILLS AND RESOLUTIONS

Under clause 1 of rule XXII, private bills and resolutions were introduced and severally referred as follows:

By Mr. HALEY:

H.R. 6646. A bill for the relief of E. Garrison Wood; to the Committee on the Judiciary.

By Mr. HAWKINS:

H.R. 6647. A bill for the relief of Guillermo Bell; to the Committee on the Judiciary.

H.R. 6648. A bill for the relief of Danella Alvarez de Bell; to the Committee on the Judiciary.

By Mr. TEAGUE:

H.R. 6649. A bill for the relief of Rocco A. Petrone; to the Committee on the Judiciary.

PETITIONS, ETC.

Under clause 1 of rule XXII,

117. The SPEAKER presented a petition of the Moorish School of Law and History, Baltimore, Md., relative to implementation of the 13th amendment with 20 sections; to the Committee on the Judiciary.

AMENDMENTS

Under clause 6 of rule XXIII, proposed amendments were submitted as follows:

H.R. 49

By Mrs. SCHROEDER:

Amendment to the amendment of the Committee on Interior and Insular Affairs to H.R. 49:

On page 3, line 21, insert "Naval Oil Shale Reserves," immediately before "the National Wildlife Refuge,".

Amendment to the amendments of the Committee on Armed Services to the amendments of the Committee on Interior and Insular Affairs to H.R. 49 (as reported from the Committee on Armed Services on April 18, 1975):

On page 4, line 1, insert "and Oil Shale" immediately before "Reserves"

UNITED STATES DEPARTMENT OF JUSTICE

WASHINGTON, D.C. 20530

Address Reply to the
Division Indicated
and Refer to Initials and Number
JSP:MWH:dvw:kg
DJ 144-35-0

MAR 17 1975

Reverend Clarence R. Reynolds-El
Sheik, Divine Minister
National Chairman
Moorish School of Law and History
Post Office Box 7063
Baltimore, Maryland 21216

Dear Reverend Reynolds-El:

We have forwarded copies of your letter of
December 3, 1974, with enclosed documents, to Dr.
James B. Rhoads, Archivist of the United States,
National Archives and Record Service, Seventh Street
and Pennsylvania Avenue, Northwest, Washington, D. C.
20408 and to Mr. Byron V. Pepitone, Director, Selective
Service System, 1724 F Street, Northwest, Washington,
D. C. 20435.

We are sure the matter will receive careful
consideration.

Any inquiries you have concerning this same
matter in the future should be sent directly to the
above named agencies.

Sincerely,

J. STANLEY POTTINGER
Assistant Attorney General
Civil Rights Division

By: *Maceo W. Hubbard*
MACEO W. HUBBARD
Supervisory Trial Attorney
Criminal S ection

Rommani M. Amenu-El

UNITED STATES OF AMERICA
GENERAL SERVICES ADMINISTRATION

Office of General Counsel
Washington, D.C. 20405

Reverend Clarence R. Reynolds-El
Sheik, Divine Minister
National Chairman
Moorish School of Law & History
4610-C Pen Lucy Road
Baltimore, MD 21229

Dear Reverend Reynolds-El:

This is in response to your letter of December 3, 1974, in which you
request access under the Freedom of Information Act, 5 U.S.C. 552,
to the following items:

> "1. A letter to Mr. Huss of the Office of the
> National Archives from Bro. Clifford Hazel-
> Bey dated September 22, 1974, inquiring into
> the relationship of the School and the Moorish
> National Bureau of Vital Statistics with the
> Federal Government.
>
> 2. The response sent to Bro. Hazel-Bey by
> Mr. Yock of the General Counsel's Office.
>
> 3. Any other inquiries and/or responses made
> regarding same."

In accordance with the requirements of 5 U.S.C. 552(a)(3) and 41 CFR
§105-60.105-1, enclosed are copies of the materials specified in requests
one and two, quoted above. In response to your third request, the Office
of General Counsel, General Services Administration has received no other
correspondence from private parties inquiring into the relationship of either
the School or the Moorish National Bureau of Vital Statistics and the Federal
Government.

Sincerely,

HAROLD S. TRIMMER, JR.
General Counsel

Enclosures

Keep Freedom in Your Future With U.S. Savings Bonds

160

The negro, the black, the Moor

WILLIAM DONALD SCHAEFER, Mayor

DEPARTMENT OF EDUCATION
OFFICE OF THE SUPERINTENDENT
3 East 25th Street, East Wing
Baltimore, Maryland 21218

July 1, 1975

Sheikess Betty Starkey-El
Chairman of the Educational Committee
Box 7063
Baltimore, Maryland

Dear Sheikess Starkey-El:

Your visit of Wednesday, June 25, 1975 was most enlightening
and appreciated. The expansiveness of the discussion was such
that it left me interested in having greater detail and further
information.

Obviously, some of what your colleagues had to say was known
to me. However, the framework in which it was placed was more
meaningful and thus led to my request that you provide me with
certain documents, for which I am willing to pay if necessary.

As I explained at our meeting the pressure of time does not
at this juncture permit a leisurely exploration. If this were so,
I would seek the documents, etc. without prevailing upon your time
and effort.

Any further assistance you might render for the purpose of
shedding new light and knowledge on the subject matter would be
appreciated.

Sincerely,

Roland N. Patterson
Superintendent

akc

BALTIMORE CITY PUBLIC SCHOOLS
BOARD OF SCHOOL COMMISSIONERS
THREE EAST TWENTY-FIFTH STREET
BALTIMORE, MARYLAND 21213

DR. JOHN WALTON
PRESIDENT
GILMAN HALL
THE JOHNS HOPKINS UNIVERSITY
CHARLES & 34TH STREETS
BALTIMORE, MARYLAND 21213

April 9, 1973

Mr. Clarence R. Reynolds-El
3826 Sequoia Avenue
Baltimore, Maryland 21215

Dear Mr. Reynolds-El:

I make reference to your recent visit to my office in which you reviewed a proposal for adding certain subject material to the regular school curriculum.

Because I have not heard from you since your visit to my office, I must assume that you remain in contact with our staff division concerning your request to have certain subject matter added to the curriculum. I would appreciate hearing from you and to know whether I can be of any further assistance. Please do not hesitate to call on me if you would like to address the Board at a public session at any time.

Sincerely,

Louis Beck

Louis Beck, Assistant to the President
Board of School Commissioners

LB/za

162

This charter was first issue to Richardson Dingle EL by F.Turner EL. Richardson Dingle El issued it to me, Rommani Amenu EL (formerly Clarence Reynolds-EL). I then issued a Charter of Warrant and Dispensation to Sheik Claud El Myrick Bey.

THE SUN, Tuesday, October 31, 1978

B1

'Mine eyes have seen the glory of Noble Drew Ali'

By Gene Oishi

"Black is beautiful" was the rallying cry during the resurgence of black nationalism and racial pride in the Sixties, but some members of the black community rejected the phrase and still find it repugnant today.

They are America's Moors, adherents of the Moorish Science Temple, who say all blacks in this country are descendants of the ancient Moabites and the founders of the Moroccan Empire.

The men usually wear fezzes, or knitted skull caps, on less formal occasions. Some wear turbans, as do the women, who dress in ankle-length gowns or fluffy pantaloons. On festive occasions, they appear like a band of Asiatic nomads, or a scene out of the Arabian nights.

They abhor the term "Negro" and "colored" and especially the word "black." Their complexion, they say, is olive, not black, which is the color of death, adding, "We are not a dead race."

When the Moorish Science Temple was started in Newark, N.J., in 1913, it was one of the first organizations to advocate what was later to be called "black nationalism," but it has been on the decline since the death of its founder, Noble Drew Ali, in 1929.

After period of relative quiescence, however, the organization is beginning to stir, at least in Baltimore, with a tax protest and the conviction of some of its members for filing fraudulent income tax returns. The Moors hope to appeal the cases all the way to the Supreme Court and make it their cause celebre.

In Baltimore, the Moorish Science Temple was started in 1927 on South Sharp street, when the movement was at its height nationally. There were temples in Newark, N.J., Pittsburgh, Detroit and Chicago and in several cities in the South.

Today, there are two competing temples in Baltimore, one at 762 West Baltimore street, in a narrow, three-story brick row house next to a fire station, and the other in a storefront at 519 North Howard street, across the street from the Mayfair Theater.

It was around World War I and in the decade that followed when the Moorish Science Temple had its greatest impact on the black community. Its founder was originally named Timothy Drew, who was born in North Carolina in 1886. Scholars who have studied the movement say that Mr. Drew was a man with little formal education, though his followers say he studied at Cairo University.

According to most commonly exhibited pictures of him, he was a tall, thin man, with delicate features and a small mustache. He is usually shown wearing a fez and a long, white robe with a broad sash. In other pictures, he has a turban, a long white tunic, bedecked with medals and sashes, and silky Persian-style pantaloons. He has his right hand over his heart in many pictures.

When he founded the Moorish Science Temple in Newark, it was one of the first movements within the black community aimed at instilling racial pride, though it did so by declaring that black people were "Asiatics," descendants of the ancient Moabites, who, he said, inhabited Canaan, part of what was later to be called Palestine.

The Moabites, Mr. Drew said, were one of the peoples driven out of Canaan by Joshua and settled in northwest and southwest Africa eventually to establish the Moroccan Empire. Part of the area later became North, Central and South America when a great earthquake formed the Atlantic Ocean. Thus, the theory goes, not all the Moabites came over in slave ships, but many were here centuries before Columbus's "discovery of the New World."

The Moorish Science Temple, which espoused a modified form of Islam, co-existed with the secular, return-to-Africa

See MOORS, B2, Col. 1

CLARENCE REYNOLDS-EL
... grand sheik of Howard street temple

NOBLE DREW ALI 3d
... founder "reincarnated"

NOBLE DREW ALI
... founder of Moorish Science Temple

R. GERMAN-BEY
... successor to Noble Drew Ali

164

THE SUN, Tuesday, October 31, 1978

Moorish refrain—'Mine eyes have seen the coming of Noble Drew Ali'

MOORS, from B1

Universal Negro Improvement Association, founded by Marcus Garvey, another important figure in the history of black nationalism, whose influence as an advocate of black liberation extended beyond the United States to the Caribbean and Africa.

The two movements were unrelated to each other, but Mr. Drew compared Mr. Garvey—much to the latter's annoyance—to John the Baptist, who prepared the way for the coming of Jesus Christ.

"In these modern days there came a forerunner, who was divinely prepared by the great God-Allah, and his name is Marcus Garvey," wrote Mr. Drew in his slim 92-page work that he entitled "The Holy Koran."

The passage, with poetic license, goes on to say that Marcus Garvey, a lifelong Christian, "did teach and warn the nations of the earth to prepare to meet the coming Prophet; who was to bring the true and divine Creed of Islam, and his name is Noble Drew Ali; who was prepared and sent to this earth by Allah, to teach the old-time religion and the everlasting gospel to the sons of men.

"We, as a clean and pure nation descended from the inhabitants of Africa, do not desire to amalgamate or marry into the families of the pale-skin nations of Europe. Neither serve the gods of their religion, because our forefathers are the true and divine founders of the first religious creed, for the redemption and salvation of mankind on earth. . . .

"Come all ye Asiatics of America," the volume concludes, "and hear the truth about your nationality and birthrights, because you are not Negroes. Learn of your forefathers' ancient and divine Creed. That you will learn to love instead of hate. We are trying to uplift fallen humanity. Come link yourselves with the families of nations. We honor all the true and divine prophets."

To all converts, Noble Drew Ali issued a "nationality card," which confirms the holder as a Moorish American, who honors "all the Divine Prophets, Jesus, Mohammed, Buddha and Confucius."

"I do hereby declare that you are a Moslem under the Divine Law of the Holy Koran of Mecca, Love, Truth, Peace, Freedom and Justice," the card states and ends with the statement in bold letters, "I AM A CITIZEN OF THE U.S.A."

Adherents were also given the suffix of Bey or El (pronounced eel) to attach to their last names and those rising to positions of leadership were given the title of Sheik and Sheikess. All Moors, moreover, were required to wear Turkish-style fezzes or turbans to reflect their Eastern origin.

In Chicago, Moors—made conspicuous by their Eastern dress and emboldened by their nationality cards—began walking the streets showing open contempt for white people or haranguing them about their misdeeds; so that the prophet eventually had to issue an admonition, stating:

"I hereby warn all Moors that they must cease from all radical or agitating speeches, while on their jobs, or in their homes, or on the streets. Stop flashing your cards before Europeans as this only causes confusion. We did not come to cause confusion, our work is to uplift the nation."

As indicated by this statement and other writings and proclamations of Noble Drew Ali, his was a peaceful and idealistic movement. Indications are that it remains so today.

The movement, however, did go through a turbulent period in the late Twenties in Chicago when the prophet began putting into positions of leadership better-educated persons of dubious integrity.

Arthur Huff Fuset, black anthropologist and author, who studied the Moorish Science Temple in Philadelphia, wrote in his book, "Black Gods of the Metropolis": "Unfortunately, they [the new leaders] proved to have questionable motives, and before long had introduced practices which the prophet had not anticipated. Various methods were employed to exploit the members of the cult, including the sale of herbs, magical charms and potions, and literature pertaining to the cult. Some of the leaders of the cult grew rich."

According to Mr. Fuset's account, supported by other scholars, when it became apparent that Noble Drew Ali was the main obstacle to further commercial exploitation of the mem-

---

there was a scattering from New Jersey, Delaware and North Carolina, there were no more than 50 persons attending at any one time, and about a third of them were children.

The sessions started promptly every evening at 7 P.M. with one of the Moorish security guards shouting, "Islam!" which, the Moors say, means peace. The word is also used as greeting and in the course of a speech or sermon Moors will frequently shout, "Islam!" in much the same way Christians might shout, "Amen!" to express agreement or approval.

The Hopkins Room, which seemed cavernous compared with the attendance, was decorated with streamers and gaily colored paper ornaments. Men, women and children, wearing turbans and Eastern-looking clothes, walked from place to place with their right hands raised and open in a gesture of peace.

On the walls were slogans composed around the five cardinal values of the movement: "Love, Truth, Peace, Freedom and Justice."

Stars and crescents were pasted throughout the room, and on the stage there were, as in every Moorish-American gathering, the American flag and the Moroccan flag, a green, five-pointed star, on a red field.

There were also several pictures of the Prophet Noble Drew Ali, including a painting, which showed the prophet coming out of the sea, holding a stricken child, labeled, "Humanity," in his arm. "Salvation" and "The Cares of the World" were also written on the painting.

The convention opened with the reading of the "Divine Constitution and Bylaws of the Moorish Science Temple of America," which are based on Noble Drew Ali's "Holy Koran," which is largely a mixture of Christian and Islamic aphorism.

The constitution and bylaws, besides setting up organizational rules of procedure, also admonish men to look after their families and women and children to be loving and obedient. The document also states that the purpose of the movement is not to overthrow the government or to cause confusion, but rather to uplift fallen humanity.

The reading was followed by the "national anthem" of the Moorish Science Temple, which is sung to the tune of the "Battle Hymn of the Republic," and starts with the words, "Mine eyes have seen the glory of Noble Drew Ali," and ends with "Glory, glory, Prophet Noble Drew Ali. . . His truth is marching on."

Two tall, powerfully built young men, dressed in white tunics, black trousers and red turbans, stood at parade rest on stage, throughout most of the proceedings. Others, similarly dressed, or in Army fatigues, and equipped with walkie-talkies, were stationed at doors and various positions about the hall.

They were members of the National Security Forces, who are said to be trained in unarmed combat, such as boxing and karate, as well as crowd control techniques.

The men, who are unfailingly courteous, have provided security for a number of public affairs, including the Afram festival in 1976 and 1977 and the annual "college day" for high school students, put on by the Direct Search for Talent, a city agency that encourages and direct students who want post-high school education.

Providing security for organizations, which prefer the colorfully dressed and polite Moors to regular police, appears to be one of the main activities of Moorish Science Temple. (The Howard street temple has a Moorish National Special Police.)

For the 1976 Afram festival, the organization provided 28 guards at a price of $5 per man hour, for a total bill of $6,000, according to Norman Ross, who was chairman of the festival committee. Largely because of the high cost, Afram did not use the Moors this year.

There could also be some legal problems, since according to the State Police, the Moors are not licensed to provide security guards. William Porter-El, supreme legal adviser and general counsel of the National Security Forces, however, insisted his was a "volunteer" force and what appears to be payments for services are actually "contributions."

Judging from the convention and a Sunday service (there are also Friday night services) at the Baltimore street temple, the movement appears, at least to an outsider, to be closer to Christianity than to Islam.

A Sunday school lesson attended by a handful of children, for

---

Sun photos—William Hotz and Jed Kirschbaum

7-week-old daughter, Anna, with her 1-year-old son, Philo Dade-el, at her side during a Moorish convention (below).

A youngster listens to scripture readings at the Howard street Moorish Science Temple (above). Sister D. Dade-el holds her

---

faction, first to Frederick avenue and two years ago to the Howard street location.

In 1975, he proclaimed himself the reincarnated prophet. He said that Noble Drew Ali 2d, before his death in 1945, had designated him as his heir. When asked what reincarnation meant, the new prophet said it meant that his successor before his death called a meeting and passed "the word" to him on a piece of paper.

Most of the day-to-day leadership at the temple, however, appears to be in the hands of Sheik Clarence R. Reynolds-El, who has the title of national chairman.

Under his leadership, the temple, which runs a Moorish School of Law and History, is pushing vigorously for a court test of the organization's position that the Thirteenth, Fourteenth and Fifteenth Amendments to the Constitution are invalid as far as ex-slaves are concerned because they have never been legally raised to the status of persons.

Sheik Reynolds-El and the organization's lawyer, Jacques E. Leeds-Bey, say the amendments contradict the Fifth Amendment's due process clause, which protects private property. The former slaveholders, they say, have never been compensated for their loss, nor have former slaves been compensated for their period of involuntary servitude as Abraham Lincoln had intended when he issued the Emancipation Proclamation.

Sheik Reynolds-El and Mr. Leeds-Bey, in fact, spoke almost sympathetically about the Ku Klux Klan, which they said was formed by former slaveholders in self-defense because their constitutional rights were being violated.

They said Congress at one point appropriated $478 million for the purpose of compensating both slaves and slave owners, but the money was never disbursed. At 6 per cent interest, they note, the amount would by now be a rather substantial sum.

The money, they said, should now be used to realize Lincoln's plan of colonizing territories "between the Alleghenies to the Rockies" with former slaves and to develop "model communities" where the Moors may recover their religious and cul-

of the leaders of the cult grew rich."

According to Mr. Fuel's account, supported by other scholars, when it became apparent that Noble Drew Ali was the main obstacle to further commercial exploitation of the membership, efforts were made to displace him. In the ensuing internal struggle one of the leaders was killed.

Though the prophet was not in Chicago at the time of the killing, he was arrested upon his return by police, to whom the Moors, because of their assertiveness, were anathema. He was released after a few weeks on bond, but did not live to face trial.

Current members of the Moorish Science Temple say that the Prophet Drew Ali died of pneumonia, but at the time the suspicion was that he died either through injuries he received while undergoing police interrogation or as a result of a beating from some members of this organization.

According to some accounts, one segment of the movement was taken over by Wallace D. Fard, who was later to split with the Moors to found the Nation of Islam, a militant, black supremacist, political cult, whose members were later to be dubbed "Black Muslims."

Elijah Muhammad, who took over the Nation of Islam, after Mr. Fard mysteriously disappeared, is also said to have belonged to the Moorish Science Temple at one time.

After the death of Noble Drew Ali, however, there appears to have been little unity in the movement, which broke up into smaller factions with individual temples in different cities going their separate ways.

In some cities, the temples are headed by persons who say they are the reincarnation of the Prophet Nobel Drew Ali. The temple on North Howard street in Baltimore, for example is headed by Prophet Noble Drew Ali 3d, Reincarnated.

Noble Drew Ali 3d used to be called Richardson Dingle-El, a former construction worker, who was the grand sheik of the temple on West Baltimore street. But for reasons that remain unclear, the temple split in 1972, and Sheik Dingle-El moved his

The money, they said, should now be used to realize Lincoln's plan of colonizing territories "between the Alleghenies to the Rockies" with former slaves and to develop "model communities" where the Moors may recover their religious and cultural heritage, as well as their sense of identity.

To press this claim, four members of the temple have avoided paying income taxes, on the grounds that they are not liable for taxes because they have never been raised from the status of "chattel" and they have never been offered naturalization privileges. If immigrants from other countries must be naturalized before they become citizens, they ask, why not those of Moorish ancestry?

Sheik Reynold-Bey acknowledged that the Moorish Science Temple has declined in membership since the death of Noble Drew Ali, but said it was on the upsurge with an increase in college-educated converts. The Baltimore temple, he said, currently has about 20 college graduates, who are being moved into positions of leadership.

Sheik Reynolds-Bey, himself, went two years to the Community College of Baltimore, where he studied political science and American government. He joined the movement in 1971 and now devotes his full time to it.

He said that in the time of Noble Drew Ali registered Moors numbered in the millions, but the current number throughout the country was only about 240,000, with only about half of them active.

The Howard street temple, he said, has registered about 1,500 persons, though at a recent Friday night service, there were only about a hundred persons present.

The service had some Islamic components such as the call to prayer, done in Arabic, and at least a portion of the congregation said their prayers in the Muslim fashion, on their knees and with their foreheads touching the floor.

Over on West Baltimore street, at the competing temple, the successor to Noble Drew Ali is Dr. R. German-Bey, a retired steelworker.

The Moorish leader is a practitioner of "polarity therapy," which, his wife, Mrs. La Aquanetta German-Bey, said originated in the Orient and consists of treating physical ailments through applied pressure to influence the flow of energy currents in the body.

Dr. German-Bey joined the Moorish Science Temple in 1927 at age 18 and helped to establish the first temple in Baltimore that year. In 1928, he said, the Prophet Noble Drew Ali, himself, came to Baltimore and tested five of the brothers.

Dr. German-Bey said he, was the only one to pass the test, whereupon, "The prophet blessed me from my head to my privates, and said, 'My son, I want you to tell my Moors the truth.'"

He was eventually to conclude that Noble Drew Ali had given him a mandate to lead the movement, for, according to Dr. German-Bey, the prophet said before he left, "The angel has come for me twice and if he comes again I will be ready to go, because my work is finished." Noble Drew Ali died the following year.

It was not until 1972, however, that Dr. German-Bey was officially elected National Grand Sheik by at least one segment of the movement. He was later conferred the title of "Prince of Peace and Successor to the Prophet Noble Drew Ali."

As National Grand Sheik, Dr. German-Bey has brought three national conventions to Baltimore. The last one lasted five days, beginning September 18, and was held in the Hopkins Room of the Civic Center. It commemorated the 50th anniversary of the first national convention called by Noble Drew Ali in Chicago in 1928.

Dr. German-Bey said he sent invitations to all nations, including one to President Carter and Mayor Schaefer. The Mayor, whose photograph is prominently displayed at the Baltimore street temple, did not attend, but for the third straight year proclaimed a "Moorish-American Week" in Baltimore.

Delegates came mainly from the Washington area. Though

are also Friday night services at the Baltimore street temple, the movement appears, at least to an outsider, to be closer to Christianity than to Islam.

A Sunday school lesson attended by a handful of children, for example, dealt mainly with the so-called missing years in the life of Jesus, which, according to Noble Drew Ali's "Holy Koran," were spent in India, Europe and Africa.

The book, which does not refer to the Prophet Mohammed, the founder of Islam, is also called "The Book of the Seven Seals," a reference to St. John's Revelation, in which such a book is mentioned.

Thus the number 7 holds a special significance for the Moors. It is seen everywhere surrounded by a circle broken in four parts, representing the four corners of the earth and their respective prophets: Jesus, Mohammed, Buddha and Confucius.

Members of the temple, moreover, say their ritual prayer, standing, facing East and with five fingers of one hand and two of the other held up. At the Baltimore street temple, the members did not pray in the traditional Muslim fashion.

Dr. German-Bey said the brothers in the East worship "in the Arabian style," noting that while Mohammed was a prophet to the Arabians, "Noble Drew Ali was the prophet to the ex-slaves of America." He said there was some resentment against Arabs because some of them sold the ancestors of Moorish-Americans into slavery.

The Moors conform to the Islamic moral code to the extent that they do not eat pork and refrain from smoking and drinking.

Dr. German-Bey's temple is also active in the prisons, where they maintain what they call preparation centers. At the Maryland Penitentiary, Warden George Collins, estimated that there were about 80 prisoners who are adherents of Moorish Science Temple.

The temple also maintains several business in Washington, including a restaurant, a health food store, a variety store and a car repair shop, called Bey's and El's Auto Clinic.

Howard Street Temple Guides Moorish Science In U.S.

By Carl Schoettler

Prophet Noble Drew Ali is said to have been moved to found the first Moorish Science Temple of America in 1913 in Newark, N.J.

And when the Noble Drew Ali passed to his physical death in 1929, the stewardship devolved on the Noble Drew Ali II, Reincarnated, who practiced Moorish Science mainly in Chicago.

The Noble Drew Ali II met his physical death in 1945 and the leadership passed to the Noble Drew Ali III, Reincarnated, who resides in his physical form here in Baltimore.

Between Noble Drew Ali II and Noble Drew Ali III, a schism occurred that led to the founding of what became the World Community of Islam in the West, known as the Black Muslims. A loyal remnant, the one based here, remained faithful to Moorish Science.

The Moorish Science Temple, The Divine and National Movement of North America, Incorporated, No. 13, is at 519 North Howard street. And there, too, is the new Moorish School of Law and History, where, in the words of Sheikess Carolyn Reynolds-El, "research has already begun in the fields of historical fact and law, both constitutional and universal."

The Moorish Science Temple is a long, bright room behind a plate glass storefront across the street from the Mayfair Theater. The walls are hung with portraits of Abraham Lincoln and Anwar Sadat, a tapestry depicting the Signing of the Declaration of Independence much as it appears on the $2 bill, maps and artifacts of Moorish Science and photographs of the Noble Drew Ali I and his successors, flanked by the flag of the United States of America and the flag of the ancient Moroccans, which is a 5-pointed green star on a field of red.

"Noble Drew Ali III, Reincarnated, our spiritual guide, our spiritual leader and adviser, has delegated the administrative part of the movement to the staff here," says Sheik Clarence R. Reynolds-El, divine minister and national chairman, a forceful and articulate man who could be seen as the Malcolm X of Moorish Science.

The twin pillars of the temple are Islamic religion and Moorish American nationality.

"The word Moorish is a nationality," Sheik Reynolds-El says. "People have a tendency to identify us as a religious movement, when we have inherited our religion along with our nationality."

Sheik Reynolds-El says Moorish Americans trace their ancestry to the ancient Moroccans.

"We mean we are descendants of ancient Moroccans who inhabited the northwest and southwest shores of Africa," says Sheikess Reynolds-El, who is the temple's director of orientation and naturalization and wife of the sheik.

"Trace it further back and you get to the ancient Moabites," says the sheik. The people were chased from the land of Moab by Joshua, he says, and given sanctuary by the Pharoahs of Egypt on the northwest and southwest shores of Africa. "We were an eastward people moving westward."

"Along the old water route," he says. That's 36 degrees 30 minutes, Sheik Reynolds-El says, a latitude obtained by a complicated formula from the Master Meridian, 30 degrees 30 minutes, defined by the Great Pyramid in Egypt, which divides the world into quarters. (Pyramidology is taught in one of the courses at the Moorish School of Law and History.)

"North, Central and South America are now what were the northwest and southwest coasts of Africa," Sheik Reynolds-El says.

"Before the earthquakes caused the split between Africa and America," he explains.

"That's why we say we're descendants of Moroccans born in America," he says. Present-day Morocco is the closest thing to those ancient shores in Africa.

Moorish Science disputes the idea that the slave ships of 1619 brought the first Moorish or African inhabitants to the Americas.

"We had already been inhabitants many thousands of years before that event occurred," the sheik proclaims.

The Moorish Americans do not like the terms "Negro," "black" or "colored." Sheik Reynolds-El dismisses them as European.

"We don't have to call ourselves Negroes. There is no country called 'Negro.' There is no country called 'black.' There is no country called 'colored.'

"We know who we are. We know from whence we came. And we know what our goals are. And we know what our contributions have been."

Moorish Science contends that Moorish Americans have never been naturalized as U.S. citizens.

"So-called Negroes have never been naturalized," Sheik Reynolds-El says, "so how can they be protected under the Constitution: A chattel that has never been recognized as a person."

He rejects the 13th, 14th and 15th amendments as defective in providing for Moorish Americans.

The Moorish Science Temple has petitioned Congress for implementation of what they call Abraham Lincoln's "executive will," the preliminary Emancipation Proclamation of Sept. 22, 1862, and the "original" 13th Amendment with 20 sections.

"If these things had been complied with then," Sheik Reynolds-El says, "we wouldn't be a beggar people. After the war we would have been properly educated, bringing us back into the human family.

"And we would have had economic security which would have eliminated the need for welfare because of the large amount of money appropriated for the compensation to former slaveholders for their 'property' and former slaves for their period of servitude."

He says $478 million was appropriated by Congress but never disbursed.

"We're pressing for compensation under the executive will of Abraham Lincoln," he says. "Reparations. We could demand our rights. Let the country decide the validity of our claim."

Even a 6 per cent return on $478 million is a lot of money over 110 years, he says.

The Moorish Americans also say they intend to petition for Congressional action, or an executive order, to restore what they call documented ancient family names. Until then, they attach the suffixes Bey or El (pronounced eel) to their "European" names—in the manner of Sheik and Sheikess Reynolds-El, or Sheik Leon Smith-Bey, the assistant director of education, and Sheikess Andrea Jones-Bey, director of health education.

Bey derives from a Turkish word for land governer, Sheik Reynolds-El says, and *El* from the Hebrew word for God.

Many of these things are taught in considerable detail in the Moorish School of Law and History, which is expanding into the second and third floors of the Howard street temple. The Moors are now seeking state accreditation for the private, post-secondary school.

A benefit for the school, the Third Annual Moorish Costume Ball, will be held at the Hilton Hotel at 8.30 P.M. Saturday.

"We'll be in our ancient dress," Sheik Reynolds-El says.

Sheikess Jones-Bey, who is in charge of the benefit, says Dr. Martha Cobb, head of the Romance language department at Howard University, will speak on the Moorish influence on European culture.

"The brothers will do a sword dance and the sisters a flag dance, with the ancient flag," the sheikess says. "And there will be a costume pagaent: all original costumes made by the sheiks and sheikesses depicting our dress throughout history from Moorish Spain to ancient Moab to the American Civil War."

"There are about 50 Moorish Science Temples in the United States," Sheik Reynolds-El says. "This is the first school. A model school. Our intent and purpose is to put a school wherever there is a Moorish Science Temple."

TEMPLE OFFICIALS—From left, Sheikess Carolyn Reynolds-El, director of orientation and nationalization; Sheik Clarence R. Reynolds-El, divine minister and national chairman; Sheikess Andrea Jones-Bey, director of health education, and Sheik T. Scott-Bey, stand before flags in headquarters.

appeared in Evening Sun January 20, 1978

Rommani Mulai EL Amenu EL
This photo appeared in the
Baltimore Metropolitan
Magazine (1979) MST of A.
The location, 519 N. Howard St,
Downtown Baltimore, MD
Rommani's Birth Certificate
Officially Amended July 17, 1979

Grand Shiek Clarence Reynolds-El

THE MOORISH AMERICANS
A NEW
NATIONALISM

PETER HARRIS

Look to the capital city. Always. There you can sense the nation's ferment; its growth, its rumblings, its strides, bold or uncertain. Especially look to the capital of developing countries. Here the groping is tinged with adventure. With righteousness. Clearer though, the interplay between their national goals—often idealistic—and the practical, yet consequential tasks of feeding and clothing, housing and caring for its people; of forging workable and peaceable relationships with other countries.

From Africa and Asia to this hemisphere's expanding nations, the explosiveness of the tension created as a result of the demands of now and the promise of tomorrow is keenly visible. Mix in the everpresent spectre of outside, imperialistic pressures applied by the industrial, developed predators and the concoction is formidable.

Cast an eye on Baltimore. You smile no doubt. But, from all available signs, this city is the seat of government for the developing Moorish-American nation. And its leaders are typically facing all the complex chores attendant to nation-building. In the face too, of a pertinent peculiarity: their country is to be raised within another nation. And if the physical implications weren't awesome enough, they also face the difficulty of promoting a philosophy unfamiliar to the majority of the people nationhood would most benefit.

These are concepts not to be taken lightly.

Nationalism is a passionate subject on whatever side of the issue your convictions place you. In America, certainly since the Moorish Science Movement began in 1913 (one year before Marcus Garvey began the Universal Negro Improvement Association (UNIA), too many people have died and been killed for discussion here to be taken lightly.

No one has.

"Some people have classified Moorish Science as being a religion. It is not a religion! and I'd like to make that specifically clear. Our religion is Islam. But the organization has national and divine principals."

Grand Chairman Clarence Reynolds-El (say eel) did not begin our two-hour interview (at his Mondawmin Mall office) with this statement. But it too crucial to lay buried. The confusion over his movement's fundamental aims has festered too long. Indeed, it was accepted by Theodore Vincent, in his book *Black Power and the Garvey Movement*. He called the organization an "... internationalist deflection in the form of escape to other worldly movements ...," comparing the Temple to the Nation of Islam (which grew out of the Moorish Move-

ment) and the "social movements of Father Divine and Daddy Grace. . . ."

Countering that assessment, Reynolds-El, who was appointed by Noble Drew Ali, 3rd (Noble Drew Ali, Timothy Drew, started the first Temple in Newark, N.J.) to "reorganize the movement all over the country," points to concrete, ongoing efforts which he insists, should dispel any confusion surrounding Baltimore's Moorish Science Temple, the Divine and National Movement of North America, Inc.

"We have organized a Moorish School of Law and History located at 519 North Howard Street," explained Reynolds-El, his voice measured and confident, his full bearded face calm. "There are 20 persons on our staff with either an A.A., B.A. or M.A. degree. Our desire is to establish a school all over the country—to eradicate the many misconceptions about what the movement was really designed to do; to provide a stimulus for better education and better character among our youth and to promote better economic security for Moors in America."

Emphasizing also "a rapport with all of the temples all over the country," Reynolds-El notes the most obvious refutation of the 'religious-kooks' tag: "I'm not saying this in a boastful manner, but ... we have taken the lead in terms of some very important (U.S.) history that we have researched in the National Archives."

Specifically, the Moors' research centers on the legislative history of the United States at its inception (we were there as Moors ... you can research this through the dissenting opinion of the (1857) Dred Scott decision of Justice Curtis ...") and the years right after the Civil War (specifically "Lincoln's initial Emancipation Proclamation and the 13th Amendment with 20 sections") That amendment incidently, has only two sections as finally adopted—outlawing slavery and, giving Congress the power to enforce that section.

Research shows "we have been classified as less than a human being, a thing," Reynolds-El submits.

The Temple's response?

A tax protest, began in 1975, which led to indictments and convictions of Temple members. "I'm sure that the public should be able to see there hasn't been much attention given to it by the national news media. Which should indicate that

Reynolds-El with instructors Micheal Baker-Bey, Charles Johnson-Bey and John C. Laboo-El at the Howard street Moorish School of Law and History

it's a very deep subject," says Reynolds-El. "We are following the judicial process and we intend to got to the Supreme Court. I'm sure the public can see (also) that it must be something very serious if we were willing to be incarcerated under the legal process rather than taking to the streets with clubs and sticks and stones . . . that we were ready to stand as men."

Predictably "confident" about the case's outcome, Reynolds-El believes a positive ruling would lead conclusively to the establishment of the Moorish nation-within-a-nation. Lincoln's plan of reparations, naturalization and colonization, between the "Alleghenies and the Rockies," as stipulated in the 20 sections of the 13th, he maintains, would assure that.

Section 17, as extracted from a copy of the law used in the School of Law and History:

Whenever any State wherein Involuntary Servitude is recognized or allowed shall propose to Abolish such Servitude, and shall apply for (cash) assistance . . . the Congress may, in its discretion, grant such relief not exceeding one hundred dollars for each Person liberated. But Congress shall not propose such Abolishment or relief to any State. Congress may assist Free persons of African descent to emigrate and colonize Africa.

Section 20, which seems to nullify the whole ballgame:

The provisions of this Article relating to Involuntary Labor or Servitude shall not be altered without the consent of all the States maintaining such Servitude.

Ultimately, Reynolds-El says the Moors "would really like to see a naturalization process set up for all persons who've become educated to the fact that they're Moorish-American. We realize that a lot of our people will never accept this on their own."

Meanwhile, because "we've been harping" on these issues

locally—rallies, lectures and man-on-the-street rap sessions— citizens are gaining "more and more" interest, Reynolds-El says. They usually ask "Do you think we'll get the money? But it's not just the money," he emphasizes. "Because if they paid all of us off in cash, the money would go right back into the system. We're talking about the money that's owed to us as a nation . . . to give us some economic thrust where we can begin to negotiate with other nations, just like other big corporations do, as other entities do."

Presumably, this is the vision of every Temple, large and small (such as the fledgling New Ark Temple, which is guided, spiritually at best, by Joseph Vaughn-El, from the Jessup House of Corrections in America.) Of course, Reynolds-El indicates that whatever tactics a Temple uses, "we all have the same" adherance to law and nationality.

So perceived split between Baltimore's other Temple—The Moorish Science Temple of America Inc., located at 726 West Baltimore St. and begun in 1927,—out of which grew the Howard Street Temple, is speculation at best, he suggests.

(Dr. R. German-Bey, director of 726, was "not interested" in talking about his Temple. Through his secretary, Dr. German-Bey said "We have many offers . . . (but) on behalf of the conflict of interest and the others who came from under this jurisdiction and went astray, (I'd) rather not deal with the matter." In 1972, Noble Drew Ali, 3rd, then Richardson Dingle-El, split from Dr. German-Bey's Temple, stopping first at Frederick Avenue and eventually landing at the Howard Street site.)

As in any nation, there are sincere differences in Moorish methodology—even if the stated goals are consistent (the Democrats and Republicans are examples). Reynolds-El says unalarmedly that the Baltimore Street Temple is "more reli-

The negro, the black, the Moor

giously oriented. In recent times we are really working closer together," he added.

It would seem that their union is necessary for the success of even everyday practical relationships. Such as those between members of the estimated 10,000 "registered" Howard Street Temple members, "not half are active," Reynolds-El says frankly. And it's certainly needed to put flesh on the visions: "We envision building an educational center and Mosque and a model Moorish community, with our own housing, medical programs, group insurance," explains Reynolds-El.

America and collective independence for African-Americans have always had a power-based relationship. And critics of the Temple's law-oriented approach to Freedom—including Marcus Garvey, who spoke of an African homeland—doubt this country's sense of fair play—even in the face of truth.

They refer for example, to the unhibited FBI-speared attack on the Republic of New Africa (RNA), which also emphasizes reparations and a U.S. land base ("... the billions of dollars now owed us for the forty acres and a mule we never got," according to RNA president Imari Obadeli (May/June 1978 *Black Scholar*). Infiltrated, with many of its leaders jailed (including Obadeli), RNA also speaks of the inadequacy of the 13th and 14th (granting uncertain citizenship) Amendments, demanding the opportunity for African Americans to choose citizenship. In fact, RNA was operating with residents of the "Black counties and parishes of Louisiana, Arkansas and Mississippi," writes Obadeli, when the local police attacked members there.

Such skepticism about tactics, combined with historical (ancient) and ideological differences, plus plain mutual stubbornness—accounted for poor vibes over the years, between the Moors and other nationalist organizations—in the U.S. as a whole. In his book, *Black Nationalism*, E.U. Essien-Udom observed: "The consequences to the disagreement among the Black Nationalists on what the central ideal shall be has given rise to sectarianism among them. Their past performance in this respect hardly justified their appeal for a 'United Front of Black Men.'"

Local relations were strained as well. Both sides, however, detect a healthy change for the better.

Kali Tacuma, at 38, has "been around actively struggling for 14 years." During that time, he says his Pan Africanist-inspired community activism has ranged from organizing baseball teams in Harlem Park to the operation of a farm-cooperative in Pennsylvania. Nowadays, he directs the Alke-Bu-Lan-Atiba Center on Edmondson Avenue and has joined forces with a member of the Moorish Temple. The project: a community conscious food coop-restaurant in the Center.

Tacuma says the reason for the interactions with Clyde O'Millner-Bdy (Kibwe) are simple. "I have never observed him doing anything not constructive for Black people," he said, sitting erect on the couch in his west Baltimore living room. He adds: "Any of the groups—Moorish, Pan Africanists, Marxists—have the same problems (with its membership): some people are just going to be members; others talkers; others are going to work, talk and think, and they are the most important people."

Tacuma observes that "every Black person who gets into any kind of group is looking for *a* way, not *the* way. If he had the way, we'd all be free by now, there's no question about that."

In the interest of harmony, Reynolds-El, calling it part of the Temple's "new image," says "we are making ourselves more accessible—it takes all kinds of people to get something moving." Still, "we try to encourage people to become affili-

ated and active because then we can depend on them. On the other hand, we can no longer block out that help, as long as the intent is clear."

The Temple's apparent 'circle-the-wagons' attitude tended to promote cynicism, causing further unproductive isolation. And it also confused more people than it informed. "Some of us through our apparel and through our manner, sometimes we're attracting people, but then, when the people come and are inquisitive, and they want to learn, we tend to freeze up on them or just feed them a little bit and say 'that's all, and you got to go through X, Y & Z changes to find out more," notes Charley Dugger, host of radio show "Voices and Choices in Ebony" on WEAA-FM. Objectively, Dugger also says the Moors "have made our people more studious and more concerned about the law. But I think there is too much secrecy—and this is with some of our other groups (too). We need to take more to the people than we are taking to the people." And, he cautions, "I don't think we can let ourselves off the hook. A lot of our confusion is because we don't take the time to dig, to read, to pursue."

Reynolds-El, whose "blood brother," Owusu Bendele, was the former director of the Timbuktu Center (now Alke-Bu-Lan,) says a lack of openness led to other nationalists believing "that we were trying to demonstrate Arab policies. The thing we have in common with the Arabs is the fact that we're Muslims," he insists. The chairman says now that "a lot of the information we had was not consolidated in such a fashion that it afforded them a true understanding of what we were all about.

"But I find that recently, my communication is open. I realize contact and communication are the essential things needed among our people in order to bring any kind of understanding about," he adds. "I recognize the fact that if one does not have the same understanding that you have, then definitely you should come to some sort of communication agreement where you can share your information and discuss it intelligently as men."

Paul Coates, owner of the PANAF Community Book Store in Park Heights, and a former member of the Black Panthers, says "recently, I've had very enlightening conversations ... with this—for lack of a better word—new Moorish thinking. Of course, my ideological outlook has changed somewhat." Coates "senses" an apparent "willingness to listen to other positions ... to work with other organizations, giving respect to their positions." This is the test, Coates believes: "Working along with others who don't necessarily agree that you have to know nationality in order to struggle for Black people." So-

Sheik Jacques E. Leeds-Bey, and attorney Robert Jay Kessler confer with Reynolds-El

berly, Coates nevertheless sees coalitions with the Moors for "specific things" as the most practical at this point.

"Certainly folks can look forward to supporting the Moors on this tax thing," he submits. "I have made a commitment to assist in whatever manner I can. That's not a specific commitment, but a definite commitment."

Similarly, O'Millner-Bey (Kibwe), cofounder with Tacuma of the "Coop Pot," values interpersonal strengthening. "Kali and myself have been through a lot of things together," he reveals. "And at this point, we don't need to be separate. (There isn't) anything stopping me from sharing (responsibilities with him;) whether I'm a Muslim or he's a Pan African. We shouldn't be attached to any organization that keeps you detached from another soul. We have to incorporate one important thing—love, whether it be the Nguzo Saba or Allah."

Besides reconnecting with other continental nationalists, Reynolds-El points to the Moorish Temple's improving bond with the African state Morocco—"repairing the bridge," the chairman calls it. Moorish-Americans say we are descendants of the "Ancient Moors, who inhabited the whole Northwest and Southwest shores of Africa," Reynolds-El says. Late last year, when Morocco's King Hassan visited the U.S., the Temple sent a formal contigent to Washington to greet him, presenting him with a plaque as well.

Reynolds-El says increased interaction with Morocco "marks great progress in history." And, along with some revising in their practice of Islam, it increases the Moor's chances for international validity.

There could be a snag, however, which would leave the Temple—indeed, the Moorish-American nation—open to question. The reason: late last year even as the King visited, Morocco was engaged in a war for the colonization of the Western Sahara (according to reports in the respected *Africa News Digest*)—against a recognized (16 nations) national liberation front (POLISARIO); even after sending 2,000 troops to Zaire to help the French quell a popular uprising against President SeSe Seko.

Beyond tactics and methods, this could offer the toughest obstacle for meaningful international relations. For in America and throughout Africa, Asia, South and Central America nationalist empathy for genuine liberation struggle is sacred.

Reynolds-El seemed to recognize the apparent discrepancy in the Moorish-American platform. Haltingly, his vague responses to questions about it underscored the delicate balance between exposing freedom (even while actually attempting to gain it) and physically (which includes the moral and spiritual) throwing your weight behind that cause.

"It's very difficult when you haven't heard both sides of the stories in a case such as this. We are going to be a very potent force whenever we're recognized as descendants of Morocco born in America. When we begin to take our place in the affairs of men, I know that we will be instrumental. Even though it has been more or less accepted that those troops did land there, there are other things that I'm not at full liberty to discuss at this juncture, concerning why this was projected in that fashion. But I'm sure that with proper input from us, something like that could be resolved with minimal efforts—once the repairing of the bridge takes place," Reynolds-El said. "Because that happened before we met with the King of Morocco."

This nation building, this coalescing of diverse people, this clamor to rely independently on ourselves is no simple task. The plans are many, some tested, others untried.

An observation from Dugger: "The goals and objectives need to be more basic and primary so the people could understand them better."

"In our structure, we want to bring more truths and facts to children at a younger age than we normally have been as a Nation of people," says Reynolds-El.

The sincerity/similarity exists. Mostly it's been the work/words that have differed. It's safe to say now that it's long past time for them all to be reconciled.

These are concepts not to be taken lightly. □

The negro, the black, the Moor

The Star of Islam, American flags, and a portrait of President Lincoln adorn the Mondawmin Mall office of Grand Sheikh Rommani Mulai El Amenu-El (left), head of the United Moorish Moslems of America. Sheikh Jacques Leeds-Bey (right) represents the group in a suit seeking restitution for all black American descendants of slaves.

University, and to reorganize the Madrassah Islami.

Discussion at the Masjid Al-Allah centered more on the topic of *zakat*, alms-giving or charity, than at any of the other communities. Mwamba and another Masjid member voiced their frustration with a city government that they said is unresponsive to the needs of Baltimore's poor and is much more interested in making Baltimore a showcase American city. "There is very little help for poor people," Mwamba said.

"We are anticommunist and anticapitalist," said Mwamba. "Yet we are the most peaceful people one earth." He said communists are a godless people while those who hoard their wealth cause other people to go hungry, an equal offense because it is an abuse of God's creation given equally to us all. Mwamba was as critical of capitalism in the nations in the Organization of Petroleum Exporting Countries (OPEC) as he was of that in any of the industrialized countries. "Many affluent Muslims do not practice charity towards poor brothers in the faith," said another member.

But for all of his frustration with the life of Baltimore's poor, Mwamba confessed feeling shock and indignation after the looting during last year's big blizzard. "They were not even the poor blacks," he said. "The looting was inexcusable."

Clothes-lookinglass. Photo: Michael Agelopas

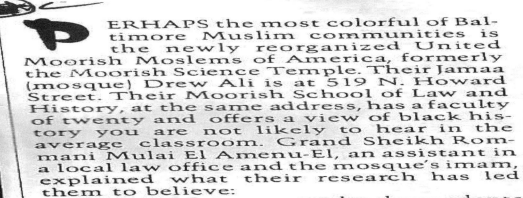

ERHAPS the most colorful of Baltimore Muslim communities is the newly reorganized United Moorish Moslems of America, formerly the Moorish Science Temple. Their Jamaa (mosque) Drew Ali is at 519 N. Howard Street. Their Moorish School of Law and History, at the same address, has a faculty of twenty and offers a view of black history you are not likely to hear in the average classroom. Grand Sheikh Rommani Mulai El Amenu-El, an assistant in a local law office and the mosque's imam, explained what their research has led them to believe:

Black Americans are the descendants of slaves taken from the west and northwest coast of Africa, where Islam has been practiced for as long as a thousand years. People in this region of Africa historically have been called Moors. Moors today, the people of Morocco, Mauritania, and northwest Africa, are a dark-skinned people with an established culture, the sheikh said.

The term *Negro*, he continued, refers to no specific regional culture and just means "black person." It also came to mean "slave," something owned, something with no standing on its own in human society. To trace American blacks to the Moors, however, identifies their past with a glorious Near East culture and its expansion from the ninth through the fifteenth centuries. This dramatic reversal of the prevailing view of black history became the theoretical basis of the black nationalist movement that began its spread through American cities in the early part of the century and eventually led to the Black Muslims. Today, most of what remains of this nationalist movement is split into factions and lives off past glories.

The United Moorish Moslem congregation looks to the future with hope, though. It uses the term Moslem to distinguish itself from the Black Muslims. Members are often conspicuous wearing the fez, a red, inverted bucket-shaped hat with black tassel. The moorish suffixes "Bey" or "El" are usually attached to the last names of members. Amenu-El estimates that there are about a hundred active local members. As part of a drive to attract members from the Baltimore community, a Moorish Ball was held at the Hilton Hotel last fall.

In 1974 four members of what was then still the Moorish Science Temple filed a brief with the Internal Revenue Service stating that they would no longer pay income taxes. Their argument: As descendents of slaves, they should not have to pay taxes until the federal government pays restitution to all black American descendants of slaves.

President Lincoln had planned to naturalize and compensate former slaves after the emancipation, said Amenu-El, sitting under a portrait of Lincoln in his Mondawmin Mall law office. During Reconstruction, however, the plan was forgotten. And Sheikh Jacques Leeds-Bey, a Moorish Moslem attorney who was also in the office, pointed out that American Indians are receiving reparation for broken treaties while former slaves and their descendants have not been considered for compensation.

Although the four tax protesters recently were indicted by a federal grand jury for falsifying income tax returns, the United Moorish Moslems of America are planning new legal action. Leeds-Bey insisted, "This is very important to us. It is not just a symbolic act. We must be returned to our original human state. The law must recognize that we are human just as it once recognized that we were not."

Other small Muslim congregations meet in Baltimore. A small remnant of the old-guard Moorish Science Temple meets at 762 W. Baltimore Street. The newest Muslim community in Baltimore, with an average of fifteen worshippers at Friday prayers, is Masjid Qaanitun Al-Quran, located at 330 Alto Road in West Baltimore.

The Baltimore Jamaat (mosque) of the Ahmadiyya Movement in America, at 4406 Garrison Boulevard in Northwest Baltimore, is the only Shiah Muslim community in town and is unconnected with any other Baltimore masjid. Its president, or *ameer*, is Abdul Hafeez, a spry, 77-year-old former steelworker.

The Ahmadiyya Movement was founded in 1890 in what today is Pakistan by a self-proclaimed *mahdi* (messiah), Hazrat Mirza Ghulam Admad. Ahmadis, as

Dr. Martha Kendrick Cobb

Martha Kendrick Cobb was a wife, mother, scholar, educator and activist who lived much of her life in Washington, D.C. A brilliant woman, she spoke five languages and after 30 years of teaching English, French and Spanish in the Maryland, Massachusetts and New York school systems, she went to Howard University to teach in the Department of Romance Languages, where she eventually became department chairperson. In the following decade she published many reviews and scholarly articles, many of which focused on Afro-Hispanic literary criticism. Her doctoral dissertation, entitled "Harlem, Haiti and Havana," compared the works of Langston Hughes, a Cuban poet and a Haitian poet, and won the College Language Association award for outstanding scholarship in 1983. Teaching at Howard for 15 years, she impacted thousands of students, many of whom became teachers themselves.

But Martha Cobb was more than a scholar. The mother of four children, she was married to the late Dr. Charles E. Cobb, who for 20 years was the Executive Director of the United Church of Christ Commission for Racial Justice. She was also an activist who supported her husbandês work, including his run for mayor of Springfield, MA in 1965 and the civil rights work of her children, especially her son, Charles Cobb, Jr., who was a leader in the Student Non-Violent Coordinating Committee. But she also challenged injustices herself, including marching in protests in Cairo, IL with her aunt, picketing stores in New England that were affiliated with Southern stores which discriminated against African Americans, and marching in the historic March on Washington in 1963. Martha Cobb was a modern-day renaissance woman.

ye site
ice/witness/wfj052002.htm

ABRAHAM LINCOLN

Lincoln was said to be the illegitimate son of a Negro by Nancy Hanks. In his campaign for the Presidency he was often referred to as a Negro by his opponents. He was even depicted as a Negro. He was called Abraham Africanus the First.

What gave strength to this was that his hair was more Negroid than Caucasian. So was his color. Of his father, he said, "His face was round, his complexion swarthy, hair, black and coarse, eyes brown." Of himself, "Of dark complexion with coarse black hair and dark eyes." Herndon, his closest friend and law partner said he had "very dark skin."

His confidential servant, William Slade, an ex-slave and a Negro, was much fairer and had straight hair. Slade looked like a white man. Herndon said, "There was something about his (Lincoln's) origin, he never cared to dwell on." Other writers agree with him. Coleman says, "All we know about President Lincoln's parentage and birth under his own hand are two brief records one an entry in the Bible in his own handwriting that he was born on February 12, 1809 and the other, a brief autobiography which he gave Mr. Jesse R. Fell in December, 1859 for a campaign sketch."

Lincoln had a secret preying on his mind. Was it his race? His enemies harped on it. Herndon says of it, "Lincoln often thought of committing suicide. Why? Did the knowledge of his mother's origin or his own press the thought of suicide upon him?" (The Hidden Lincoln, p. 412, 1938).

Jacobson mentions a "Cathechism" by a "western author adducing evidence" that Lincoln was of Negro ancestry. He also mentions another "Cathechism" by Chauncey Burr, who said, "It would not rebound to Lincoln's honor to have it proved that he is part Negro.

8

ABRAHAM LINCOLN

Cartoon of 1860. Original source not known now. Appears in David Browder's "Ordeal of the Presidency." Note his wooly hair.

7

The above picture and text is taken the book entitled "The Five Negro Presidents" by J.A. Rogers. A good question for the readers viewing the picture would be –why is Lincoln depicted as a Moor?

Rommani M. Amenu-El

IN PRINCE GEORGE *Virginia*

Moor Colony Flourishes

By Thomas Howard
Times-Dispatch News Bureau

PRINCE GEORGE, Dec. 22—Deep in the heart of Prince George's woodland country is a community where the greeting is "Islam" and the parting is "peace."

The men wear the fez and the children wear turbans. Over the doorways and windows of homes and buildings are the symbols of their Moslem faith —the star and crescent and the "circle seven."

It is the Moorish Science colony, the only one in the South, and home for 25 families of Moors.

F. Nelson Bey, founder of the colony, is the grand governor and secular head of the settlement. "Some people call me the "supervisor," he said.

The 80 persons who live on the 200 acres owned by the colony term themselves Moors by virtue of descent from North African Moabite tribes brought to America as slaves in the 18th and 19th centuries.

Although their religion is that of Mohammed, the Moorish Science Temple of America makes Chicago its mecca, where the order was founded in 1913 by their late prophet, Drew Ali.

Bey, a North Carolinian and a graduate of North Carolina Agricultural and Technical College, joined the movement in 1927 in Detroit. He was sent to Prince George county in 1939 as a missionary and he and three others cleared the 200 acres of dense woodland purchased by the Chicago group.

"We found the people in the area curious but receptive," said Bey. Gradually a few persons joined the colony and it has developed slowly but steadily since. Some try it and move on, but others come and stay. Bey said no evangelizing is undertaken. A person is free to join and just as free to leave.

There are 28 buildings owned by the colony, nearly all of them residences. Most are small and some crudely built, but others are masonry. Property is owned communally, but Bey said "a man builds his own home with the help of the colony and lives in it as long as he wants."

The temple, the community meeting hall, and several of the dwellings are of Moroccan architecture—with square, flat roof, and jutting roof timbers. The temple is the center of the colony. The settlement also owns a garage and store.

Most of the males are away during the day, as farm or factory workers. "Friday is the Moslem's holy day all over the world," said Bey. "But we have to live with the customs of America, so we work on Friday." The weekly temple service is held each Friday evening, conducted by the grand sheik, the colony's spiritual head.

Fundamentally the religion is the same as the eastern Islamism, said Bey. "But we have to modify it to meet the circumstances." The faith as established by Drew Ali follows a modified version of the Koran. Bey explained they believe Jesus was one of the holy prophets and his instruction is a fundamental part of their doctrine. Jesus, Mohammed, Budda and Confucious were all the same reincarnated spirit, born and chosen by plan by "the great God of the universe, Allah," said Bey.

All families have either Bey or El as the surname. "They are the names of the Moabite tribes from whom we are descended," explained Bey. A newcomer arbitrarily selects either tribal name.

The colony celebrates two holidays, January 8, the birthday of Drew Ali, and September 17, the birth of supreme counsel C. Kirkman Bey. Pilgrimages are made to the Chicago temple.

Bey's own philosophical guidance has done much to make a place in Prince George for the colony. As an organized group, the members have been called on to help fight forest fires, get crops in or lend a helping hand wherever needed.

Bey said his instruction from Chicago when he first came down was simple. "Make friends at all costs, and once you have made friendships, hold them."

—Staff Photo
F. Nelson Bey, Founder of Moorish Colony
Prince George Colony Is Only One in the South

178

In the above picture Is the Prophet Noble Drew Ali in the center sitting in the affirm position. To his immediate left is Oscar Stanton De Priest. (See the short bio below) seated directly below the Prophet on the first row is said to be either Sheikh Mealy El, Lovett Bey, Small Bey or Sheik Foreman Bey. To the far left of the Sheik is said to be Claude D. Greene

Oscar Stanton De Priest

From Wikipedia, the free encyclopedia
(Redirected from Oscar Stanton de Priest)

Oscar Stanton De Priest (born 1871 in Florence, Alabama - 1951) was a lawmaker and civil rights advocate.

Oscar Stanton De Priest was the first African American elected to Congress in the 20th century. He was elected to the U.S. Congress in 1928 as a Republican. During his three terms (1928-1935), as the only black representative in Congress, De Priest introduced several anti-discrimination bills. He spoke at the first Moorish Science Temple convention in October 1928 in Chicago. He joined the organization and moved through the ranks to become a ranking member and chamber member.

His 1933 amendment barring discrimination in the Civilian Conservation Corps was passed by the Senate and signed into law by President Roosevelt. A second anti-lynching bill failed, even though it did not make lynching a federal crime. A third proposal, a bill to permit a transfer of jurisdiction if a defendant believed he or she could not get a fair trial because of race or religion, would be passed by another Congress in another era.

Civil rights activists criticized De Priest for opposing federal aid to the needy, but they applauded him for speaking in the South despite death threats. They also praised De Priest for telling an Alabama senator he was not big enough to prevent him from dining in the Senate restaurant and for defending the right of Howard University students to eat in the House restaurant. De Priest took the House restaurant issue to a special bipartisan House committee. In a three month-long heated debate, the Republican minority argued that the restaurant's discriminatory practice violated 14th Amendment rights to equal access. The Democratic majority skirted the issue by claiming that the restaurant was not open to the public, and the House restaurant remained segregated. De Priest was defeated in 1934 by Democrat Arthur W. Mitchell, who was also an African American. De Priest was also defeated in 1936. He was elected to the Chicago city council in 1943 and served until 1947.

His house in Chicago is a National Historic Landmark.

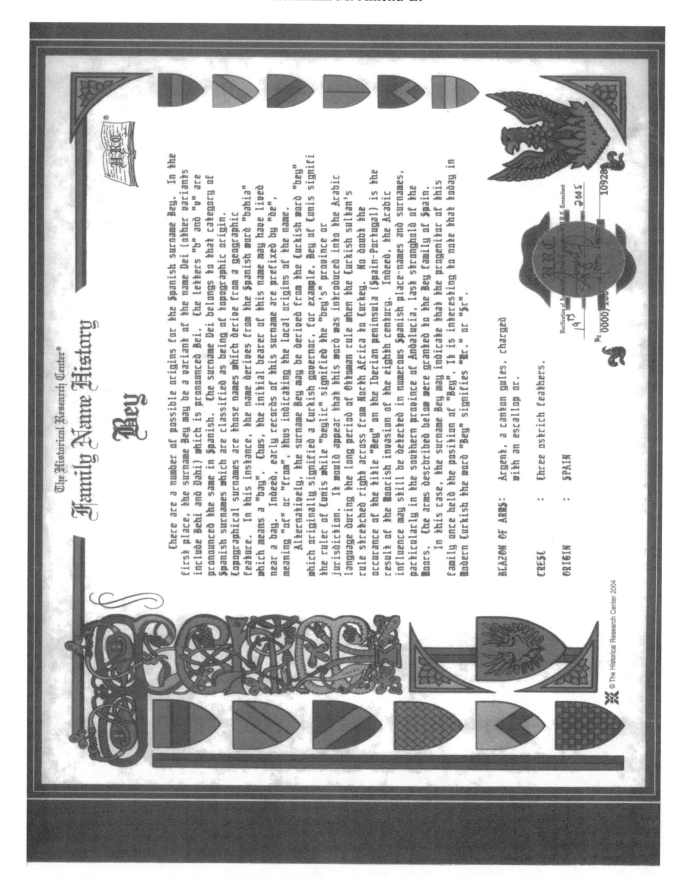

The Historical Research Center®

Family Name History

Bey

There are a number of possible origins for the Spanish surname Bey. In the first place, the surname Bey may be a variant of the name Vei (other variants include Behi and Dahi) which is pronounced Bei. The letters "b" and "v" are pronounced the same in Spanish. The surname Vei belongs to that category of Spanish surnames which are classified as being of topographic origin. Topographical surnames are those names which derive from a geographic feature. In this instance, the name derives from the Spanish word "bahia" which means a "bay". Thus, the initial bearer of this surname may have lived near a bay. Indeed, early records of this surname are prefixed by "De", meaning "of" or "from", thus indicating the local origins of the name.

Alternatively, the surname Bey may be derived from the Turkish word "bey" which originally signified a Turkish governor, for example, Bey of Tunis signifi the ruler of Tunis while "beylic" signified the "bey's" province or jurisdiction. It would appear that this word was introduced into the Arabic language during the long period of Ottoman rule when the Turkish sultan's rule stretched right across from North Africa to Turkey. No doubt the occurance of the title "Bey" on the Iberian peninsula (Spain-Portugal) is the result of the Moorish invasion of the eighth century. Indeed, the Arabic influence may still be detected in numerous Spanish place-names and surnames, particularly in the southern province of Andalucia, last stronghold of the Moors. The arms described below were granted to the Bey family of Spain.

In this case, the surname Bey may indicate that the progenitor of this family once held the position of "Bey". It is interesting to note that today in Modern Turkish the word "Bey" signifies "Mr." or "Sr".

BLAZON OF ARMS: Argent, a canton gules, charged
                 with an escallop or.

CREST   :   Three ostrich feathers.

ORIGIN   :   SPAIN

© The Historical Research Center 2004

November 12, 1999

Popular New King Has a Goal: A Modern Morocco

Map
- Morocco from Microsoft Encarta Concise
Encyclopedia

By CRAIG R. WHITNEY

ABAT, Morocco -- King Mohammed VI succeeded to the throne in July when his father, Hassan II, died after reigning for 38 years. As crown prince, Mohammed had been dismissed by some as a bachelor playboy.

But in only three months, the 36-year-old king has emerged as a powerful advocate of social change in a region that is witnessing a generational shift in monarchies from Morocco to Jordan.

Already popular among this country's 30 million people, Mohammed VI, close-cropped and unshaven, looks more like a movie star than a monarch. On a recent 10-day tour through the country's north, hundreds of thousands lined the streets to cheer him. Schools closed, ancient markets shut down and entire families trooped to the roadsides to see the young king, who arrived, wearing a white suit and a black tie, standing up in a white Cadillac stretch limousine with a sunroof.

Diplomats here in the capital and ordinary people

LEFT HADJ AHMED BALAFREJ EXECUTIVE SEC'Y GENERAL OF INDEPENDENT PARTY OF MOROCCO AND SPOKESMAN FOR HIS MAJESTY MOHAMMED V KING OF MOROCCO AND HEAD OF MOROCCO ROYAL DELEGATION TO THE UNITED NATIONS. RIGHT MOHAMMED EL MANDJRA MEMBER OF MOROCCO DELEGATION TO THE UNITED NATIONS. GRAND SHEIKH F TURNER-EL HEAD OF MOROCCAN UNITED ORGANIZATIONS FEDERATION AND SPOKESMAN FOR ALL MOROCCAN AMERICAN PEOPLE. ALL THE ABOVE PARTICIPATED AT THE COMMEMORATION OF THE ACCESSION TO THE THRONE OF MOHAMMED V KING OF MOROCCO WHICH TOOK PLACE AT HOTEL PLAZA 59TH STREET 5TH AVENUE NEW YORK ON NOVEMBER 18, 1952.

16e anniversaire de l'accession au Trône de S.M. Hassan II

This is a photo of then Crown Prince of Morocco (Sidi Mohammed) and his brother
Rashid. The Crown Prince is now King Mohammed VI. Pictured on the right of Grand
Sheikh Rommani Mulai El Amenu-El (dark beard) is Colonel Khaldoun? Top religious
scientist of Morocco. To his immediate right are Abdelkadir Mondir (Moroccan Muslim
coordinator) and other embassy officials. King Hassan II arraigned this meeting with his
son the Crown Prince and Grand Sheikh Rommani Amenu-EL to express his appreciation
of his arrival reception at Andrews Air force Base and subsequent participation by a
delegation of the Moorish School of Law and History at his address at the National Press
club Washington DC.
The photo was taken at the Madison Hotel, Washington DC on November 15th 1978.

BBC News | Africa | King Hassan: A life in pi...

BBC News Online: World: Africa

Front Page | World | UK | UK Politics | Business | Sci/Tech | Health | Education | Sport | Entertainment | Talking Point | High Graphics | Feedback | Help | Noticias | Newyddion |

Saturday, July 24, 1999 Published at 08:05 GMT

King Hassan: A life in pictures

BBC News | Africa | King Hassan: A life in pi...

King Hassan: A life in pictures

Muhammad Ali and King Hassan

World Contents

- Africa

BILALIAN NEWS

NOVEMBER 24, 1978

King of Morocco
His Majesty
King Hassan II
on official visit

(United Press International)

Though still young, his Majesty, King Hassan II of Morocco, has proven himself as one of the most dynamic leaders of emergent Africa. King Hassan is one of the architects of his country's independence, and he has already emerged as a leader of outstanding ability and intelligence.

His Majesty, Moulay Hassan, was born in the Royal Palace at Rabat July 9, 1929.

Educated in French and Arabic in Western civil law and Islamic religious tradition, King Hassan began learning statecraft while not yet 14 at the Casablanca Conference of 1943 between United States President Franklin D. Roosevelt and British Prime Minister Winston Churchill.

AS AIDE TO HIS father, Sultan (later king) Mohammed V, he heard the monarch explaining Moroccan aspirations for independence to the anti-colonial Roosevelt.

After taking a French law degree, King Hassan found himself in exile with his father in 1953 while the French contended with a growing war for

his father that he pressed his father to make no concessions with France, and insisted that his father's return to the throne and independence were the only bases for future French-Moroccan relations.

The war ended in 1955 and the Sultan returned from exile in 1956 as King, designating Mr. Hassan as Crown Prince.

The slim, handsome young prince became his father's ambassador at large.

Taking the throne at his father's death in 1961, King Hassan married Lalla Latifa, daughter of a court official. They settled down to a quiet life.

HE HAS THREE daughters, Lalla Meriem, 16, Lalla Asma, 13, and Lalla Hassan, 10; and two sons, Crown Prince Sidi Mohammed, 15, and Moulay El Rashid, 5.

OVER THE YEARS King Hassan has survived two assassination attempts and three abortive coups.

He wrote in his memoirs, "Le Defi" (The Challenge):

"No chief of state is immune to fanaticism, or plain simple stupidity. I am perfectly aware of this. They are all

His Majesty, King Hassan II

anti-colonial Roosevelt.

After taking a French law degree, King Hassan found himself in exile with his father in 1953 while the French contended with a growing war for Moroccan independence.

While in exile, he became so close to

He wrote in his memoirs, "Le Defi" (The Challenge):

"No chief of state is immune to fanaticism, or plain simple stupidity. I am perfectly aware of this. They are all occupational hazards."

Bustling city of Rabat with modern hotels and busines Ocean.

Royal Grand Rabat, during a state ceremony.

PRESENTING RECENT gift from Muslim world to the WCIW is Mondir Abdelkader, a Moroccan Muslim who has offered his services to the Community for many years in helping the overall Muslim world to better understand the works and efforts of Imam Wallace Deen Muhammad to propagate Al-Islam. Receiving the gift is Sheikh James A. A. Shabazz, (right) Senior Imam of Masjid Elijah Muhammad in Chicago, and Mu-min Muhammad (center).

THREE BERBER musicians and one female dancer, un "celebrate" Moroccan life while performing at Carso during MEDITERRANEA.

The Berbers, the oldest tribe in Morocco, live as they of this exotic land. Their music and ritual ceremonies w and suburban locations.

King Hassan Of Morocco

City Doctor Has A Royal Patient

By Sue Miller

A Baltimore doctor travels 3,710 miles several times a year to see a patient.

The gastro-intestinal specialist flies to Paris, Madrid or Lisbon, where he is then picked up by royal jet for the last leg of the journey. That may take him to Casablanca, Rabat, Fez, Marrakech, Skirat or even to the skiing country of Ifrane.

"I've found out," says Dr. Marvin M. Schuster, "that there are a lot of palaces in Morocco."

His patient is King Hassan II, who moves from palace to palace as he governs the country located on the northwest coast of Africa.

Until recently, Dr. Schuster, who is chief of the digestive disease division at City Hospitals and is a professor of medicine at the Johns Hopkins Medical School, had managed to keep his professional tie of a year and a half with the King quiet.

But, the King will be at the White House in Washington December 7 and 8 and may even slip over to Baltimore for a reception or two, so the word has leaked out.

The 48-year-old King has a stomach disorder, according to Dr. Schuster, who says he would be violating ethics of a doctor-patient relationship if he were more specific.

Dr. Schuster, who is widely known for his work with biofeedback—a process which enables one to control body functions by concentration—says this controversial treatment is not part of the King's therapy. Drugs are, but he would not say which ones.

The Baltimore specialist says he has declined a fee, but has accepted a block grant, "a generous gift," the amount of which he would not disclose, from the

[Continued, Page C 2, Col. 5]

Baltimore Doctor Has A Royal Patient

[Continued from Page C 1]

King for digestive disease research being conducted jointly by City and the Hopkins.

The doctor's air fares back and forth from Morocco are paid by the King, who also has given Dr. Schuster and his family "gifts such as rugs."

The local doctor shares the responsibility of keeping the King's intestinal problems on an even keel with Dr. Joseph Kirsner, his former professor at the University of Chicago Medical School.

Dr. Schuster, who studied under Dr. Kirsner, says he also was recommneded for the post by Dr. Donald Frederickson, of the National Institutes of Health in Bethesda, Md., who had been contacted by the Moroccan government.

The King is "now in excellent health," according to Dr. Schuster, and pictured as a vibrant, courageous man, who golfs, plays tennis, sails, hunts and flies.

The King is further described as "extremely well read, not only in a general way, but in medicine." Prescribing a simple medication can take 20 minutes, Dr. Schuster says, because "the King wants to know its effect physiologically, pathologically and pharmacologically."

On one of his visits to Morocco, says Dr. Schuster, the King told him that he respects "teachers and physicians more than anything else in the world."

And, he adds, "The King wants what he considers the best of medical attention."

King Hassan's prime internist is Claude Betourne, the dean of the University of Paris Medical School. Some 50 doctors, several of each kind, says Dr. Schuster, attend the royal family and are guests at the King's annual New Year's Eve party.

Dr. Schuster and his family have a standing invitation to the New Year's party and to the celebration of the King's birthday July 7, and have gone to both.

He finds Morocco a country of "marked contrasts—it has one foot in antiquity and another in the modern era." On one hand, he says, one sees women wearing veils who avert their heads when a picture is taken, and yet 25 per cent of the country's medical students are female.

The King, he says, is "on a strong push to modernize the country."

He has a large ongoing road- and home-building program, he has made education compulsory on all levels, and because of massive screening programs he has initiated, diseases such as tuberculosis and tricoma, which causes blindness, have virtually been eliminated.

Dr. Steven Mueller, the president of the Johns Hopkins Institutions, and Mayor Schaefer have planned receptions for King Hassan, if he can make the trip to Baltimore.

KING HASSAN
May Visit Baltimore

'MOORISH' REGIME OPENS OFFICES, ASKS STATUS

The establishment of a Moorish Republic provisional government in the United States was announced yesterday by Col. Hassan Jeru-Ahmed Bey, commander of the Black Man's Volunteer Army of Liberation.

At a press conference in the organization's newly painted row-house headquarters, which is to be the provisional government's embassy at 1642 Newton St. NW, Hassan said he would go to the State Department tomorrow morning to seek diplomatic recognition for his military regime.

He said the Moorish Republic, to which "every black, either consciously or unconsciously," belongs, will "deal with governments as a government," to secure the benefits of self-determination, land and freedom for its people.

It owns 2,000 acres of land in several African countries, Hassan said.

SUNDAY, JANUARY 17, 1971

WASh. D.C. NEWS PAPer

In the above article then Colonel Hassan Jeru Ahmed Bey (known to most as Colonel Hassan) first manifested the concept of the United Moorish Republic. Later in 1974, Colonel Hassan was Ordained and subsequently promoted to General of the United Moorish Republic Army at the Moorish Science Temple, Divine and National Movement of North America Incorporated # !3 in Baltimore Maryland.

Far left: Rommani Amenu-El in his younger days, next to him is Michael Onefuru-Bey
Standing: Grand Sheik Richard Dingle-El

Sheikess Carolyn Reynolds-El – Grand Sheik Richardson Dingle-El

Members of the Moorish School of Law and History in support of His Royal Majesty, King Hassan II of Morocco in front of the National Press Building in Washington, D.C. 1978

This is a photo of King Mohammed V Grandfather of the present king of Morocco (King Mohammed VI). This picture was taken in 1955 while the King was in transient from exile in Madagascar back to Morocco. The person with the Fez in the back ground is Grand Sheikh F. Turner-EL.

MST of A, 519 N. Howard St., Baltimore, MD 1977

This photo was taken the 1950's at the Moroccan Homestead, New Haven Connecticut. It is said this homestead was part of the Thomas Edison/Dr. Todd Estate. Pictured at the far right is Grand Sheikh F. Turner-EL. To his left is Hadj Ahmed Balafrej, Executive Secretary General of the Independent Party of Morocco as well as other United Nations Representatives. To the far left are two Moorish American representatives from the Moroccan United Organization Federation.

Rommani Amenu El (seated) Wajid Bey (far left) 1978 Washington, D.C.
during visit of King Hassam, Morocco

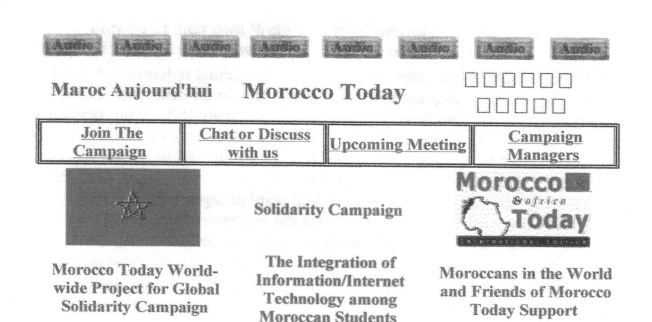

| Join The Campaign | Chat or Discuss with us | Upcoming Meeting | Campaign Managers |

Maroc Aujourd'hui   **Morocco Today**

Solidarity Campaign

Morocco Today World-wide Project for Global Solidarity Campaign

The Integration of Information/Internet Technology among Moroccan Students

Moroccans in the World and Friends of Morocco Today Support

Moroccan people is keenly aware development is unattainable as long as layers of the populations are not entitled to decent living standards
-said Our Young King Mohammed VI -

>p/□   >p/□   >p/□

Invitation
To join the Solidarity Campaign for the Poor: Launched by H.M. King Mohammed VI
Moroccans Abroad Chapter
The Goal: Full Integration of Information/Internet Technology Environment for Moroccan Educational System

The new generation of Moroccans Abroad is making the most beneficial use of the Information Technology and Internet to serve their country.

King Mohammed VI

198

"Prophet Noble Drew Ali Reincarnated" Founder of the Moorish Science Temple of America Aug. 1934

Noble Drew Ali in
Panama

Prophet Noble Drew Ali

The ordination and Promotion of then Colonel Hassan Jeru Ahmed-Bey (center) to Minister General of the United Moorish Republic Army. To the left of General Hassan) as he came to be known) is Col. Rafiq Bilal-EL. To the right of General Hassan is Col. Mahdi Nur EL-Haqq-EL. On far right is Rommani M. Amenu-EL known then as Chariman Clarence Reynolds-EL.

This picture was taken directly across the street from the Blair House in Washington D.C. during President Anwar El Sadat's visit.

REFERENCES

Bancroft, George. <u>History of the United States From the Discovery of the American Continent.</u> New York: Brown & Little, 1860

Carroll, Charles. <u>The Negro A Beast or In the Image of God.</u> Miami: Mnemosyne Publishing Co., Inc, 1969

Commager, Henry Steel. <u>Documents of American History, Volume I to 1898, Ninth Edition</u>.

Hurd, Charles Codman. <u>The Law of Freedom and Bondage Volume I.</u> New York: Little, Brown & Co., 1858.

Logan, John A. <u>The Great Conspiracy</u>. New York: A.R. Hart & Co., Publishers, 1886

Moore, Richard B. <u>The Name Negro: Its Origin and Evil Use.</u> Baltimore: Black Classic Press, 1960

Morison, Samuel Eliot and Commager, Henry Steel. <u>The Growth of the American Republic Volume I Fifth Edition.</u> New York: Oxford University Press, 1962

Rogers J.A. and Helga Rogers. <u>Five Negro Presidents</u>. New York: 1957

<u>Webster's Collegiate Dictionary, Fifth Edition.</u> G&C Merriam Co, 1942

INDEX

A

Abraham Lincoln, ii, 33, 68, 92
Alexander Haig, iii, 100
Alfred Collins-El, ii
American Indian, 80

B

black, iii, v, vi, vii, viii, 2, 8, 11, 12, 13, 17, 33, 39, 47, 48, 80, 83, 92, 100, 102
Bobby C. McQueen-Bey, ii, 100
Bro Clifford Hazel Bey, ii
Bureau of Vital Statistics for the State of Maryland, 83

C

Carl Albert, 92
Carolyn L. Reynolds-EL, ii
Charles Glen-El, 92
Charter of Warrant and Dispensation, 168
Chefreen El Ontu-El,, ii
Claud Myrick -Bey, ii
Claude D. Greene, 50
Clayton, Ralph, 22
Colonel Campbell C. Johnson, 68
Colonel Swartz, 62
Compensated Emancipation, v, vi, 35, 39, 68, 73, 100

D

Department of Mental Health and Hygiene, 83
DHMH, 83, 88
Dred Scott, iii, vi, 10, 13, 14, 16, 25, 73, 102

E

Elaine Myrick-Bey, ii
Emim Ankh Unu-Bey, ii

F

F.Turner EL, 168
Foreman Bey, 50
Fourteen Amendment, 102
Fourteenth Amendment, 10, 88, 102

G

General Hershey, 62
Grand Sheik Hommett Anderson El, 60
Grand Sheik Richardson Dingle El, 61, 62, 69
Grand Sheik Richardson Dingle-El, 60, 68, 80
Grand Sheik Richardson El, 60

H

Herbert Joiner-Bey, ii, 84
Hispanic, 80

I

IRS, iii, v, 100
Isisara Adolemiua Bey, ii

J

Jacques E. Leeds-Bey, ii, 101
Jacques E. Leeds-Bey, Sr, 101, 177
James and Helen Richardson-El, ii
James C. Evans, 68
James C. Evans El, 68
Judge C. Stanley Blair, 101

K

Kessler, Robert J, 94
Khalil Adolemiua-Bey, ii
King Hassan II of Morocco, 196
King Mohammed VI, 201

L

Leon Smith-Bey, ii
Lovett Bey, 50

M

Malbert Brown-Bey, ii
Mark Stout, 92
Martha Leeds-Bey, ii
Mealy El, 50
Micha-El Oneferu-Bey, ii
Mongoloid, 80
Moorish National Bureau of Vital Statistics, 62, 81, 84, 88
Moorish School of Law and History, ii, iii, v, vi, vii, 33, 39, 50, 61, 68, 73, 80, 83, 100, 196

N

National Archives, 62
negro, iii, v, vi, viii, 8, 11, 12, 13, 16, 17, 18, 25, 33, 46, 47, 80, 83
Noble Drew Ali, i, vi, 50, 56, 60, 62, 68, 73, 203, 204
Noble Drew Ali Reincarnated, 60

O

Oscar Stanton De Priest, 183
Our Authority, 62

P

Parren J. Mitchell, 92
Peter Rodino, 39, 92
Prophet Noble Drew Ali III, 69

R

Richardson Dingle El, 62, 168
Richardson Dingle EL, 62, 68, 168
Richardson Dingle-El, ii, 80
Richardson Dingle-EL, 68, 84
Richmond Fourth Circuit Court of Appeals, 102
Robert C. Nix Jr, 92
Robert J. Kessler., 101
Rommani Amenu El, 200
Rommani Amenu EL, 168

S

Sarah Ferrell-EL, ii
Selective Service, iii, 62, 68
Selective Service Act, 68
Sheik John Givens EL, 60
Small Bey, 50
Supreme Court, v, vi, 16, 17, 25, 73, 102

T

the Moorish School of Law and History, v, 73, 83, 100
The Moorish Science Temple, Divine and National Movement of North America Inc, #13, 60
thirteenth amendment, 33
Timothy Dingle-El, ii, 68

U

UCC, 92
Uniform Commercial Code, 92
Unto Thee I Grant, 56
US Federal District Court, 101
US Justice Department, 101

W

Wajid Bey, 200
Wajid Ebenufu-Bey, ii
White, 12, 80
William Wellington Bey, 68
writ of Mandamus, 101